TRANSFORMING THE ACADEMY

TRANSFORMING THE ACADEMY

Faculty Perspectives on Diversity and Pedagogy

EDITED BY SARAH WILLIE-LeBRETON

RUTGERS UNIVERSITY PRESS

New Brunswick, New Jersey, and London

This publication was supported in part by
the Eleanor J. and Jason F. Dreibelbis Fund.

Library of Congress Cataloging-in-Publication Data

Names: Willie-LeBreton, Sarah, 1963- editor.
Title: Transforming the academy : faculty perspectives on diversity and pedagogy /
edited by Sarah Willie-LeBreton.
Description: New Brunswick, New Jersey : Rutgers University Press, 2016. | Includes
bibliographical references and index.
Identifiers: LCCN 2015028623| ISBN 9780813565088 (hardcover : alk. paper) |
ISBN 9780813565071 (pbk. : alk. paper) | ISBN 9780813565095 (e-book (web
pdf)) | ISBN 9780813572956 (e-book (epub))
Subjects: LCSH: College teaching—Social aspects—United States. | Education,
Higher—Social aspects—United States. | Education, Higher—Curricula—United
States. | Education, Higher—Aims and objectives—United States. | Minorities—
Education (Higher)—United States. | Educational equalization—United States.
Classification: LCC LB2331 .T727 2016 | DDC 378.1/25—dc23
LC record available at http://lccn.loc.gov/2015028623

A British Cataloging-in-Publication record for this book is available from the British
Library.

Visit our website: http://rutgerspress.rutgers.edu

Manufactured in the United States of America

For Jonathan and Jeremy,
and those who continue to teach me

CONTENTS

ACKNOWLEDGMENTS

This collection has never been mine. It is ours. Our hope is that it serves as a springboard for conversations among colleagues and friends, students and administrators, legislators, board members, parents and co-workers—all those who care deeply about education, and higher education, in the United States. Nonetheless, getting an edited volume from ideation to publication depends on particular individuals. I am indebted to the three people who asked me to serve as discussant for their presentations at the American Anthropology Association—Cheryl Jones-Walker, Anita Chik-katur, and Dela Kusi-Appouh. After them, I am indebted to the authors who made themselves vulnerable by their willingness to contribute essays to this volume. The candid conversations that we have had with colleagues on our various campuses have helped us to be continually engaged in the creation and re-creation of institutions that are intellectually exciting, invigorating, and more just and inclusive.

The Michener Funds at Swarthmore College allowed me a full-year sabbatical, but it is the community of colleagues, co-workers, and students that have made coming to work, more often than not, an experience I cherish. My *alma mater* offered me the chance for a friendship with Joan Cotellessa, the editor with whom I worked privately, and I am grateful for her generosity, speed, care, and good humor; she became a true partner in a matter of days and stuck with me. The thoughtful comments and encouragement from reviewers of an earlier draft of the volume were crucial, as were the insights and suggestions of an excellent team at Rutgers University Press, including Peter Mickulas, Katie Keeran (no longer at RUP), Marlie Wasserman, Carrie Hudak, Kimberly Guinta, Romaine Perin, and Kristen Bonanno. I am fortunate to have had the support of friends, family, and colleagues, the deepest support having come from my spouse, Jonathan.

INTRODUCTION

The Challenges of Diversity and Pedagogy

SARAH WILLIE-LEBRETON

College students today face serious challenges, but so, too, do the faculty who teach them, the boards that govern their institutions, and the administrators who—with greater or lesser success—translate everyone to each other. Along with concerns about student debt, sexual misconduct, and assessment of student learning and whether skills learned translate to the workplace come concerns about diversity, inclusion, and navigating the campus when one is the first in one's family to attend college. This volume assumes that education is more of a process than a product, and that the concerns students have and raise while they are enrolled are central to the educational mission. Diverse faculty members, once students themselves, are unusually well positioned to participate in the national conversations on these issues and to offer insights and wisdom about the college campus as a workplace.

If these essays represent in any way the thousands of college and university faculty on today's campuses, it is a wonderful moment to be students in their classrooms! In large leaps or small steps, faculty, students, administrators, and staff are finding their way toward shared governance, wise investment and spending, technological creativity and innovation, and moving the boundaries of knowledge. The faculty and staff who share their stories in these pages struggle to be accountable to their students and their colleagues, to their own ideals, and to the larger goals of education for life. These same faculty and staff are likewise cognizant that with new possibilities—such as tablets for all first-year students, online learning, and loan-free financial aid packages—we still face challenges. College is currently beyond the reach of many, those who begin college do not always finish it, and many students leave college with large amounts of debt. College is also a moment when students have an opportunity to interrupt the prejudices with which they may have been raised, since it's often the first time students have lived with those who come from very different backgrounds.

A few years ago, three scholars, at the start of their careers, gathered at an annual professional conference. The scholars spoke to the challenges of teaching about difference when they represented difference to both their students and their colleagues. With various identities, which included having been born in and outside the United States, being queer and cisgender (straight), being single and married, raising children and being child free, they took what had been private conversations about their experiences, held them up to the light of analysis, and began—with an apparently all-white audience assembled at their session—to engage in a larger and more public conversation. Their presentations inspired and, somewhat revised and expanded upon, are included in this volume.

Adding to their reflections, nearly a dozen academics join them in this collection, each speaking from a different position. Some of the contributors are persons of color, others identify as white; some were born in this country, some outside it; some are queer, others straight; some grew up poor or working class, others middle class or affluent; some are at the dawn of their careers and others at the dusk. They represent a range of disciplines in the social sciences, arts, and humanities, and their experiences have informed their pedagogies, career choices, and scholarship, shaped by the campuses on which they work.

None of the contributors to this volume attempts to represent all perspectives. We acknowledge that the subject of higher education is polysemic, meaning we interpret it in multiple ways. We're aware that higher education has itself become a lightning rod, standing in for so many of the social challenges that the United States faces. And yet it's clear that we all benefit from the excitement and new knowledge that grows in diverse settings, with learners from a variety of backgrounds.

The authors in *Transforming the Academy* offer their experiences from the perspective of onetime outsiders who are now faculty and staff at predominantly white, American institutions of higher learning. Some of our institutions are public, others are private; some are universities, others are colleges; some are small, others are large; and thus, implicitly, the broader concerns about higher education in the United States are ones with which these authors wrestle every day. In one sense, this book reflects macro changes—the social transformation of the American academy as difference has come to be rhetorically celebrated, and, at a number of colleges and universities, actually realized. In another sense, the authors wrestle with micro realities—the quotidian challenges of being faculty members who represent diversity in the curriculum, in the department, and on the faculty. As such, we share lessons we have learned that are both specific and general.

WHY DIVERSITY, WHY NOT JUST RACE?

As I described to a number of colleagues and friends this project of hearing from diverse faculty, several people expressed concern: "The issue is racial diversity, Sarah. Institutions use other forms of diversity to avoid working on racial diversity, especially to avoid recruiting working-class Black and Latino students to campus." Indeed, recruiting faculty and full-paying students from other countries who, once here, are forced to contort themselves into the United States' racial categories can make our campuses more colorful and culturally diverse while simultaneously allowing us to avoid conversations about inequality specific to this country since its inception.[1] As a multiracial person who identifies as African American, I am particularly moved by this concern.

Several colleagues argued that the real problem is class and income inequality. If we pay attention to class, then we will help all financially insecure Americans who want to attend college. Fewer poor and working-class students are able to afford college, and they need funding options. To be sure, affordability and access to higher education for poor and working-class students are serious issues. I am wary, however, when concern for poor and working-class students becomes a concern for policy makers only when middle-class or affluent students experience challenges to their class privilege or when white students sense a challenge to their racial privilege. We need to be vigilant to ensure that focusing on one aspect of inequality does not become a way to avoid talking about other aspects.

Another colleague worried that "if you keep adding subaltern statuses, no one will know what your book is about." Let me address this one straight on: When we focus on difference, rather than race, class, gender, disability, or sexuality only, we come to understand how each of these characteristics fits into the oppression/privilege paradigm much more clearly. We also expose ways that none of us experience our identities singly. Political philosopher Iris Marion Young (1990) argues that with every experience of oppression—a systemic experience that targets one's association with a group—there is a corresponding experience of privilege, whether or not one's privilege is conscious or chosen. Because many societies, including our own, have denounced formal inequality, such as segregation, those who benefit from informal inequality are often unaware of the ways in which they are privileged in relation to someone else's oppression. This is just one of the ways that well-meaning people who benefit from social inequality can participate in reproducing it (Bonilla-Silva 2013). The approach of this volume, to ask folks about how their identities intersect with their pedagogy, can lead us to both empathize with those who have different experiences and to appreciate the complexity of our lives.

Focusing on specific experiences of those who lift up one aspect of their identities and those who interpret their lives at the intersections of several identity statuses is both useful and necessary. There are, incidentally, scores of books published about single or even double identity experiences. Those insights give us empirical evidence against which to judge and to interpret the salience of one aspect of our experiences. With instrumentality and clarity, we must begin to understand how an insistence on one approach may inhibit our commitment to challenging oppression against many categories of people.

In an op-ed critique of what we might call official diversity in the *Chronicle of Higher Education*, Lennard J. Davis (2011) shows the importance of such multilayered analyses of diversity. Davis reminds us how quickly hegemony—the rule of a small, powerful, dominant group by coercion and consent rather than by outright domination—can integrate tendencies that oppose it, usurping the powerful ideas that had previously challenged its oppressive ways (Gramsci 1971).

What does this have to do with the topic at hand? As recently as the 1980s, *diversity* was a radical term that challenged the homogeneity and unquestioned segregation of college campuses along gender, race, sexuality, ability, and religious lines. The concept and watchword of diversity just a few decades later has been absorbed as a stated goal of higher education, making its way into nearly every mission statement, onto every college and university website, and into every catalog. And while that is mostly a good thing, such rapid integration of the concept without concomitant real changes has come at a cost.

Today, Davis (2011) argues, although most proponents of diversity would reject "the idea of normal ethnicity," they may have "no problem with the notion of normal in a medical sense, which means branding some bodies and minds as abnormal." He worries that as long as diversity and its officially designated proponents understand it only as including "the categories of race, ethnicity, and gender," and as long as it is constructed superficially as any identity that "we all could imagine having, and . . . is worthy of choosing," then disabled identities will not fit this paradigm. Indeed, the current construction of diversity fits into the ideological paradigm of neoliberalism. A central feature of neoliberalism is the importance of choice. For Davis, the characterization of choice as the apotheosis of empowerment is deceitful: "The screen of empowerment . . . conceals the lack of choice and the powerlessness of most people." Moreover, such a screen obfuscates the ways that many identities are more complex than celebrations lead us to believe, and most identities involve neither choice nor fantasy. It is here that the genuine inclusion of disabilities within diversity may facilitate a more effective critique of the ways in which the once-inclusive concept has been hijacked from its ability to transform the academy more fully.

Clearly, embracing the concept of diversity opens up a range of serious issues, and it is precisely this interplay of issues, raised by the variety of experiences that the faculty and staff contributors to this volume have, that allows us to compare their similarities and differences. Structures of domination, oppression, and privilege are interrelated. Understanding the structural reasons one group is denigrated or excluded may provide important insights into why other groups also are excluded and denigrated. It is precisely why I have chosen to include a range of experiences among the identities of contributors to this volume, to begin the difficult work of analysis and the applied work of finding pragmatic solutions. As esteemed anthropologist James Clifford has observed, "The language of diversity [can] mask persistent inequalities" (2012, 421). *Transforming the Academy* reveals that the analysis of diversity can also be revealing and liberating.

THIS VOLUME

Young reminds us why it is so important to listen carefully to the voices of those who have been oppressed or marginalized, who labor in the interstices, and those who do the work of cultural translation and mutual interpretation and reconciliation:

> When the more bold of us do complain of these mundane signs of systemic oppression, we are accused of being picky, overreaction, making something out of nothing, or of completely misperceiving the situation. The courage to bring to discursive consciousness behavior and reactions occurring at the level of practical consciousness is met with denial and powerful gestures of silencing, which can make oppressed people feel slightly crazy (1990).

When we take the complaints of our fellows seriously, it changes the way we do business, changes our attitudes, and changes the institutions in which we study, work, learn, and co-create knowledge.

Two themes characterize the essays of these diverse scholars writing about their experiences as teachers, their memories of themselves as students, and their continuing and shifting identities as individuals and members of groups. Part I is titled "Challenging Classrooms." Each of the authors in Part I share what it means to have one's classroom authority challenged, or accepted, because one belongs to a subdominant group. These authors make their classrooms sites that challenge their students' preconceived ideas while engaging their charge by the college or university where they work to convey subject matter. They reflect on what it means to be challenged and to be challenging. The authors in this section are Michael Smith, Eve Tuck, Dela Kusi-Appouh, Mark Ellis, Cheryl Jones-Walker, Pato Hebert, myself, and Anita Chikkatur.

Part II is titled "Witnessing Protest." As college professors, we are often in the position of doing more than teaching the subject matter. Moments of crisis on campus and off can throw us into situations in which we witness our students' pain and their triumphs, and we may even mentor them through decisions that are academic, political, or personal. Sometimes we are the ones transformed, other times it is our students, and still other times, we play the role of witness for colleagues who are naming their experiences. The authors who reflect on these issues include Kristin Lindgren, Anna Ward, Betty Sasaki, Aurora Camacho de Schmidt, Daphne Lamothe, and Theresa Tensuan, all represented in Part II.

In both parts of the volume, some of the authors name and analyze the structural contradictions of the academy, for example, articulating the ways in which American higher education was never intended to be as inclusive as it has become. As people who are working in the academy, we often wrestle with the ways that higher education has been exclusive, even as it has become inclusive over time and in response to protest. Several of the authors bravely face the contradictions that define their lives and discuss some of the moments when they and their students are pushed and pulled in more than one direction.

THE PRESENT AND FUTURE

Each contributor to this volume takes his or her role as a teacher, scholar or mentor, administrator or advisor seriously. In this collection, we share some of our most profound challenges and hard-won insights. What unites the essays is the shared agreement among the authors that this is the time for making what had been private conversations more public. Indeed, as parents make decisions with their children about whether and which colleges or universities to attend, the care and seriousness with which members of today's professorate take the challenges of diversity should offer tremendous optimism for what students will find on campus.

Making public the conversation about diversity and its challenges accomplishes three things, reflecting our goals in this volume. First, it exposes parochialism, allays anxiety, and undermines mean-spiritedness. The privacy of closed doors may inadvertently protect dominant group behavior that would change in the light of exposure. Closed doors certainly protect organizations from the fresh air and transparency that make for more genuinely shared governance, clear rules, and mutually arrived at expectations. We do not deny that discretion has saved many careers, but sometimes discretion and protection call for speaking loudly enough for everyone to hear.

Second, when more than one or two people talk publicly about their experiences, institutionalized aversions to difference that are taken as part of the normative (and therefore nonnegotiable) culture of higher education are revealed as both oppressive and vulnerable to challenge and change. Most people don't want their workplaces to be bastions of patronage and special treatment (unless, of course, they think they are getting the special treatment). It is not unusual for employees on college and university campuses to be convinced that they are surely part of the group that is left out! A community can come together in the spirit of shared values if they know that when unfair treatment happens, they can be part of stopping it.

And third, through this volume, it allows us to celebrate our advocates and allies—some vocal, some quiet—who have listened to our stories, made arguments for our promotions, read drafts of our scholarship, helped us to negotiate contracts and appeal decisions that went against us, celebrated our successes, comforted us in failures, kept us from feeling crazy, been willing to change their own minds over time, and offered their best advice about our careers.

Above, I quoted Iris Young, who wrote that when those who are marginalized try to voice their complaints, they are often made to feel crazy. *Iatrogenesis* is a term in medicine that means physician-induced illness. There is also a level of neurosis among faculty and staff from previously excluded groups on college and university campuses that is the result of an academy still making its way out of dysfunction. When academic institutions do not name the challenges they face and the work still left to be done, the persons who work there can suffer from all kinds of ills that result from institutional disease. This is a lesser version of the "total institution" Erving Goffman (1961) described in his famous study of asylums, but the ramifications for tenure track faculty in particular who are different in some way from the majority may be just as severe. If one suffers microaggressions on a daily or weekly basis, if one is never socialized into the culture of the organization because one is not truly trusted or included, if one is undermined or questioned regularly after having won a position and then not given clear or adequate information about how to win reappointment and tenure, then that can lead to all kinds of responses that further undermine one's success socially and professionally at the college or university.[2] I think of those responses as the iatrogenesis of the academy, and it's an illness that can be reduced or eliminated with attention and a willingness to change ideas about how our institutions work.

A great deal has changed since I began my own graduate career in the 1980s, and we still have much work before us. One change we need to make is to bring the privately held conversations about our most egregious and painful experiences into the light of day. Each person who integrates the student body, the staff, or the faculty experiences the pain of being the first outsider to join the group, and usually many members of the organization experience the growing pains of living with difference as well. Some of those growing pains are unavoidable, but with increasing numbers of different kinds of people with different histories, learning styles, identities, experiences, and priorities come opportunities to remember the values we do share, to admit the experiences that we do not share, and to figure out together how we move forward to make higher education as rigorous, fruitful, inclusive, and intellectually exciting as it has ever been.

NOTES

1 "In ruling narrowly, the [Supreme Court] reaffirmed earlier decisions allowing for a limited use of race-conscious public policies. 'The attainment of a diverse student body serves values beyond race alone, including enhanced classroom dialogue and the lessening of racial isolation and stereotypes,' wrote Justice Anthony Kennedy in the majority opinion. But Kennedy said that such admissions programs must withstand close review. Kennedy said the 'university must prove that the means chosen' to attain diversity 'are narrowly tailored to that goal,' adding that the highest level of legal standard must be met before institutions use diversity programs. 'Strict scrutiny (of the policy) imposes on the university the ultimate burden of demonstrating, before turning to racial classification, that available, workable race-neutral alternatives do not suffice,' he said" (Mears 2013).

2 The term *microaggressions* was coined by a psychiatrist, Chester Pierce (1970), and defined by psychologist Derald Wing Sue (2010) as "everyday verbal, nonverbal, and environmental slights, snubs, or insults, whether intentional or unintentional, that communicate hostile, derogatory, or negative messages to target persons based solely upon their group membership" (3).

PART I CHALLENGING CLASSROOMS

1 ◆ DECENTERING WHITENESS

Teaching Antiracism on a Predominantly White Campus

MICHAEL D. SMITH AND EVE TUCK

White supremacy . . . has made the modern world what it is today. And yet you will not find this term in [political theory] texts. . . . This omission is not accidental.

—Charles Mills

Whiteness is the immovable mover, unmarked marker, and unspoken speaker.

—Zeus Leonardo and Ronald K. Porter

In recent decades, institutions of higher education have worked (with uneven results) to increase the diversity of faculty and expand the diversity of curricular ideas offered to students. These efforts have been made, however, without simultaneous attempts to decenter whiteness as anthropocentric normal. In other words, colleges have attempted to diversify students, faculty, and curriculum without interrupting white supremacy.

Life on predominantly white college campuses for both students of color and faculty of color includes a mixed bag of racial microaggressions and racialized aggressions. Julie Minikel-Lacocque (2013) defines racial microaggressions as "derogatory acts that are most often unconscious on the part of the perpetrator, as commonplace occurrences, and as offenses that have alternative, non-racially motivated explanations that often cause the targets to feel conflicted and invalidated" (459). The author contrasts these acts to racialized aggressions, or overt intentionally racist acts. As reported in a recent collective case study of six Latino/a students' transitions from secondary school to a prestigious predominantly white university, their first semesters were crowded by painful experiences of what scholars have called racial microaggressions, evidenced in cold stares, isolation, insensitivity, online bigotry, name-calling, and refusals by bus drivers to stop for them (Minikel-Lacocque 2013).

In this essay, written by two early career scholars who are also members of underrepresented groups on their campus and within the larger academy—one Black cis man and one Alaska Native cis woman—we present collective autoethnographic accounts of teaching diversity courses in a predominantly white small state college. In fact, the courses we design to teach about race and racism are simultaneously and perhaps paradoxically sites that undermine racism and ideologies of white supremacy as well as sites of racial aggressions, microaggressions, and laboratories in which to study such phenomena. Patricia Williams (1991) describes antiracist work, such as that highlighted in this essay, as boundary crossing from "safe circle to wilderness," as "the willingness to spoil a good party," as knowing that "everything has changed and yet that nothing has changed" (130–131). At the heart of this essay is a desire to interrupt the politics of representation as usual, a willingness to forgo the relative safety of keeping quiet.

We discuss many of the features, dips, and turns of teaching about white supremacy at a predominantly white institution. In the first section, we share our approach to theorizing whiteness in our courses. The second section considers the challenges that take place when one attempts to decenter whiteness only to find it recentered by students through various forms of resistance. We share organizing metaphors and pedagogical strategies we have used to help negotiate these challenging situations. Finally, we close the essay with a discussion of implications for policy and practice in the university.

THEORIZING WHITENESS

In our courses, we specifically engage issues of power and privilege, and it is impossible to discuss race without discussing whiteness. (We have capitalized nonwhite groups because they have often arrived at these designations as part of social movements of liberation. At the same time, there are places where the word *black* is in lowercase because it is only a description.) This is usually a new thought for white students taking a race and racism course for the first time: they often think that *race* refers to only people of color—people who are Black, Latino, Native American, or Asian. Of course, the fact that white people see themselves as having no race or as being race neutral is a central premise of critical race theory and critical whiteness studies (for an extended discussion, see Kendall 2006). But for the purposes of our classes and for the purposes of this essay, we draw attention to the perennial newness of this thought for white undergraduate students; though some might make claims against the contemporary relevance or need for courses on race and racism in undergraduate liberal or general education, the reality that, year after year, white students discover the reality and privileges of whiteness and their investment in it is evidence of the absence of conversations about race and racism in K–12 schooling and the necessity for these conversations in higher education.

We hold that to theorize whiteness is to theorize white supremacy and its disavowal. We agree that "there is no 'race' outside of the historical genealogies and multiple political derivations of white supremacy, and to posit race without an essential and critical engagement with its structuring white supremacist genealogies is (at the very least) a profoundly ahistorical gesture" (Rodriguez 2011, 48). Indeed, part of the labor of our courses is to help both white students and students of color recognize whiteness, see its societal position as both superior and normal, learn the history of how race has been constructed, notice the unearned privileges that accrue to whiteness, and take steps to interrupt white supremacy and decenter whiteness and white ideology as normal.

Interestingly, many of our white students and students of color come to our classes having never had formal instruction on race but already weary from talking about it. That is, they have had no opportunities to discuss race in settings in which there was an expert facilitator to help craft the shape of the discussion, but they already feel like experts on the subject without much to learn. As noted, many white students enter our classes thinking that this course is about other people—about people of color (a term they usually encounter for the first time in our courses and need lots of practice and coaching to adopt). They are surprised and maybe even a little nervous to learn that they will be learning about whiteness and white ideology.

When we meet students, they are frequently firmly attached to the virtues of color-blind ideology, meaning they are invested in the idea that racism will go away only if it is not discussed, and that it is impolite or even offensive to speak openly or directly about (a person's) race. Thus, the two primary ideas that students grapple with in the first days of class are (1) it is OK and necessary to talk about race and racism and (2) white people have a race, and how white people are raced has implications for everyone.

Students in our classes are learning about race and racism in a historical moment that has all the markers of being unprecedented: the United States has elected a Black president, the U.S. population is increasingly diverse, and much formal discrimination is illegal. But these new realities have done little to change substantially racial hierarchies that filter access and opportunities in the United States. The president has enacted policies that harm communities of color in the United States and around the globe, urban and rural communities are increasingly segregated, and outlawing formal discrimination has not meant the eradication of informal racist practices (Winant 2004). Winant talks about this as a historical moment in which white people's lives are made dual:

> On the one hand, whites inherit the legacy of white supremacy, from which they continue to benefit. But on the other hand, they are subject to the moral and political challenges posed to that inheritance by the partial but real successes of the black movement (and affiliated movements). . . . Obviously, they did not destroy the deep structures of white privilege, but they did make counterclaims on behalf of the racially excluded and subordinated. As a result, white identities have been displaced and refigured: They are now contradictory, as well as confused and anxiety-ridden, to an unprecedented extent. This is white racial dualism. (4)

White racial dualism can be a departure point for the behind-the-scenes theorizing of whiteness that informs our work with students. White students enter our courses espousing a variety of (false) truisms (everyone is a little bit racist; wanting to stay with your "own kind" is human nature) that represent the ways they have heard other white people in their lives— parents, teachers, other trusted adults, friends—deflect recognition of unearned advantages and unfair social arrangements. At the same time, they know that there are many potentially wrong things that can be said in conversations about race and that their words can not only harm others but also ruin their own reputations. The resulting strategy usually is to say as little as possible, both to minimize harm and to conceal the gaps in their knowledge. We agree that when white people engage in racist speech and acts, "they demonstrate a profound misreading of the subjects they encounter," but they are also demonstrating a profound misreading of their own whiteness as at the center of human experience (Holland 2012, 2).

A common thread across our teaching is the framing influence of critical race theory. Among critical race theorists, racism is theorized "not as isolated instances of conscious bigoted decision-making, but as larger, systemic, structural, and cultural, as deeply psychologically and socially ingrained" (Matsuda et al. 1993, 5). Critical race theory prompts an analysis of how racism produces its own categories and institutional operations, such as the granting of citizenship and other legal rights. It traces how "rights," practices, material benefits, and forms of knowledge are constituted as white property (Ladson-Billings 1995). Cheryl Harris (1993) theorizes whiteness as property, observing, "In ways so embedded that it is rarely apparent, the set of assumptions, privileges, and benefits that accompany the status of being white have become a valuable asset that whites sought to protect" (1713). Harris explains that race, the racialization of identity, and the subordination of black people and indigenous peoples provided the justification for both slavery and conquest (1715). Although the strategies of domination used against both groups were markedly different, "the former involving the seizure and appropriation of labor, the latter entailing the seizure and appropriation of land" (1715), these strategies worked together to form the basis of what is now widely understood as "property rights." Indeed, the origins of property rights in the United States are rooted in racial domination. Even in the early years of the country, it was not the concept of race alone that operated to oppress Blacks and Indians; rather it was the interactions between conceptions of race and property that played a critical role in establishing and maintaining racial and economic exploitation. . . . The hyper-exploitation of Black labor was accomplished by treating Black people themselves as objects of property. . . . Similarly, the conquest, removal, and extermination of Native American life and culture were ratified by conferring and acknowledging the property rights of whites in Native American land. . . . These distinct forms of exploitation each contributed in varying ways to the construction of whiteness as property. (1716)

Harris insists that whiteness is property in all senses of the word; it is a traditional form of property in comprising all of a person's legal rights, defining one as free (and not a slave), and affording tangible and material benefits (1726). It also meets modern definitions of property and expectation-based definitions of property. Although Harris locates the construction of whiteness as property at the intersection of both the enslavement of black people and the conquest of Indigenous people's lives and land, most critical race theorists have focused on the invention of race as a justification for chattel slavery (Ladson-Billings 1995). At the same time, scholars in the field of settler colonial studies have focused on the creation of the settler colonial nation-state and its attempts to erase Indigenous people's lives and claims to land (see Wolfe 2006). These scholars contend that "white supremacy's most excessive and extensive violences never quite displace or truly depart from the massive historical ambitions to which they are attached, whether Manifest Destiny, democracy, or the making of white 'modernity' itself" (Rodriguez 2011, 51). More recently, scholars bridging both fields have been working to theorize the relationships that Harris outlines in her 1993 article, attending to the nexus of a white supremacy that transforms both Indigenous people's land and Black people's bodies into property (Tuck and Yang 2012; Wilderson 2010; Byrd 2011).

The construction of whiteness as both superior and normal, or white supremacy, has required the attempted erasure of Indigenous peoples. For settlers to make a new home on stolen land, they must disappear the Indigenous inhabitants, first through violence, then through assimilation, economic strangulation, and changing the historical narrative of the land (Tuck and Yang 2012). This is why it is so common to hear that there are no real Native people anymore, that Native people have no legitimate claims to their lands, and that those who persist are on the verge of extinction. None of these statements is true, but they are the narratives that circulate.

The formation of white supremacy has also required chattel slavery, the enslavement of black bodies that could not run away and disappear into the free population. In chattel slavery, it was not the person but the body that was valuable—for labor and for labor only. The person was extra, was punishable, was murderable. The person, who might escape, who might seek revenge, had to be made into a monster, a danger, a threat, someone determined to cause harm (Tuck and Yang 2012). Again, these are the untruths that circulate. These constructions of blackness have lingered and been resurrected long since the abolition of slavery. They are evident in the exorbitant number of black and brown youth stopped by police officers in the former's own neighborhoods (4.3 million of the first 5 million stop-and-frisk encounters in New York City were conducted on youth of color); the disproportionate number of black men in prison; and the question of whether Trayvon Martin, a black adolescent visiting family in a gated community in Florida, was a threat to Neighborhood Watch volunteer George Zimmerman, who identified as white and Hispanic and who would kill Martin even after police instructed Zimmerman to leave Martin alone.

Black people are thought to be suspect when moving outside the implicit and explicit spatial boundaries enforced by white supremacist society.

> It is precisely because the black subject is mired in space and the white subject represents the full expanse of time that the meeting of the two might be thought of as never actually occurring in the same temporal plane; yet the desire to get over such a meeting is immediate and the recovery is often swift. Exactly how does one move beyond a nonevent? (Holland 2012, 18)

This is what can be so frustrating when students and colleagues insist that racism is less prevalent now than it was in prior generations. Applying a relative temporal measure—better now than it was before—ignores the spatial constrictions enforced on black life and the material benefits accrued to whiteness because of those racialized spatializations (Lipsitz 2011). How is it possible to say that now is better than before when there are more black people incarcerated now than ever were enslaved (Alexander 2012)? Who does it benefit to say now is better than before? Why is time the measuring stick and not space, not freedom?

What is important in this discussion is the need to analyze the interactions of whiteness and white supremacy with blackness and its interactions with Indigeneity in tandem—not collapsed into a kind of multicultural critique of abstract oppression—but with a nuanced specificity that attends to the reasons and results of myriad differentiations between the racialization of African-descended people and the racialization of people indigenous to what is now the United States of America. For example, Patrick Wolfe (2006) has theorized the competing, historically simultaneous logics of the one-drop rule that was attached to blackness, and the blood quantum policies attached to native peoples in the United States (see also Tuck and Yang 2012). Both logics work to protect white supremacy, requiring the proliferation of black bodies as property and the accumulation of land as property, land stolen from peoples indigenous to it, which has been cleared of those peoples (Tuck and Yang 2012). These considerations of the inventions of race and its justifications, the roles of the state and law in protecting whiteness as property and the property of white people, and the strategic ascendancy of whiteness throb at the center of our teaching. They help us to make choices on what to emphasize as key concepts. They also help us to understand the resistance and disavowals students make of whiteness.

ENGAGING WHITENESS

As professors in a school of education, we address the lessons learned as we have attempted to decenter whiteness in our courses—reading together, thinking together, and holding each other accountable. Many of our students are aspiring and practicing educators. Thus, one facet of our discussions about race and whiteness specifically is the role of schools in maintaining and promoting racial discrimination and hierarchies. In our courses with students not majoring in education, we also discuss the roles of schools in reproducing racism, especially as students begin to wonder aloud why this is the first time they have ever encountered a course on race and racism.

Here, we attempt to make sense of our personal and professional roles by simultaneously looking back at and remembering our many journal entries, lunchtime conversations, and personal reflections since we began teaching at the same university a few years ago and sharing some of our present insights. Several themes recur: understanding safe and unsafe spaces, refining the role of text, (dis)locating the self and disclosure of self, and managing resistance. Below, we provide a brief overview of each of these themes, with some of the questions that continue to linger for us.

Most likely as a result of changes in the discourse made available to K–12 students in the past decade, many undergraduate students come to college courses expecting these courses to provide a "safe" space for discussion. Applying even a basic understanding of Maslow's hierarchy of needs, educators understand that fundamental concerns such as safety must be attended to before one can hope to draw a student's attention to more abstract concepts. That said, of course, we agree that no one should ever feel humiliated or dehumanized in a classroom; nor should anyone ever be physically harmed. Nonetheless, cultivating a course environment that remains a fertile ground for meaningful exploration of race and racism involves an alchemy of personal, interpersonal, psychological, and emotional elements that undulate between centripetal and centrifugal forces. At times, thoughtful attention to some course details serves to unify and draw students in, yet these same course elements can push other students away.

In a typical course, we might set general guidelines for course participation and set about the task of teaching. One might assume that "by virtue of formal and procedural guidelines, safety has been designated for both white people and people of color. However, the term 'safety' acts as a misnomer because it often means that white individuals can be made to feel safe. Thus a space of safety is circumvented, and instead a space of oppressive color-blindness is established. It is a managed health-care version of racism, an insurance against 'looking racist'" (Leonardo and Porter 2010, 147). Further, in courses that focus on topics preloaded with psychological and emotional valence, even a "standard" rule for interpersonal conduct like the "golden rule" might be second guessed (Kendall 2006, 51, 122).

What remains for us, even after reflection, conversation, and consulting the literature, is a nagging set of questions introduced by a single fundamental shift in thinking about our course environments. Besides considering the absolute and physical safety of the learning environment, one might also think about the relative and emotional safety of the environment. In this context, one might reasonably wonder, What aspects of the environment are a priority and at whose expense does our attention or inattention come? Further, while most thoughts of safety locate students at the fulcrum, considering the relative safety of the learning environment also requires faculty members of color to consider personal factors that might have implications for their professional interests.

We do our best to create the best environment for this work while also reconsidering privately, and now publicly, many of the following questions: (1) How is safety defined in this context and to what degree can it be safeguarded for *everyone*? (2) How differentially safe is the learning environment for white students, students of color, or the faculty member? (3) What if a white student feels "unsafe" when her long-held beliefs are challenged? When she realizes she has benefited from the dispossession of others, or when she is confronted by the implications of her own white privilege? Should that lack of feeling of safety foreclose those important conversations? (5) What if what makes her feel safe is what makes others, including faculty of color, feel unsafe? (6) How might maintaining her feelings of safety make it feel unsafe for students of color in the room? To the last question, Leonardo and Porter (2010) are skeptical about the degree to which a safe space can exist in most mainstream, mixed-company dialogues about racism. In their view, such dialogues are arguably "already hostile and unsafe for many students of color whose perspectives and experiences are consistently minimized." (140) Further, the strictures of some safe spaces that favor white students might create double binds that present untenable choices for students of color whereby "either they must observe the safety of whites and be denied a space that promotes people of color's growth and development or insist on a space of integrity and put themselves further at risk not only of violence, but also risk being conceived of as illogical and irrational. [This happens] even in [spaces] that aim to critique and undo racial advantage" (149).

In our classes on race and racism, we have found that course texts play a surprisingly powerful role. Neither of us would necessarily rush to defend the inherent authority of text; on the contrary, a central message contained in each of our courses is the challenge for the students to question received knowledge and evaluate the text and context with a more discerning eye. Through the products and the process of our teaching, we hope to provide a more liberatory educational experience. That said, understanding the value that students place on the authority of texts and the multiple (un)spoken messages communicated by the presence (and absence) of narratives in a curriculum, we are strategic and intentional about the texts we use.

Teaching in predominantly white spaces has put us in the unusual position of designing primarily text- (and media-) based courses. In these predominantly white spaces, class texts are often the only sustained encounters with the voices and perspectives of peoples of color (other than our own) that white students can engage. Although many students enter these spaces with the belief that this generation is far more "tolerant" than generations past, a second look into their lived experiences, particularly in school and social domains, will reveal a quite segregated experience and a dearth of meaningful relationships with people from backgrounds that differ from their own. Consequently, multiple voices are needed to keep the focus on the lived realities of racism for a range of individuals instead of their viewing racism as, more or less, an intellectual abstraction.

Attending intentionally to the representation of texts in our courses also communicates the value placed on social justice education by scholars who embody multiple social identities. That is, we hope that including scholars from multiple backgrounds helps to disabuse students of the idea that social justice and equity pedagogy are issues that are relevant for only people of color. As we assign texts by white authors on race and racism, it is sometimes hard not to get frustrated when students respond positively to the "reasonable," "insightful" messages of white authors such as Gary Howard or Frances Kendall and negatively to the "defensive," "angry" messages of Black authors such as Lisa Delpit or Gloria Ladson-Billings (even when their messages are strikingly similar). Sometimes making this observation in class leads to fruitful discussions about how our (un)conscious assumptions about the messenger influence the degree to which we can receive the message; and on rare occasions a white student will admit, "I could just hear it differently from someone who is also white."

Because white students are so reluctant to see and hear the lived realities of racism, we challenge them to interact with course texts that provide accounts that cannot be denied. Then, in our teaching, we ask them to quote from the text, point to important passages, discuss key concepts, and put ideas into conversation with ideas from other texts, so that they cannot avoid the perspectives shared. In Michael's class, students are asked to note passages from the text that provided them with "aha" moments (that is, passages that provided insight or elicited strong agreement), "uh-uh" moments (that is, passages that elicited strong disagreement), and "huh?" moments (that is, passages that were confusing). These collected segments of text can then serve as the departure point for large- or small-group discussion. Such practices may seem corny to students but they provide a structure for how they can begin to interact with the text and each other.

Despite spending time carefully considering text selection, we still sometimes wonder privately, and now publicly, about the implications of these choices. We ask ourselves: How does teaching in this setting compel me to change the way that I teach? How has anticipating students' resistance to course concepts shaped my pedagogy? Finally, an important question for each of us remains: What strategies might I explore if students' resistance was not one of my core pedagogical preoccupations?

One major difference between Michael and Eve concerns the degree to which students are encouraged to interpret course material through the lens of their personal experiences in our classes. In one introductory course that we both teach, Michael takes an inward-out approach, while Eve takes an outward-in approach. That is, Michael's version of the course asks students to begin with their own biases and assumptions (what might be thought of as a psychology-based approach) in order to build a social analysis. Reflecting on the sites of recognition in and (dis)connections with the text becomes instrumental in shining light onto previously unexplored blind spots in students' consciousness. Further, an assumption is made that the thorough and critical exploration of the biases, beliefs, and expectations of the other can lead to insight that may subsequently influence professional and personal behavior. Eve's version of the same course invites students to study racism as a social phenomenon, to identify it "out there" (what might be thought of as a sociological approach), and then eventually to reflect on personal biases and assumptions "in here."

These different approaches have, along with differing results, yielded much discussion and insight. Each approach has accompanying benefits and challenges. The dependence on students' willingness and ability to draw connections from the text to their lives can be frustrating—especially in instances when Michael feels that the students are able but unwilling. When it all comes together, however, the results can be transcendent. In some ways, the differences reflect our professional training but also our personalities and interests. More than anything, we have found value in the opportunities we have had to peer over each other's pedagogical fences and trade recipes for helping young educators to develop more critical habits of mind. We still sometimes wonder privately, and now publicly, how effective each approach is in interrupting white supremacy and decentering whiteness, and how one approach might help to refine the other.

Another difference between our approaches concerns how much of ourselves we disclose in class. We each wonder, as (sometimes) the only nonwhite person in the class, Is my life another text? Sometimes Eve comes out of her classes feeling like she has given too much of herself away, whereas Michael is more willing to make his experiences an open book. There are certainly benefits to this form of disclosure in class. Being willing to openly share related life experiences and reactions to the text can help to make this form of text engagement normative in the class. If we presuppose that we have chosen readings that are both provocative and evocative, we would not be immune to experiencing something personally, emotionally, psychologically, or intellectually in the process of reading a text and preparing to teach the class. For Michael, sharing these insights and moments of recognition in the text serves as symbolic gestures of his investment in participating in the group process, similar to the way he is asking his students to participate. Along the way, he hopes that he is also modeling the ways in which we actively engage texts to make text-to-text, text-to-self, and text-to-life connections. Also present in this form of engagement is the assumption that students can think critically about the negative space created when they lack direct lived experience with concepts presented in the text. That is, a student who never directly experienced the more oppressive consequences of racism might reflect instead about the meaning that can derived by examining a life lived in the absence of such a reality.

On the other hand, doing the work of decentering whiteness as faculty of color can make all parties feel more vulnerable—the degree to which we truly are more vulnerable is another question. In part, this is because theorizing race and whiteness "stabilizes identity for those who impose it and those who work to expose it" (Holland 2012, 6). That is, when we enter into conversations on race and whiteness with students, our own racial identities are immediately on display and on the table for discussion—whether that discussion takes place in class and in real time, after class walking back to the dorms, or on our teaching evaluations. To be sure, understanding that the bare representation of our cultural selves in the way that we talk about race and respond to students is never far from our consciousness. What is less clear, sometimes, is students' understandings that the ways in which they engage in the discourse is also culturally determined and certainly not race neutral. Their experiences of privilege, power, and oppression inform the lenses through which they interpret the course texts and the manner in which they (dis)engage with the course discourse.

There is also the inherent vulnerability that comes with offering a piece of our personal lives in a setting where we cannot be certain how that offering will be received. Although the risk and opportunities to disclose personal encounters with racism will on some level always be there, we still sometimes wonder privately, and now publicly, about some of the following things: How will the narratives Michael shares about his race and culture be deconstructed and cross-examined? Will students experience him as being the "angry black man," for instance, who incorrectly sees race and racism in everything? Perhaps, most important, will his lived experience be invalidated once it is offered for public consumption?

Despite efforts to decenter whiteness in our courses and provide alternate interpretive frameworks and other counternarratives, there are inevitable instances during a semester when students either will consciously reassert the dominant paradigm as the proper and preferred way to interpret race and racism or, in some other manner, reveal just how difficult it is to untangle the intellectual and psychoemotional knots that prevent them from making room for a new perspective. In such cases, instructors have to make strategic decisions about how to address issues in a different way.

Regularly presenting course material that interrupts common popular narratives on race and racism elicits a range of responses from students. Discussing texts in class, students often remark about the "aha" moments that they experience as an author presents an idea or way of looking at an idea that is altogether novel. At other times, students remark about the ways in which an author offered language to something they felt in the past but did not have the words to express—the insight that was hiding in plain sight. Frequently, though, we also have to manage the resistance that comes with presenting ideas that create an uncomfortable cognitive dissonance as students are challenged to reconcile our texts' discussions of race, privilege, and oppression with a lived experience that has, in many ways, sheltered them from having to do such critical self-reflection. To reconcile this cognitive dissonance, we see students deploy a range of psychological and emotional strategies. A potentially useful conceptual framework for understanding student resistance, in this context, might focus on the active and passive dimensions of their responses to course material.

We have identified some ways in which students demonstrate active, passive, and, even, actively passive forms of resistance in our classes. Active resistance to course material is a fairly self-evident concept, in practice. It can be seen in the most overt, explicit, conscious attempts to oppose, circumvent, or derail meaningful exploration of course material. In time, one begins to understand when reasonable student questions about a reading have turned into a more entrenched exchange, disputing either the merit or the content of a text. Sometimes active resistance is expressed by devaluing and disrespecting the author ("This reading was dumb . . .") and other times with annoyance at the discussion of race ("Are we still talking about race?"). When active resisters are in the class, they can be toxic to the safe and thoughtful classroom learning environment that instructors are attempting to cultivate. Active resisters have a way of silencing other students, slowing creative and critical momentum, or reducing the likelihood that others will take risks in the classroom.

Although active resistance happens from time to time, we find that it is a more rare occurrence in most of our undergraduate and graduate classes. After describing the course expectations during our first meeting and delving into race and racism headlong in the second meeting, Michael lets students know that this is what is typical for this course over the semester. If the course is not what students thought or hoped it would be, he will happily sign a drop or withdrawal form so they can find a course that is a better fit. Should they decide to stay in the course, however, he lets them know that he expects committed engagement in the material. There are typically at least a couple of people who, at that point, choose to withdraw from the class. The conscious and explicit choice to withdraw from the class is preferred to withdrawing consciously and explicitly within the class.

The failure to see a large proportion of active resisters in this class might also have something to do with the current way in which racism is manifested in our present society. For the most part, people are no longer allowed to participate in mainstream society and openly make racially disparaging comments. As we understand contemporary expressions of racism, "racism a.) is more likely than ever to be disguised and covert and b.) has evolved from the 'old fashioned' form, in which overt racial hatred and bigotry is consciously and publicly displayed, to a more ambiguous and nebulous form that is more difficult to identify and acknowledge" (Sue et al. 2007, 272). This "more ambiguous and nebulous" form of racism also reduces opportunities for students to practice a more uncritical form of race consciousness. To resist actively in a way that draws attention to oneself as someone who "has a problem with diversity" contradicts the postracial color-blind narrative and experience of self that many students claim at the beginning of the semester. To resist this work, yet not draw explicit attention to oneself, requires another tactic: passive resistance.

Passive resistance, by definition, is necessarily a more subtle, implicit, and, perhaps, even less conscious response to interactions with course material that challenges one's beliefs and questions one's worldview. We might see passive resistance in superficial engagement with course materials and activities, as well as in the more critical and reflective course elements—even when engaged directly. This is not to suggest that every student who chooses not to participate in large-group discussions is practicing passive resistance. In every class, there may be numerous students who are fully engaged intellectually but experience anxiety about speaking in front of the entire class. Often, these students can be very active and productive participants when offered the opportunity to share their reactions in small groups. Instead, when we refer to passive resistance, we are referring to students who have a repeatedly conspicuous lack of opinion—in large groups and in small groups and even when they are engaged directly by the instructor.

The primary identifying feature of the passive resister is silence. There is silence in their (lack of) contributions to large- and small-group discussion, relative silence when they are asked to discuss and share with a partner, and limited response when they are directly addressed by the professor.

Their heavy silence seems more an enduring "trait" than a transient reaction (Yalom 2005). Michael identified with Ladson-Billings (1996) when she stated, "In the past, I had not considered my students' silences to be acts of resistance or defiance (although I have witnessed silences used as powerful weapons of young children in inner city classrooms). Often, I interpreted [the silence] as the appropriate response to their lack of knowledge about particular subjects" (80). In the absence of student contributions, he sometimes felt compelled to make up the difference by filling the void with his own stories, opinions, and interpretations of text. Reflecting on his frustration one semester, he began to think more about what the students were saying in their silences. Attempting to fade into the background by minimally participating in the public forum of the course (passive resistance) can, in some ways, be seen as a by-product of one's having previously participated in a color-blind cultural ideology and finding that this ideology leaves one ill prepared to participate meaningfully in a more critical discourse about the actual lived experience of race for oneself and others. Lewis (2008) notes, "For many of us, lacking the language to talk about confusions concerning race and its meaning in our lives, any discussion of race becomes dangerous territory—we worry about making a mistake, saying the wrong thing, being 'misinterpreted' as racist" (76).

A class with multiple passive resisters can have dire consequences for faculty who teach these courses. Faculty members may find themselves in the curious position of responding (or failing to respond) to the mixed messages communicated by the students.

> In those classes where teachers depend on hearing what students are thinking and feeling, the silence can inhibit growth and understanding. This use of silence can result in miscommunication. When students do not raise questions or challenge ideas, teachers can be led to believe that there is agreement and common understanding about what is being read and discussed. (Ladson-Billings 1996, 82–83)

Hearing no questions or objections, an instructor may assume that the class is on the same page and continue moving in the wrong direction. Worse yet, the silence that was held may turn into a loud retributive evaluation at the end of the course when a conversation might have helped things along the way—a particularly precarious outcome for untenured faculty members who participate in this work. Viewing silence as a form of passive resistance to engagement has created an impetus in each of us to explore and to actively respond to it more directly in class. Working to understand silence within the dynamics of the classroom may prove effective in improving participation.

Silence can be used as a way for one to defend oneself, but it can also be used to declare disengagement and disapproval. This active resistance, even if it is silent, is a more offensive weapon, a wanton disengagement or declarative gesture that seems to say, "I'm not going to learn from you and you can't make me." Ladson-Billings (1996) makes a similar observation, "I have seen students decide not to learn as an act of defiance against the teacher. This refusal to talk is often the only way a child has to fight against the authority and power of adults"—though in this context we are not talking about adults who have a deeper cache of communication skills than children (82).

Reflecting on instances when we have felt that students were flaunting their disengagement from the course, presumably in response to the instructor or the course material, it called to mind what might be the clearest illustration (and subversion) of Kohl's (1994) distinction between a failure to learn and choosing to not-learn. "Failure is characterized by the frustrated will to know, whereas not-learning involves the will to refuse knowledge. Failure results from a mismatch between what the learner wants to do and is able to do" (6). In this context, there are times when a student's frustration or misunderstanding of a text seems to be more about the student's a priori rejection of the content and decision not to expend the cognitive resources necessary to engage fully with it.

We can recall asking students what they thought about a reading and being met with the reply "I don't know. I didn't get it." "OK," Eve might respond, "What didn't you 'get' about it? Point us to a passage. We'll figure this thing out together." Silence. Then, "I don't know. The reading was just hard. I didn't like it and don't get it." Are the readings challenging? Sometimes, but certainly not above the reading level of undergraduate and graduate students. Are the readings boring and unevocative? Their authors certainly have a perspective that one can disagree or agree with; we do not think there is a reading in the lot about which a student would have absolutely no opinion. Instead, reading these encounters as sites of resistance, we view such instances as students' making an active decision to disengage from learning: a willed choice to do nothing to interact with ideas that might challenge or clarify one's worldview. Herbert Kohl's (1994) work tells us that

> learning how to not-learn is an intellectual and social challenge; sometimes you have to work very hard at it. It consists of an active, often ingenious, willful rejection of even the most compassionate and well-designed teaching. . . . Deciding to actively not-learn something involves closing off part of oneself and limiting one's experience. It can require actively refusing to pay attention, acting dumb, scrambling one's thoughts, and overriding curiosity. (2, 4)

The willed choice to be a flagrantly passive participant can be identified in practice. "I realize that many youngsters who ask impertinent questions, listen to their teachers in order to contradict them, and do not take homework or tests seriously are practiced not-learners. The quiet not-learners sit sullenly in class, daydreaming and shutting out the sound of their teachers' voice" (28).

This choice to participate in silent active resistance may be an ego defense against a perceived attack on something that is very precious and fundamental: one's worldview. Sometimes, there is a paradigm-shifting moment when such an individual makes room for new ideas and welcomes a new way to see a world that was hiding in plain sight. For others, the reaction is to retreat and disengage, perhaps, because the implications are too difficult to face directly. Given such a choice, one might see a student choose to participate in active passive resistance and to reject the competing worldview, thereby keeping the previously more comfortable worldview intact. That is,

> not-learning tends to take place when someone has to deal with unavoidable challenges to her or his personal and family loyalties, integrity, and identity. In such situations there are forced choices and no apparent middle ground. To agree to learn from a stranger who does not respect your integrity causes a major loss of self. The only alternative is to not-learn and reject the stranger's world. (6)

CONCLUSION: CAN WE REALLY TALK ABOUT RACE?

In a recent book, Beverly Tatum (2007) explores the question, Can we talk about race? Unpacking this question leads Tatum to ask other related questions about our society's collective will and preparation to engage in such a discourse. Can we talk about race and racism critically, honestly, and comprehensively so that we may better understand how the dynamics of this social institution influences our lived experience? Tatum asks, "Can we get beyond the fear, our sweaty palms, or anxiety about saying the wrong thing, or the wrong words, and have an honest conversation about racial issues? What does it mean in our personal and professional lives when we can't" (xiii)? For us as faculty of color who teach courses about race and racism at a predominantly white institution, these very fundamental questions constitute critical tensions in our pedagogical principles and essential elements grounding that which we ask of our students (and ourselves). Reflecting on the ideas presented in this essay and this essential question, the answer is "Yes, we can talk about race . . . but it's complicated."

This answer is intended to draw attention to the interactions between personal, institutional, and cultural factors that make talking about race challenging personally, and complicated professionally. In the personal domain, we might assume that the politics of identity contribute to the (un)conscious assumptions and expectations about the "other," influence our interpersonal interactions, and inform the narratives we construct to interpret our experiences. In our classroom contexts, we might assume that students' reactions to and interactions with us, in some measure, are mediated by the glut of cultural messages about young black men or the dearth of experiences with Native American individuals. Without personal experience, some scholars suggest, individuals default to representations to fill memetic space of the other (Thompson 1996). Often these popular representations present unsophisticated notions of its subject, a matter exacerbated by the limited range of representations of people of color in popular culture, literature, curricula, and other media. In many instances, our students report that we are, if not the first teacher of color they have experienced, certainly one of a small handful. In short, sometimes the degree to which we can talk about race in class is complicated by students' assumptions, expectations, and relative (dis)comfort with people of color.

Personal identity factors complicate the degree to which we can talk about race in a second important way. For us as faculty members of color, engaging the topic of race and racism with predominantly white classes, it would be naive to assume that our races are neutrally evaluated by students. That is, one might wonder about the degree to which being a black professor inhibits (or facilitates) the conversations about race. To what extent do the stereotype-ridden or uninformed perspectives about Indigenous peoples shape students' impressions of class material? In the subject matter we cover, all things can never be equal, but we still wonder, How would the contours of the conversation change if a white colleague were similarly engaging the class in the very same conversation? Exploring this very notion directly in class, Michael has found that students will sometimes sheepishly acknowledge the discomfort of being asked by their black professor to take risks and delve honestly into the issues. In Eve's experience, students from the same class have chastised her on course evaluations for connecting course ideas to issues of Native identity both too frequently and too infrequently. Talking about race is already an anxiety-provoking endeavor, according to these students, without the additional concern of, perhaps, (un)consciously offending the very individual who has the power to determine their grade.

One of the biggest cultural components complicating our capacity to engage in critical conversations about race is the pervasiveness of the *color-blind narrative* with which many students enter our courses. The color-blind narrative is a default position for many, and interrogating this ideology is often a precondition for having an authentic conversation about the ways race and racism interact with power, privilege, and oppression. Oddly enough, participation in a discourse about racism while adhering to the rules of color-blind ideology is a peculiar paradox necessitating talking about *racism* but not really talking about *race*, acknowledging that racists are "*out there*" but not "*in here*," or being comfortable talking about racism as something that *happened* but not something that is currently *happening*.

The degree to which we can really talk about race is certainly complicated by institutional factors. For instance, the (un)spoken value placed on diversity is important. Are courses on topics like race and racism experienced by students as outside the *real curricula* or are these courses represented as central to disciplinary and global understandings? In education, where the teacher population is predominantly white, monolingual, middle class, and female, at the same time as the student population grows increasingly culturally and linguistically diverse, programs wrestle with the uneasy tensions between using a sole *diversity course* to train teachers, infusing the *diversity content* throughout the program, or some combination of the two. That said, the implicit messages about the place and value of such courses seem to influence students' expectations about course content and rigor, and the degree to which they enter these curricular spaces ready and willing to fully engage the material. Administrators play a vital role in ensuring that the stated value for diversity in marketing and accreditation literature is also plainly evident in the ways in which degree programs and general education requirements reflect diversity content. This cannot be a value that is fought for primarily by faculty of color and a few white allies. Collective effort, buttressed by individuals with power and access, is needed to create and sustain systemic change.

Institutionally, we can talk about race if we establish and adhere to some common understandings. Without this set of understandings, authentic, critical, and useful conversations devolve into hollow platitudes about our common goodness and humanity while never addressing the far trickier spaces involving the ways in which race is used to divide, privilege, and oppress. Singleton and Linton (2006) attempt to provide individuals who would do this work with "four agreements" necessary for participation in "courageous conversations about race." They suggest that participants in such conversations agree to (1) "stay engaged" in the conversation, (2) recognize that there will be moments in which they will "experience discomfort," (3) "speak [their] truth" and honor others' truths, and (4) expect and accept that such conversations may not end with "closure" (58). Michael uses these four agreements as a departure point for establishing ground rules for how his class will talk about race and racism over the course of the semester. Sometimes students will add other agreements to the list such as "keep an open mind," "ask questions when confused instead of making assumptions," and "be aware of your assumptions." As with most principles based on ideals, however, these four agreements and our class addenda are well intentioned but hard to maintain continually throughout the course of a full semester when the persistent topic of each class meeting presents perspectives that challenge the dominant worldview many students bring to class with them. Intellectual and psychological persistence, as well as unflinching honesty, are required to do this work.

Critical conversations about race that occur in (racially) *mixed* company appear to be fairly rare in our students' daily lives. Although the demographics of our university would suggest that there is a diverse student body, our students' lived experience of this diversity suggests a far more segregated experience. In their personal lives, the experience of social self-segregation seems to be fairly high. Not having meaningful engagement with people from different backgrounds in less socially charged circumstances raises the psychological stakes when one is asked to talk about race in mixed company in class. Indeed, some students have reported that while a racially diverse class offers an opportunity to hear multiple perspectives, it also creates an anxiety about stepping on an invisible mine of racism.

Administrators might consider more critically the lived experience of the persons who embody the demographic data used to extol the virtues of the diversity on campuses. Assuming the validity of Allport's (1954) contact hypothesis—that interpersonal contact is the best way to reduce prejudice between minority and majority groups that are in conflict—(and we do believe in the validity of the hypothesis), we would add that mere proximity to difference does not ensure a meaningfully integrated experience. Crucial to Allport's hypothesis is the phrase "under appropriate conditions." And we would describe such conditions as those with power and authority using their responsibility to structure opportunities that facilitate more meaningful interactions between groups. We can certainly participate in this task within the sphere of influence of our classrooms; clearly this is a value at the center of our personal and professional lives. We call on administrators to support these efforts within their spheres of influence.

At the intersection of myriad interconnections between our social identities and those of our students lies an important question: How do we prepare course curricula that explores race and racism comprehensively and critically for an audience that (a) has not thought about the function of racism in their lived experiences with much depth, (b) has not developed the habits of mind to understand many of the fundamental issues, (c) holds and maintains unsophisticated schema for race and racism, and (d) has uncritically ingested popular cultural postracial notions? That is, how do we have conversations about race knowing that a key conceptual component of such a discourse (i.e., understanding the role of whiteness in dominance, power, and privilege) directly challenges the lived experience, dominant world-view, and cultural narrative that many students bring to class with them? We know how *we* will continue working in this direction; the question we ask ourselves and each other privately, and now publicly, is, What will others do to join us in this work?

2 ◆ IS THERE A SILVER LINING?

The Experiences of a Black Female Teaching Assistant

DELA KUSI-APPOUH

My skin color was not a criterion for being selected as a teaching assistant (TA) for the course Race and Public Policy. The White female professor who taught the course had worked with two other TAs before me: a White female from California and a Filipina. Nevertheless, race became central to my experiences as a TA in spring and fall 2009. While I carried my experiences with me and casually contemplated them, it was not until I participated in a fellowship program for future faculty that I discovered the challenges faced by all female faculty of color, particularly those in predominantly White institutions (PWIs). In this essay, I draw upon existing literature as I reflect on, narrate, and place my experiences in context.

Patricia Hill Collins (1990), an eminent scholar and pioneer of Black feminist thought, encourages African American women to respect their subjective and specialized knowledge. This includes the process of consciously making of our experiences a narrative, or *narrativizing* personal experiences, allowing us to know, construct, and understand the reality of the world we live in (Munro 1998; Polkinghorne 1995). Kishimoto and Mwangi (2009) further explain that narrativizing involves analysis, self-reflexivity, and making judgments. Narrativizing, therefore, represents a critical means through which to reveal the oft-ignored complexities of women faculty of color and their (re)actions. The body of research on the teaching experiences of women of color in predominantly White institutions of higher learning has grown over the years, yet these experiences have not fed into mainstream feminist pedagogy. What research does exist points to the fact that the challenges women instructors of color encounter in the classroom result from the unique intersections of characteristics such as gender, race, personal history, course content, and pedagogy (Niemann 2012; Sampaio 2006; Brown, Cervero, and Johnson-Bailey 2000; hooks 1994). Furthermore, the instructor's characteristics are amplified by students' own sensibilities, especially since for many of them, this is their first time taking a course in which they engage in a scientific inquiry of subjects such as race (Sampaio 2006).

The Race and Public Policy course is generally offered every other semester to third-year students and examines social inequalities in the United States through a historical lens and explores the role of public policies in amplifying or redressing these inequalities. I applied for a TA position to the Department of Policy Analysis and Management for fall 2009. I was offered the position after the professor reviewed my application and deemed me a good fit based on our overlapping research interests and academic disciplines. Prior to the beginning of the course, the professor and I spent a few days discussing the topics covered in the syllabus as well as her assigned readings and assignments. She explained that the course usually attracted students studying in policy analysis, education, and sociology, many of whom aspired to law careers. Less common were students in engineering and the biological sciences. The professor explained that discussion would be accommodated in class, and I would be expected to prepare for and coordinate review sessions for the midterm and final exams.

The professor had been trained in sociology and demography, and her course design emphasized a pedagogical approach whereby students were encouraged to engage in open discussion, based on the reading materials, following class lecture. The students' learning experience was enriched by their completing five major assignments: an autobiographical essay on personal racial/ethnic identity; a reflection on social position and situational access to power and privilege; and a three-part assignment using state-level demographic data to analyze race/ethnicity/nativity, residential segregation, and educational attainment patterns.

Several of the students had never taken a class that focused entirely on theories of and evidence about race and ethnicity in the context of the United States, race as a social construct, racial identities, and the impact of immigration on racial interactions. Even fewer had been presented with critical analyses of the institutionalization of race through policies—or what Omi and Winant (1994) call racial projects—such as affirmative action, blockbusting, and residential redlining. A pivotal moment for the majority of students—regardless of background—came from their reading Peggy McIntosh's "White Privilege: Unpacking the Invisible Knapsack" (2003) in the first week of class. The article garnered fiery reactions that led me to believe that students would benefit from separate discussion sessions to unpack the contents of the reading(s).

By default, my most engaging interactions with students occurred during the scheduled midterm and final review sessions, during which I aimed to create a safe space for discussion. Feminist pedagogy suggests that safe classroom spaces are created by the instructor, where no one voice dominates, and where students are encouraged to find their voices (Lee and Johnson-Bailey 2004; hooks 1994). The scholarship of Maher and Tetreault (1993) guided much of my thinking. With voice, those in the classroom are able to represent their own interests and speak for themselves. My main goal during these review sessions, therefore, was not only to review the course material thoroughly but also to create a classroom environment in which students could feel comfortable enough to reflect openly on what they were learning and to have voice. The extent to which voice carries in the classroom, however, is related to one's position in it. The latter highlights the concept of *positionality*, which recognizes that people's backgrounds and identities may be fluid and informed by relations and context. In the classroom, identities such as age, race, ethnicity, gender, class, physical ability, sexual orientation, religion, and social status are reinforced by the positionality of both the instructor and the students (Lee and Johnson-Bailey 2004; Brown, Cervero, and Johnson-Bailey 2000). As such, the level of intellectual engagement and dialogue can be affected by the positionality of the instructor and the composition of the class (Maher and Tetreault 1993; Brown, Cervero, and Johnson-Bailey 2000). The fall 2009 class comprised students from varied racial and ethnic backgrounds. The first assignment also revealed multiple descriptors that students used: first generation college educated, of first- and second-generation African or Caribbean origin, working class, and upper middle class. Depending on the topic under discussion, students tended to form alliances across socioeconomic backgrounds and racial/ethnic identities.

A series of events underscore why and how my positionality—as a TA as well as a young, Black, able, and straight female—affected dialogue and interactions. Despite my attempts to foster an interactive environment, I quickly realized that most students talked directly to me, rather than to each other. I found myself having to disclose parts of my personal history, serving to validate my experiences as a Black person in America as well as my ability to speak from a scholarly and objective perspective. In their autoethnographic critique of safety in feminist pedagogy, Kishimoto and Mwangi (2009) describe how by being confronted with hostile and skeptical academic climates in a predominantly White institution, they continually felt the need to justify and defend themselves and often felt that disclosing their personal lives was inevitable. Whereas Mwangi (a professor of African origin) associates self-disclosure with authenticating her presence in the classroom, Kishimoto (an American-born Asian) explains how using self-disclosure and intentional humor helps ensure that students do not question her qualifications for teaching about people of color in the United States (Kishimoto and Mwangi 2009). In my case, I discussed how my identity as an African and subsequent racial identity as a Black person had been challenged numerous times during my college years in the majority-Black city of Atlanta, Georgia. Because of the curious looks and sometimes direct questions, I also disclosed how and why I became a sociologist interested in studying race as well how I "ended up" at an Ivy League institution. The irony of these disclosures and justifications is that pursuing graduate education at highly ranked academic institutions met the *least* of my African family's (and perhaps even societal) expectations. Meanwhile, I had slowly come to find that in the United States, a Black graduate student at an Ivy League institution was even less expected. I felt that I had to bare my soul to get students to trust my abilities and qualifications. Nevertheless, disclosing these experiences prompted some students to start sharing their own.

As I posed course material review questions to the class, some students answered them with a delicately placed "right?" at the end of their responses. It appeared to me that the students were trying to figure out where I stood on issues of race. It seemed these students were less interested in discussing their honest reactions to the readings and more interested in answering the question to please my convictions, which in their mistaken opinion would then lead to a favorable grade. Several students assumed that disagreeing with my views would affect their grade more than if they presented a convincing argument reflecting a mastery of the class readings.

Students were able to talk to each other during discussions on how their varied trajectories had led them all to the same institution of higher learning; they quickly learned, however, that they faced remarkably different experiences based on their social position. Such instances generated rich discussions about privilege, access, and inequality among the majority of students. A heated discussion in class had ensued when a White male student expressed dismay at a Black student's "taking his spot" at another university, leaving him no option but to attend Cornell University. His comment divided the class, but not necessarily across racial lines. I called on a Black female who had grown up in a well-to-do family in a wealthy neighborhood to contribute to the discussion. "Clearly, I don't agree with what he said. I have my opinions, but I'd rather not offend anyone," she stated. I explained that she could discuss her opinions without having to offend anyone, to which she responded, "I feel that people wouldn't understand where I am coming from . . . not even you." During a one-on-one meeting, this student explained to me that she had yet to meet other Black students who opposed affirmative action and she assumed the same applied to me "as a person, but not as a TA."

While I had spent hours structuring the review session in ways that would help students articulate the connection between the theories and empirical evidence in their own words, I felt that my teaching abilities and ability to be objective were under scrutiny. Such scrutiny may be explained by results from a survey and focus group conducted in a university setting, which revealed that a substantial proportion of college students believe that "professors teaching subjects that directly reflected their race or gender are more biased and less likely to teach objectively" (Sampaio 2006, 919). Johnson-Bailey and Cervero (1998) affirm that for women of color, positionality forces these women into daily negotiations in which their White counterparts, both male and female, are much less likely to engage.

The credibility of women faculty of color is frequently questioned (Brown, Cervero, and Johnson-Bailey 2000; Johnson-Bailey and Cervero 1998). Given that students in predominantly White institutions are seldom taught by women faculty of color, many students do not see them as capable of generating or producing knowledge (Lee and Johnson-Bailey 2004). The resistance I encountered when I introduced new information made it clear that some students questioned my credibility. Indeed, when I discussed the projected shift in racial/ethnic demographics and that by the year 2050, African American, Asian American, and Latino students would constitute approximately 57 percent of all U.S. students, I received some blank stares and puzzled looks. One White student blurted out, with much skepticism, "We didn't talk about that in lecture, did we?" to which a Black female retorted: "Yeah, but it's still relevant to what we are talking about here." I then smiled and asked the class to contemplate how this "majority minority" demographic shift (U.S. Census Bureau, 2008) could affect the issues we had been discussing thus far. Some students view the classroom as a space for faculty of color to perpetuate their personal (Kishimoto and Mwangi 2009) or political agenda (Lazos 2012), rather than as space in which racial and gender issues can be addressed as legitimate areas of study. Juanita Johnson-Bailey, an African American professor, explains how she is often faced with students who confuse her critique of Whiteness, the ideology of white supremacy, and her examination of oppression with a hatred of Whites, particularly White males (Lee and Johnson-Bailey 2004). Reflecting on this exchange after the session, it occurred to me that some students either perceived my additional information beyond the scope of the readings as having a hidden motive or didn't consider it valid because it didn't come from the professor. Or both. From talking with my immediate predecessor, it was clear that as TAs we shared similar problems regarding student work and complaints, but she could not relate to the implicit interrogation that I felt. I didn't have anyone with a similar background with whom to compare notes or commiserate over these teaching experiences, but I did have several opportunities to share them with the professor, who had a keen appreciation of the underlying meanings I was drawing from these classroom experiences.

Related to credibility is authority. Over the course of both semesters, I distinctly remember three cases in which I felt that my authority in the classroom was undermined. Three students demanded to know why they received lower-than-expected grades and the criteria for my grading rubric. In all three situations, the low grades were because the students did not sufficiently demonstrate their understanding of the assignment and lacked critical analyses. In my correspondence with all students, but especially those who were sure they deserved more merit, I felt the constant need to be strategic in how I responded to them, especially when e-mailing them or writing comments on their work. I was careful to use well-constructed sentences and avoided any colloquialisms or mundane language, for fear of being misconstrued or taken out of context. In one of the three cases, a White female student registered her dissatisfaction by contacting the professor directly. After reading the assignment, the professor pointed to several shortcomings and delivered her verdict: she would have given an even lower grade. It may be that many students are fixated on getting the highest grades and meeting graduation requirements, but contacting the professor directly to complain about my grading style was for me an overt interrogation of my authority as well as an affront to my competence in assigning grades that fairly reflect the quality of work submitted. Such presumed incompetence has been documented as part of the daily experience of women faculty of color (Lazos 2012).

Fortunately, not all issues of credibility and authority are undermining or require the baring of souls. As a female African American postsecondary mathematics instructor describes, "As far as my own race is concerned, I think they admire the way I present myself in the classroom, being of the Black race" (Brown, Cervero, and Johnson-Bailey 2000, 281). On his way out of the final review session, a White student thanked me for being a great TA and concluded, "I am sure it was not easy teaching this kind of stuff." After everyone left, a Black female student added, "I am in the sciences, so I usually don't see Black TAs and even fewer Black female TAs. I liked the way you handled the affirmative action discussion. I usually get so mad when it comes up, but you kept us on task. I think it's good that you are the TA for this class." Similarly, a White female student expressed out loud that she liked the way I organized the final exam review session and felt more comfortable talking about these "difficult topics" with me. Her comment generated agreement among some students, when a Latina student explained, "It helps that you are a TA *and* a person of color. *Plus* you know your stuff, you know?" Several students nodded enthusiastically.

After the first semester of being a TA for this class, I was left with mixed feelings and unsettled questions about the weight of my positionality on the types of interactions I had with students. It was unusual for the course to be taught two semesters in a row, but being offered the TA position again for the next semester represented an opportunity to try things differently. Now that I was more familiar with the course material, I proposed to the professor that we include a voluntary weekly discussion section as well as an ongoing group project. I felt it was important to help students address issues of power and structural inequalities that they likely took for granted, or had never needed to confront. Perhaps if students knew each other better through their group work, they could engage in these conversations earlier on in the semester. I also hoped that the weekly discussions would serve as a space for collective debriefing and self-reflection for those who wanted it. The professor for the class responded positively and these changes were implemented.

The second time around proved positive on multiple levels. First, since opportunities for dialogue were spread out over the semester and students got to familiarize themselves with each other, discussion sections engendered an even more enriching learning environment for the students and for me. Second, the following semester's class included more Asian Americans, athletes, sorority sisters, and middle- to upper-class students from minority communities. As with the previous semester, however, it was some students' first time engaging in analytical inquiries about race and related policies. They also struggled to articulate their relationships with privilege and access and their reactions towards structural inequality. Also similar were the students' perceptions of me as a TA and the importance they attached to my race. A Korean American student expressed that it made sense to her that I would be the TA for this class because I was probably "more familiar with this kind of material." A Black female student confided that once she realized that I (and not the White professor) was grading the homework, she was more open about her feelings towards group positioning, residential segregation, and how long-standing policies had negatively affected neighborhoods like the one she currently lived in.

The impact of the course appears to have had long-lasting effects. To date, the professor and I have received requests for recommendation letters from past students as well as e-mails about the transformative nature of the course and their experiences during and after the course. One student from fall 2009 wrote to say that he had recently been appointed as the director of employment equity programs and affirmative action plans at a large research university. He also stated that what he learned from the course had shaped his outlook and that he was grateful for the opportunity to "freely make contributions during the course." He described the course as "definitely illuminating."

My experiences as a Black TA for a course on race and public policy, with a racially, ethnically, and socioeconomically diverse set of students have been well informed by the literature on the experiences of women faculty of color. Finding similarities in their experiences helped to contextualize and validate my own. What I did not expect, however, was the profound effect that describing and reflecting on my experiences would have on me. The process of narrativizing and meaning-making was as cathartic as it was burdensome. Still, these experiences are only a precursor to the many challenges encountered by women faculty of color, challenges that include the structural impediments maintained within the academy (Niemann 2012; Johnson-Bailey and Lee 2005). Indeed, as several of my graduate school colleagues enter the tenure process and confront its challenges, I ponder the experiences they are having as minorities among minorities: They teach courses with an explicit focus on race, gender, or both; they sometimes face harsh classroom environments, harassment, and negative course evaluations; they encounter insensitive or unresponsive university administrations; and they attempt to use pedagogies that may marginalize their own lived experiences. These realities hit me while I contemplate becoming a professor. Then I remember that the majority of my colleagues are still at it, sharing stories of resilience and overcoming challenges. I hope it means that this cloud has a silver lining.

3 ◆ RADICAL LEFTIST OR OBJECTIVE PRACTITIONER?

Perceptions of a Black Male Professor

H. MARK ELLIS

As an African American male teaching sociology at a predominantly white state university for the past eighteen years, I have experienced a wide range of reactions to my presence as a professor and person of color. While many of my encounters and interactions both in and out of the classroom have been rewarding, some have not. Sociologists question social arrangements and examine privilege, power, and the practice of social justice and equality. When engaging students in this mission, I reflect on who I am as a sociologist and person, who others think I am, who they would like me to be, or who they think I should be in these learning moments.

As a professor tasked with helping students build a better world, I experience tension between maintaining an optimistic attitude in the classroom while being viewed as "a problem." This, of course, makes reference to W.E.B. DuBois's famous rhetorical question with which each Black American must wrestle, "How does it feel to be a problem?" Do I enter the classroom with the mindset that I am indeed a problem, or do I reject those historical pathologies and projections? Reject them as I might, there is no avoiding the fact that some of my students automatically read me as militant, radical, incompetent, or antiwhite; this is the inescapable issue I must navigate. As administrators, faculty, and graduate students read these reflective testimonials derived from my teaching experiences, I hope they consider seriously what it might mean that (1) faculty on their campuses may be considered problems simply because they are persons of color and (2) persons of color, and other previously excluded groups, may perceive some institutions of higher education as antebellum plantations, with prescribed roles and intransigent inequality.

My pedagogical delivery, course content, references, and presentation of objective data have been greeted with resistance, suspicion, doubt, and shock by many, respected by some, and viewed as transformative by others. Is this range of responses indicative of anyone teaching any behavioral science or is it reserved for just professors of color? Perhaps it is both.

In this essay, I share accounts of how race and identity politics—my own and those of my students'—are mediated by empirical evidence, subjective evaluations, objective data, and critical analyses. I have chosen examples of how the presentation of high-affect material interacts with race and plays out in the classroom. I examine how messages, messengers, and message receivers exchange and acquire knowledge. While many faculty members see the mission and role of the social sciences as potentially transformative, messengers of transformation can also be viewed with contempt, moral objection, and resistance. I close by offering theoretical solutions on how intellectual roadblocks can be removed by suggesting phenomenological approaches to examining commonalities in the shared human experience.

First, we need to understand how students in general and especially majority students perceive the role(s) of the college professor in the classroom. These perceptions often act as barriers of resistance to critical exploration in social science courses. Students must first understand the three primary intellectual burdens in social sciences: (1) to gather empirical data through observation (what people *do*), (2) to explain their behavior (*why* people do what they do), and (3) to predict social behavior (*when* and *how* might people behave under *which conditions*). Many students resist hard evidence whether it be from the Bureau of Labor Statistics, the Bureau of the Census, Uniform Crime Reports, the Gini index, or the Centers for Disease Control on how the historical evolution of systemic oppression and the disenfranchisement of marginalized people are produced and maintained.

The reasons behind students' rejections of objective facts are at least twofold. First, many students see the presentation of such data as evidence of what their parents or talk radio might refer to as a leftist agenda. Their perceptions of how I perform and present race, ethnicity, and gender identity politics interacts with the ideas they arrive with when the class begins, and I am often construed as antiwhite. Female colleagues assure me that this is also true for them; their performance of gender interacts with ideas about women with which students arrive, and they are often construed as anti-male. Many students filter the race, ethnicity, sex, or social class of their professors before they consider the material being presented. Do their professors who are different from them have a hidden agenda? Are they credible purveyors of knowledge? Is this professor coming from a nefarious place with the mission of demonizing white people? Some students see these data as corrupt and reinterpret them through lenses of suspicion that focus on me rather than the facts.

On the other hand, when some of my white male colleagues present the same data and concepts their students view them as inspirational professors and awesome presenters of eye-opening objective facts. I recall a comment on a student evaluation from a course I taught on the sociology of police work in which the student said, "The professor spends way too much time on race issues. What does race even have to do with police work?" Connecting intellectual information takes time and open minds. While the many working-class students at the university where I teach may not always have the same level of academic preparation as do middle-class students, they are nonetheless just as capable of connecting the dots. It is one of the rewards of teaching—to be present the moment they begin to see the larger picture and begin to see structured inequality. Compared with their more affluent counterparts, they are less invested in avoiding an investigation of systems of privilege.

The second reason why some students reject objective findings is that they may see their own subject positions in these data and see where they personally sit in relationship to power and privilege. Some may feel that I am blaming them personally for the past. Despite my efforts to interpret data by offering multiple theoretical frameworks, examining not only individual behaviors but also macro forces, some students see me as a moral engineer trying to influence how they think about, see, and act in the world. As for the accusation of moral engineering, changes in values and belief systems may occur during the learning process, and I have no direct control over that transformation. I can't change someone in a fifteen-week semester. I can model for them critical thinking, offer them analytical tools, and provide evidence with which to understand the world better. I am unapologetic if students leave my courses and become change agents for the social betterment of all.

Discussing and learning about difficult and sensitive social issues is not always easy but they remain a necessary piece of our broader cultural conversation. Day one of my Sociology of Police Work course, I had twenty-five white male students who were also pursuing a concentration in criminal justice. I asked them to write down on a note card five reasons why they or someone they knew would want to go into law enforcement. The first and second reasons on *every* note card I collected were (1) "I can carry a gun" and (2) "I can kill someone with a gun." I immediately redesigned that course the same night when I went home and had to rethink what it might mean to them that I am Black and not a police officer. More important, I knew that I had to put race, class, gender, and history at the core of this course. These are categories of human existence that we all share but that are not neutral identity markers and are difficult to discuss. As difficult as these conversations are, students need to know how these categories affect crime, victimization, the prison state, and judicial outcomes. Prisons represent varied social concepts, including prisons as gender-policing institutions; students need to know why men of color are disproportionately incarcerated compared with white men and women in general. (For an excellent discussion of the role that prisons play in social inequality, see Michelle Alexander's [2012] *The New Jim Crow: Mass Incarceration in the Age of Colorblindness.*)

After presenting feminist theories that shed light on the sexism inherent in capitalism, imperialism, and colonialism and on the social construction of identity, in an interesting twist, I have been accused of being racist and of spending too much time on such race and gender issues. When we discuss racial, gender, and sexual orientation integration in the U.S. military, we examine historical events and how policies on unit integration are formed. Again, my students have said I am spending too much time on irrelevant issues. After discussing organizational accountability and oversight in the military, I ask students how police hold themselves accountable. I ask them how the military does this. What happens when a male member of the armed services sexually assaults a female service member? I have them examine organizational practices and in the end, some students ask me, "What does this have to do with criminal justice?" A well-designed liberal education is supposed to facilitate an answer to that question or at minimum allow students to see the relevance of this line of intellectual inquiry.

Throughout the years teaching at my current institution, students have articulated some of the following comments during in-class discussions: "Obama is president; there is no more racism . . . We now live in a postracial society . . . Our generation didn't cause slavery . . . No one in 2014 should have to pay for slavery . . . Slavery was in the past and if you don't make it today, it's because you are not trying hard enough . . . Stop harping on the past. It has nothing to do with how things work now . . . The Trayvon Martin and George Zimmerman case was an isolated incident. Besides, George Zimmerman is a White Latino and most violent crimes are Black on Black or minority on minority . . . Blacks disproportionately commit more crimes than Whites . . . Whites are not the problem . . . White-collar crimes are not as bad as violent crimes and they don't affect anyone but the individual who commits the crime . . . Women have equal rights . . . Hillary Clinton was secretary of state and so was Madeleine Albright and Condoleezza Rice. [In fact, some think that the secretary of state is the unofficial female position in the president's cabinet.] . . . Sarah Palin ran for vice president . . . Anyone can achieve what he or she wants to and there is no more discrimination . . . If Black women learned to close their legs and didn't have corrupt morals, they wouldn't be eating out of my back pocket . . . It's sad when a government rewards such careless behavior . . . What do you mean, there is no hierarchy of oppression? Of course the Holocaust was worse than slavery. What? Do you also have a problem with Jews too? . . . and, Stop blaming us [I assume they mean white people] for the past . . ."

Many white students see my lectures and discussions as personal attacks at some point during the semester. I try to look beyond the claims and ask myself how they may view my personal positions on these matters. I want them to examine these types of issues as rigorously and critically as possible, and I wonder if they are able to do so in the classes of my white colleagues and if they make these same kinds of comments. I also wonder if they ask their white professors the questions that I have been asked: "Do you have your doctorate? Is your doctorate real? Where did you go to school? Is that graduate program even ranked?"

Our discussions of privilege, power, and social class are neither linear nor simple issues. When thinking and designing my courses, I ask: (1) What questions or set of issues, ideas, arguments, agreements or disagreements in the field am I addressing in this course? (2) How are those issues related to other courses of study or other ways of knowing? (3) What do I want my students to know and be able to do when they leave my course? The simple answer is, I want my students to be able to discern between fact, fiction, and opinion; to be able to present an argument, draw sound conclusions, consider the unknown, think of ways these issues can be solved or resolved. If they question my competency even to lead this discussion, I worry that we will never approach my learning goals for them. I do not want my presence to be an impediment to their success, yet I suspect that my presence—if they accept it—probably offers different ways of approaching evidence.

We want our students to question facts and be able to draw valid conclusions based on objective evidence. Two plus two will always equal four. But an African American male running down the street at 2 A.M. equals what? The facts are not in dispute, but the conclusions drawn can be varied and need to be understood in situational contexts. There are as many ways to interpret behavior as there are to arrive at the number four. It is this sort of intellectual stretching in which I want my students to engage while in my courses. My challenge is to focus on the relationship between theory and data, but I am certain that much of my students' focus is on how to avoid the wrath of "the angry Black professor who is out to get white students" (as I have been described in my teaching evaluations), and I am constantly working to reframe that focus.

For some students this is the first time that they are being taught by an African American male teacher. A student once wrote on my teaching evaluation that it was her first time having a Black teacher and that she was "pleasantly surprised" that I was so "smart and articulate." She went on to admit that she could not hear a word I said for the first few weeks in the semester because what was coming out of my mouth didn't match what she expected to hear from a Black person. For those students who experience this type of cognitive dissonance, they do not necessarily reject the messages and facts because *I* am Black; rather *their* stereotypes about Black intellectual inferiority profoundly limit their ability to hear and see the material I'm teaching. Once they have processed all their assumptions about me, they then have to grapple with the material.

A White female student once told me during office hours that she never knew that there were so many Black and Latino/Latina students in the sociology major, a fact that became clear to her once she began to take upper-level courses in the major. I asked her what sense she made of that observation. She thought at first it was because the minimum GPA for graduation for this major was not as high as for others. Her next thought was in distinction to the first and she went on to say that the issues in sociology are issues to which she could not personally relate and that the minority students seemed to have an advantage in this respect. And, she continued, while it pained her to learn about societal organization and its inequality, she was nonetheless glad to be majoring in sociology because she wanted to make a difference.

While this student came from an economically advantaged background, many white students in this state university are not economically privileged and do not feel as if they have power. Some students begin to listen when they see themselves in what we are studying. On average, white students are better able to process social class than they are race. I have also noted that white females process gender first, then social class, and then race. I am careful to present comparative data for them to see how race, class, and gender are interrelated. You may be White, but if you are also from a working-class family and the first generation in your family to attend college, you may have insights that others lack when we discuss wealth distribution and life chances.

Although I try to present an accurate view of who cuts the American pie and how big the pieces are for different groups, if I mention Blacks and Latinos more than once during a semester, many White students perceive the course as being too much about racism. I show students how these issues are found in our daily encounters at work, at school, at home, with friends, and all the way down to the racist packaging on the most popular brands of pancake syrup, frozen waffles, and rice we buy and eat, to the sexist campaign that manipulates us to buy our clothing. Each individual lecture needs to pose a question that anticipates the conclusion of the syllogism. I wonder whether a critical mass of professors of color would keep students from being distracted from the work of understanding the myths of racial incompetence and inferiority (when they fear their professors of color are incompetent and inferior). On the other hand, I wonder whether white faculty might be more successful in communicating some of these materials to both majority and minority students. I invite the reader to ask him- or herself: Who is best suited to teach this material and why? What are the latent consequences of staffing these courses with persons who occupy subaltern social positions? One solution that has its dangers would be to teach high-affect material in online courses where all parties do not have to encounter face-to-face comments and reactions in real time. But we must ask ourselves, What happens to presence, voice, mutuality, and affect when lectures and discussions move online? The pros and cons of these issues are addressed in my research on teaching sociology in online learning environments (Ellis, forthcoming).

Many students of this generation see comfort as a right of the college experience, are as adept at online games as reading, and have led overscheduled lives. They also, therefore, may expect to be entertained more than did their counterparts from previous generations. I have observed when some of my students felt discomfort in the discovery of new facts or were required to become active learners, the blame for their discomfort is ascribed not to the facts or to the style of pedagogy, but to the messenger. When the focus is on minorities and not on people in control and in power, some students feel more at ease. In a society rife with narratives of individual responsibility, personal blame, and personal triumph, explanations make students feel comfortable. For example, when I ask, "Why do Black and Latino students drop out of college?" some of the White students are quick to offer a long list of personal-blame explanations. When I rephrase the question as "Why aren't historically White institutions able to retain Black and Latino students?" they have a more difficult time answering the question. The idea that there are causes above and beyond individuals (what sociologists refer to as social structure) usually eludes them. Other such questions I ask include: Why are there so few African Americans in professional classical music? Is the Summer Olympics for people of color and the Winter Olympics for white people? Is there a difference if we ask, "How many women were raped and assaulted last year?" as opposed to, "How many men raped and assaulted women last year?" Talking about privilege, power, and issues that are "personal or private" silences some students but allows others to join the conversation. No matter how much data I provide, some students do indeed leave my courses unable or unwilling to see social patterns for a variety of reasons.

My colleagues and I ask our students to become temporary strangers in worlds that are familiar to us but unfamiliar to them while they are taking our courses. This consideration includes having students walk in the shoes of others. My focus in this essay has been on majority students, and in my experience many of them feel guilty for histories that were out of their control. It is a challenge to move them beyond feelings of guilt to an appreciation of the circumstances that have led to and continue to reinforce modern-day structured inequality.

While these discussions are a part of understanding complex social arrangements, I do present white ethnic immigration history in terms of systematic sociopolitical exclusion from the American way of life. In that discussion, students learn that all groups have experienced discrimination, and we need to understand how some racial and ethnic groups have overcome the denial of full participation in the American Dream, while other racial, ethnic, gender, religious, and sexual orientation groups have not achieved similar levels of opportunity, access, and equality. When I discuss marriage equality and same-sex rights, many of my African American students tune out and do not want to hear or have this conversation. They are more comfortable discussing racial, class, and gender discrimination, but same-sex rights issues are fraught. During one class discussion an African American male student said, "I can understand equal rights for African Americans and I suppose some more equal rights for women, but not for same sex. It's a matter of self-control and weakness. You don't have to submit to those desires. You can choose. What comes next, allowing people the right to marry their pets?" I try to explain to my students that, as a culture, we have defined the worth of a person's life in our policies, laws, and practices and how a person is (re-)presented in our culture. Some majority students begin to see shared historical struggles of ethnic whites and people of color, and for others, it might take them longer to understand and make these connections. Some students have both eyes on me throughout the entire semester because they have to watch this radical Black professor who "hates" white people and is ultraliberal. When I move on to gender-related issues, some women momentarily join me and lift their veil of suspicion; however, the White males further disengage with these sets of conversations. To them, I am not only anti-White, but I am anti-White male specifically. The question is, Is it that I am a Black male professor or is it how I/we teach and present race, class, gender, and other interlocking systems of oppression?

In our daily encounters and interactions, do we first see and process a person's race, gender, age, ethnicity, religion, social class, and perceived sexual orientation or do we simply see the totality of a person? What is most salient about the people with whom we interact? The categories for our interactions are pre-scripted and encoded in our cultural ways of doing things and in our language. Is my dentist a female? Is the college president a woman? Perhaps when minorities occupy those positions that have previously only been occupied by white males, their race or gender becomes noteworthy. Did people refer to President Bill Clinton as our 42nd White male president? When students describe their professors do they say, "I'm taking Econ with the White guy"? However, when they describe me, *race* and *sex* are usually two of the descriptors they use. Course titles and departments seem to announce or suggest an agenda to some students. It's a course in women and gender studies, a course in sociology, a course on sex equity and gender politics, a course on social stratification; therefore these courses must have a subjective agenda. Rather than title a course Race, Class and Gender, why not name it Human Intercultural Relations? Students might sign up for the latter where an apparent agenda is not implied by the course title. This becomes a real issue in terms of course registration, if departments can survive in terms of majors and last-minute course cancellations and with departments that are forced to compete for students becoming majors, taking general education courses, students selecting minors, double majors, and students taking free electives. Some of this also becomes disciplinary turf wars in which the collegiality of the conversation is undermined as faculty are pitted against each other to argue about which courses are most important for students. We plant ideas. Where these seeds end up may be well beyond our observation and arrive in a different time and place.

Here is some advice for faculty colleagues: Establish clear course objectives and student learning outcomes on your syllabi. Make sure that your syllabi have clear classroom norms, including rules about classroom discussions, talking, electronic devices, attendance, etiquette, and academic integrity. In the biological and natural sciences, once a class completes a lab experiment, there are protocols for disposing of hazardous materials. In the social sciences, we do not have the same luxury. We stir up all kinds of social toxins, bring students face-to-face with societal ills, and students have to just walk away from classes with these issues still running in their heads and attached to their hearts. We don't have incinerators to dispose of these ideas that can affect students on many levels when they leave our classes. We want our students to be able to hear these messages and ideas and to be able to process data and discuss ideas. The learning environment must be inclusive, where the professor's voice is as important as the students' voices, the texts, and the films. The professor voice unites with the student voice along with the voices of the text to create the voice of collective understanding. No one voice should be more important than another. We currently offer language tables in our cafeterias; perhaps more colleges and universities should offer similar out-of-class spaces in the residence halls or cafeterias to continue the conversations begun in our classrooms. These would be difficult to join for returning adult learners who are not able to participate as fully in residential life, but it's worth thinking carefully about. The use of online discussion boards is another approach that can be explored to present and discuss contentious and high-affect material. A downside to online discussions is that prejudice and stereotypes are not being necessarily minimized.

If I were to offer advice to colleagues on how best to maximize critical engagement in the classroom, it would be to create learning spaces that are intellectually malleable, supportive, and guided by facts, mutual respect, and a mission to consider social betterment for all. I would never tell my colleagues how to teach hot-button issues; each of us walks in his or her own shoes and has his or her own realities and experiences. Whether we present race, class, and gender as separate ideas or as interlocking systems of domination, we are faced with the uphill challenge of making sense of social structures. Perhaps rather than focus on our differences and how otherness is socially constructed, we could focus on our similarities through a phenomenological approach. Rather than point out differences based on these polarizing and dichotomous distinctions that are often binary, oppositional, and unequal, perhaps we should focus on shared lived experiences in terms of work, possessions, our bodies, our thoughts, and our voices. Why do we say, "Good morning, ladies and gentlemen. Welcome to Principles of Sociology"? Why that binary and unequal descriptor? Why not "Good morning, students"? We want our students to examine our world and problematize the mundane and what seems obvious. Ultimately, we want them to take these ideas and see how the world could be better organized. The pedagogical insights and tools in my teaching arsenal did not develop overnight. As a graduate student at an elite, private, Big Ten university in the Midwest, I had the opportunity and privilege to participate in and be a program assistant on the Preparing Future Faculty grant funded by the Pew Charitable Trusts. This allowed graduate students in physics, chemistry, biology, history, English, and sociology from our PhD-granting institution to work with four area colleges and universities, which included an elite small liberal arts college, a comprehensive state university, a predominantly first-generation and African American–serving university with many single mothers, and a two-year junior college. Graduate students from these six departments had the opportunity to work with and shadow faculty in the four types of institutions and to learn what it is like to be a professor in terms of classroom expectations, faculty research, and the challenges of service and committee assignments each kind of school required. What was eye-opening for me was to learn that I have to develop multiple scripts to deliver the same material to different audiences. We know that even when we teach two sections of the same course at the same institution, each class is different. You must know when showing a documentary, on a particular issue, made by someone with different attributes from yours is more effective than your giving a lecture on that topic. I have learned how showing useful documentaries such as *Killing Us Softly: Advertising's Image of Women* based on a lecture by Jean Kilbourne (Lazarus et al., 1979, updated through 2010) on how women in advertising are depicted is extremely successful along with showing *True Colors* with Diane Sawyer (1991) on how race works in American society or Lee Mun Wah's documentary *The Color of Fear* (1994) on how men of color talk about race and the American identity or Jackson Katz's and Sut Jhally's *Tough Guise* (1999), which addresses the connection between masculinity and violence in the male social script. I use many similar documentaries, excerpts from popular films, YouTube video clips, poems, census data, and the like to help me tell these stories and to present these ideas so that students can see others who look just like them asking the same questions and grappling with these issues.

Just as I have recognized that I am not nor should I feel I am the sole messenger to students, no one should feel that they have to play this role or shoulder this burden alone. You can find support and validation by incorporating effective material and multiple perspectives into your courses. You should also feel free to use multiple modes of delivery, including debate; presentations; guest lectures; writing on the board; handouts; small groups; inviting students to join you in the presentation of tables, charts, and graphs; video projects; journaling; ten-second summaries; and questions at the end of each class. These have been effective ways to help students see themselves as co-creators of the learning experience.

I have gathered and developed these types of teaching resources and ideas through participating in campus workshops on race, class, and gender, on teaching excellence and writing across the curriculum, and on our online course management system. My message to administrators is that campuses need centers and resources for both junior and senior faculty so that we can continue to learn from one another. Faculty need time and support not only to attend conferences on their scholarship but also to attend trainings and institutes to explore pedagogies that are relevant to students' lives.

Our students are not blank slates. They come to us with lived experiences, their own realities, understandings of the world and notions of how it works, and often a defensive posture to protect themselves when they feel attacked or vulnerable. We have to give them time to process new ideas that are introduced during class discussions and lectures. Many times, they feel put on the spot and that they are being watched by their classmates and the professor. When you pose a question to an online class, students have a few days or hours to think about their responses; this is not true in face-to-face classes. Even if you give students a few days to prepare for an in-class discussion, we are asking them to engage in high-stakes discussion topics. For some, they have no problem telling the professor what they think, especially if they feel that the professor is attacking them, blaming them or people like them, denigrating a student, or trying to manipulate them into accepting a particular belief. My challenge is to provide an environment where students can understand how social systems work; how individuals navigate in those systems; how power, wealth, and prestige work and are distributed; and what all this means for the quality of life for all.

4 ♦ TEACHING DIFFERENCE IN MULTIPLE WAYS

Through Content and Presence

CHERYL JONES-WALKER

This autoethnography is focused on my experience teaching two courses, ones that present unique cases through which to examine my role as a teacher of color at a small predominately white liberal arts college. The terms *diversity, difference,* or *examinations of social inequality* are not mentioned in the title of the core introductory course for the department, although these are some of the key themes. Introduction to Education is a collaboratively designed course that has nearly identical class readings and assignments in the two or three sections offered each semester. The second, a course on urban education, is one that I have taught at the college twice independently, and I also cotaught with a white male colleague who like myself was a junior faculty member at the time. Teaching the same course material as that of my white colleagues, and having different interactions with students related to intersections of race, gender, and class, is fertile ground on which to examine how teacher identity informs classroom processes. Similarly, coteaching a course that explicitly takes up unequal educational opportunities, the role of race/racism, nationality, language, and class in American schooling yielded compelling narratives about difference.

The cultural accounting of the relationship between my students and me aids in my meaning making and in the identification of future instructional adjustments. At the same time, the questions raised are central to my main research interests: (1) developing better theoretical frameworks with which to understand identity construction in the context of classrooms and (2) creating safe spaces in educational contexts to expand identities and explore social inequity.

Having been trained in majority white institutions similar to the college where I teach, I find that there is much about being in these settings and negotiating my identity as a black middle-class woman that is second nature to me. Also, my philosophy of teaching and learning is my touchstone when I design curriculum, plan class, and structure a learning environment so that there is a productive space that will foster honest and challenging discussions. While I study the influence of race/ethnicity, class, and gender in education, there are so many incidents that go unexamined in the day-to-day life of a college—particularly when it comes to interactions within the classroom. The method of autoethnography is defined by Tami Spry (2001) as a "self-narrative that critiques the situatedness of the self with others in social contexts." This autoethnography provides me with an opportunity to explore how students understand my goals, my expectations, and the content of the course and how this may be influenced by my social identities, specifically my race.

MY BODY CHANGES EVERYTHING

During the second year in which I offered the introductory level course, I realized that students experienced the class differently because of my background and identity. The introductory course has a common syllabus with variations in some readings and activities, depending on the instructor. The course enrolls more than half of students who graduate, so the class ranges in terms of departmental majors and class years.

"Intro" has the reputation among students for being both rigorous and illuminating. Students often report that the class changed not only how they looked at schooling and education but also how they viewed the social and political structures within the United States. For example, one student reported, "I can't begin to say how this class has opened my eyes, both personally and in terms of how I think about education" (course evaluation, December 2009). Our department aims to have the course taught by our core faculty, although occasionally adjuncts will teach it. Educational

Studies had an all-white faculty until I joined the department a few years ago, so as I write this (2010), it is fair to say that I am the only person of color who consistently has taught the Intro Education course. Many students perceive my white colleagues as progressive and committed to changing social inequality. A number of indicators led me to imagine a stark difference between these categorizations and the way I was perceived. While presenting the same material, my white colleagues could be seen as crusaders for justice and I, perhaps not by the majority but by a handful of students, as an angry black woman who was constantly forcing them to confront their privilege and their participation in systems of inequality.

INTRODUCTION TO EDUCATION, WEEK 2: A VIGNETTE

During the second week of the course (September 2009), I challenged students' use of the term *low-tiered* schools. An article we read that week by Jean Anyon (1980) identified four categories of schools, with two named as "working-class schools" (71), Students quickly substituted the phrase *low-tiered schools* for *working class* and used language that might suggest that the individuals who attended these institutions were less able, less worthy, and less competent. This perspective runs counter to Anyon's central theoretical point that school curriculum, activities, and culture are dictated by the social class of the community and "knowledge and skill that will lead to social power and reward are . . . withheld from the working classes" (67). I made an on-the-spot decision to employ a strategy I have borrowed from facilitating diversity work with adults—if someone says something that offends, the offended person can say "ouch." During this conversation, I took the opportunity to introduce the "ouch" rule. As class continued, there were many questions, and I soon realized that students assumed that I had encouraged them to rethink their use of the phrase because I must have been personally offended. I deduced that they also assumed I had attended schools that could be classified as low tiered. I was peppered with questions from students (one in particular) about the type of secondary school, college, and graduate school I attended and also those that were attended by my parents and siblings! I chose to answer, although I could have (and possibly should have) probed to get underneath their questions and refocus our discussion on the texts at hand. Part of the reason I addressed the questions was because I knew that my responses would play against their expectations. Subconsciously I also might have wanted to demonstrate my elite educational background (to borrow Anyon's terms) to win their confidence, but I felt certain that students did not expect that my parents would have attended Mount Holyoke College and Boston University in the 1950s. They were not sure what to think when I told them that my five sisters and two brothers attended Dartmouth, Wesleyan, Princeton, Yale, Brown, and Boston Universities for their bachelor degrees and Harvard, Princeton, and Berkeley for graduate degrees. When I left class that day I did not know what to think, but I felt very uncomfortable because I was not certain what had transpired. Also, while I think it is important for me to acknowledge my class privilege, I was worried that I unconsciously wielded it in order to combat racial stereotypes.

When I had a moment to reflect on this exchange, I began to assume that some students were demanding to know how I had arrived to teach at this selective institution and if I was in fact smart enough to teach them. As Roxanna Harlow (2003) argues, "Black professors' identity performances may involve providing 'proof' in any number of ways to justify their presence in a high-status position" (350). There is no question that my choice to challenge students in the second week of class, during what was for many of them their first semester at the college, contributed to a tension that became palpable. Perhaps I made a poor pedagogical choice because I did not take the analytic categories presented by Anyon and place them more explicitly within the frame of her larger argument. Students' questioning of my formative experiences and of educational background (and credentials) and those of my family may have had nothing to do with my age, gender, race, or class status, as my previous experiences in the world would lead me to believe.

My colleagues might rightfully say that students' questions were the result of my response in the moment or how I introduced the class material. While there are multiple meanings we can derive from any one event (Gee 2005), what is of interest here is how my students and I (independently) constructed meanings related to our social identities. The crux of the narrative is that my experience teaching about race, gender, class, and power in educational contexts while being a person of color has very particular ramifications: (1) how and what students learn from the course content and (2) how I am viewed and evaluated. Ultimately, I want to take stock of such classroom exchanges and my student comments and feedback in order to develop a deeper understanding of these interactions.

NAMING DIFFERENCE: A VIGNETTE

It was the first time I was teaching Urban Education at the college, and I had a fairly large and diverse group of students. I felt the class discussions were sometimes stilted and at other times volatile and I assumed that many of the students had not found their voice in the classroom space. There was a handful of very strong students who remained silent and I heard reports of a group of students of color who were so angered by statements of their student colleagues that they debriefed for hours each Monday after class. During the midsemester break, I talked with a colleague about the tenor of the class and she recommended an article by Elizabeth Ellsworth (1989), "Why Doesn't This Feel Empowering?" I decide to add the article to the syllabus, and to have students discuss it in affinity groups (race/culture, home language, class/first-generation college). They selected an identification that was most salient to them, at least for this conversation, and were given a few guiding questions to discuss. My goal was to talk with students about how using affinity groups within the space of the class felt and how it informed their learning. (I also had intended to capture the different foci of conversation of each group and how the themes differed by group but time did not allow for this part of the activity.) What I learned was that students of color were excited by their conversation and the opportunity to talk with students who were like them in one significant way. A student shared that it allowed her to voice things that she may not have ever surfaced in other small-group or whole-class discussions. Many of the white students felt just the opposite; they expressed discomfort and stated that they saw little value in such an activity. One student said that she preferred having a diverse set of voices to help her think more broadly about the material. This issue is raised in the following section; what is valuable for majority students may come at the price of not adding value or meeting the needs of students of color. And what is valuable for students of color will probably not harm and may even help majority students.

The article and the activity were informative for a number of reasons: the article for its content and the activity for what it revealed about our classroom processes. The article provided us with a common definition of *critical pedagogy*—a movement designed to create political consciousness as well as an important critique of the method related to authority, voice, and the impartiality of knowledge. The text also allowed us to read about another college class that had a similar focus and makeup. In Urban Education, we had talked extensively about how to provide equal access to quality education to all students and the issues this raises for K–12 public systems. One student captured the key themes for the first half of our class as "race, class, messages students receive through their classrooms [and] their communities, differential treatment of students [and] the underlying causes of this treatment" (midterm feedback, 2009). We had also talked about the benefits and disadvantages to remedies that relied on integrating schools to improve educational options.

What we learned firsthand from our class exercise was that the more diverse the group of students, the more varied the student experiences; therefore, students needed (and required) different things within the space of the classroom. For example, there are ways that integration and color-blind polices in higher education privilege white students and disadvantage students of color. Susan Sanchez-Casal and Amie MacDonald (2009) argue that often "underrepresented minority students are construed as 'cultural ambassadors' who provide white students with valuable knowledge about racial and cultural 'others'" (13). These authors point out that in higher education we often focus on how white students can benefit from more diverse contexts in and outside the classroom and we lose sight of how the intellectual needs of students of color are met. A black female first-generation college student in the class was aware of this dynamic and felt that it was an impediment to her learning. She wrote, "I think there are two levels of discussion in this class: (1) people struggling/adapting to the paradigm shift that removes whiteness from [the] center of discussion [and] (2) people who are really trying to grapple with urban education [issues]." She suggested that I work toward challenging and engaging learners in the second group and prioritizing their growth while allowing the students who were struggling with their voice or experience being decentered to work through these issues without getting in the way of other students.

Herein lies the key challenge for educators: how do you do all this at once? Certainly we can't privilege one group of learners over the other, but perhaps some of the needs and expectations students bring because of privileges they have been afforded throughout their educational experiences should not be attended to in the same way. Some white students and students of color want and expect minority faculty to be radical and to disrupt their fellow students' ideas about the course content and the world. It is a tightrope that we walk because we have to approach competing demands and at the same time weigh how our instructional decisions will affect assessments for tenure and promotion. One student wrote, "It is really intimidating to speak about such loaded and controversial topics in a relatively large group, so I think that there are a lot of students with good ideas who aren't speaking up because of that" (student midterm feedback, 2009). As an educator, I believe it is critical to decrease this feeling of intimidation and that it is incumbent upon me as a facilitator to surface a wide variety of voices. This feedback read alongside the comment that "some people, especially white people, are afraid to speak their minds because they want to be 'PC' and are scared of offending others" (midterm feedback, 2009) raises questions about power and privilege that as a black female professor I need to address carefully. Many students suggested that I needed to be a better facilitator, needed to increase the level of trust, needed to make people feel more comfortable. And while I take these assessments to heart, it felt as though my ability to accomplish these tasks was compromised because students with different backgrounds wanted different, and often opposing, things from me. This dynamic is documented by the following observation: "The minority teaching in predominately white colleges and universities may find herself confronting a hotbed of white student hostility, and on the other hand, the expectation, on the part of minority students, that she show her allegiance to students of color by putting white students on the defensive" (Sanchez-Casal and MacDonald 2009, 25). The diversity in the room and my presence as a minority faculty led both white students and students of color to be critical in ways that may not be experienced by my white colleagues.

SAME TOPIC, DIFFERENT PLAYERS

Because of our experience negotiating all the needs and expectations of learners in Urban Education in previous semesters and feeling that the classes never met their full potential, the colleague with whom I would coteach the course in fall 2009 decided to begin the course by naming explicitly the challenges the previous group of students had experienced. It was a heavy introduction, and because students didn't know us, or one another, they stared at the floor in silence. Later in the semester, we chuckled about these introductory remarks and wondered if it was even necessary given the group we met that September day. There were a number of key differences in the class this time around: first, I cotaught it with a white male faculty member; second, it was a smaller group—twelve as opposed to twenty-three students; and third, there were only three students of color, compared with ten the semester before.

My colleague and I spent countless hours revising the syllabus, designing each class period, and scaffolding every student assignment. Students were appreciative of the coherence and organization this brought and made statements such as this: "I felt that [the professors] definitely played off each other's strengths in terms of areas of expertise and experience. They were always prepared and well organized" (course evaluation, fall 2009). Coteaching requires that your goals are explicit because if they do not make sense to your colleague, they will not make sense to students. Working with my colleague brought increased organization, clarity, and a different energy to the Urban Education course. The student feedback we received was completely different from my students' comments the previous semester, and I wondered if my status was elevated by the presence of a white male colleague. After reading my evaluations from the introductory course (and his feedback from the same course) side by side, I was led to believe that other factors were at play. For example, I think the size of the group and the lack of diversity in the course during the following semester made teaching the course completely different. In spring 2010, there was greater commonality among student experiences, and two of the three students of color were from families who had emigrated from Africa, which brought a very different perspective from that of American-born students of color.

While students expressed frustration with the ambiguity the class raised and the lack of clearly definable solutions to improving urban education in the

U.S. context, there was not the same amount of anger or silence. One student requested that my colleague and I focus more on closure at each class because, as she said, "this stuff is super upsetting" (course evaluation, fall 2009).

The fact that there were two of us and that we had different entry points into the field of urban education provided students with a model for how to engage in difficult discussions, how to disagree respectfully, and how to provide evidence to support your perspective. It also revealed how our identities might inform our positions, often in unpredictable ways. While we tended to agree on more issues than not, students somehow identified us as being on opposite sides of the issues embedded in our curriculum. One student wrote, "It was great to hear both sides of each issue. I found that my preconceived beliefs were frequently upended during class discussions" (course evaluation, fall 2009). While we did have intense debates during our planning time, I felt that few such displays were brought to class. Students, on the other hand, saw and appreciated the intensity and difference we brought to discussions as evidenced by the comment, "You both were extremely knowledgeable and threw down when you needed to." Interestingly, coteaching issues of race, class, gender, and structural inequalities with a white male colleague allowed me to take more nuanced positions on policy issues such as "teacher matching" (course evaluation, fall 2009). My colleague presented his point of view that white teachers in urban schools will never be positioned to be as effective as teachers of color. I countered with the fact that the teaching population in urban schools is largely white, middle class, and female and we should focus on what would make this group the most effective instructors for students in urban public schools. I wanted students to claim their whiteness but also to let go of this difference so they could focus more on what they needed to learn and understand to work in urban communities. He pushed students to consider teaching in the communities they came from and to think about how whiteness and teachers' backgrounds were likely to create barriers when teachers work in communities where racial minorities are in the majority.

It was clearly different for white students to be challenged about their social identity and position by a professor who shared that identity, so in some ways this teaching partnership made my role in the classroom less risky. I was not forced into a position of neutrality, because there was another body, a counter voice, and in this instance he was assuming a position that could be construed as more hard line than my own. I had to worry less about students' tendencies to assign a radical position to me simply because I am a faculty of color or, more understandably, to feel uncomfortable because my stance challenged their positionality. That being said, as I indicated at the start of this essay, the implications for my white male colleague being viewed as radical were very different from what it meant for me.

This coteaching experience makes me reflect on a study by Harlow (2003) that found that black professors work to prove their competence, while white male faculty tend to downplay their intellectualism in order to make themselves more approachable to students. So while I reactively played my cards (or credentials) when prodded by first-year students during the second week of Introduction to Education, my white male colleague would sometimes talk about attending a state college; he might neglect to mention the Ivy League institution from which he received his PhD. He presented this to me as an intentional choice because he rightly assumed that his race and gender led students to assume that he has always occupied privileged status, including attendance at elite institutions, which was not the case.

Students sometimes assume that I have a lived experience in urban communities or that I have faced the same kinds of conditions or hostile displays of racism as the youth that we study, and I have not. In this case, it may simply be my race that lends credibility to my authority rather than my years of work in urban schools or the fact that urban education and the construction of identities in these contexts are my main areas of research. For better or worse, one colleague commented about the number of black seniors who wanted to work with me on their thesis projects. She felt that, either purposefully or subconsciously, all the black students were assigned to me. I appreciated her willingness to raise explicitly an important (and loaded) departmental issue but it was complicated in this particular case because my research interests did align squarely with students' proposed topics.

POSSIBILITIES

In the way of an introduction, I pointed to the importance of a cultural accounting of the interaction between my students and me. I imagine that it will help me make sense of my work in the classroom and suspect that it will guide the pedagogical adjustments for courses in the future.

Given the research related to instruction about social inequity and studies about faculty of color at predominately white institutions, a tension arises for me. How do we appropriately read student interactions and student evaluation of our work when we understand them to be laden with power issues and occasionally to have undercurrents of racism, classism, and sexism? And for me, someone who argues about the centrality of student and teacher identities and interactions to the teaching and learning process, how could I possibly suggest that we dismiss or diminish the veracity of certain types of feedback because they might be tinged by racism or sexism? I must listen carefully and at the same time take into account that *specific* factors beyond my control play a role in how students experience my courses and this often connects to how my role, knowledge base, and authority as a young, female, junior faculty of color is viewed.

College teaching in general requires a significant amount of "emotional labor and management" because instructors are expected to suppress their emotions while evoking those of their students (Harlow 2003). This emotional labor is also affected by the content of what we teach, as well as the diversity of students and our positionality. As discussed, students of color may expect us to validate their voices and let their experiences stand on their own. These students may imagine that they have the status of expert because of their racial or cultural identity. I disrupt this stance because it is counter to my instructional goals and my understanding of identities, and how they operate. While I do not want underrepresented students to use their racial identity to discredit their white student colleagues, I do want to acknowledge how their lived experiences can be used to inform the conversation and to challenge commonsense understandings. While I want to be reflective and self-critical, I do not want to mistake all students' discomfort or their inability to find their voice as the limitations of my facilitation or the organization of the class but rather to make sense with students about how such feelings might be connected to a different framework, a diversity of voices represented in class readings and by classmates, and my presence as the primary voice of authority in the classroom.

RECOMMENDATIONS FOR POLICY AND PRACTICE

Faculty and staff members at colleges and universities must become educated about how various course content requires a different kind of teaching, affecting workload, student engagement, and how students evaluate their experiences and learning during the course. Additionally, faculty and staff need to understand that these factors inform the way that courses, and more important, individual instructors, are evaluated. As we move to diversify our faculties and transition members from junior ranks to tenured professors, we need to consider how one's status as minority faculty, and the likelihood of more student diversity in classes offered by underrepresented minority faculty, are likely to surface particular and subconscious biases on the part of students.

Finally, I note the work of Sanchez-Casal and MacDonald (2009), who present a critical access model in the introduction to *Identity in Education*. They define critical access as "creating academic worlds and campus communities that are responsive to the pervasiveness of white privilege and that transform all areas of educational life in ways that acknowledge, support, and develop the intellect and full humanity of students of color" (12). My autoethnographic account supports the need for such work for students *and* faculty. Minority faculty at predominately white institutions continually walk a tightrope, while our colleagues' feet might rest on more solid ground. In addition, the senior colleagues who evaluate us must understand that the stage on which we teach is different. Recognizing this should provide a safety net (institutional policies and resources) so that everyone can remain safe and members of the college community are afforded continual support in the practice of teaching under such challenging conditions. I would expect that, with the recognition of what is at stake, with policies that attend to the context and the needs of different communities, and with purposeful mentoring, faculty will more consistently meet success.

5 ◆ WHAT YOU MAY NOT SEE
The Oscillating Critique

PATO HEBERT

Teaching presented in isolation from student experience risks student detachment.

—Robert Boice

When thinking about writing for this collection, I was tempted to belabor something akin to "Greatest Hits of Institutional Alienation." I considered the ways I am most frequently constricted and contested, namely, through both tokenization *and* illegibility. I recalled representing one of the places where I have taught in very public, bilingual discussions of international community partnerships replete with press, consulate dignitaries, and potential donors. I also recalled that, immediately after the event, the white university president shook my hand vigorously and, perhaps overzealously, whispered job support that never materialized. Or the time a colleague of color glibly called me white in a meeting full of mostly white colleagues. Or the ignorance and the awkward tiptoeing around queerness and polysexuality, as potential colleagues try to glean from vitae, recent projects, or simple inflections what they may not legally ask during job interviews. Or countless times reminding well-established senior faculty and administrators what they have forgotten: that the cost of urban housing is exorbitant and the lack of start-up funds a genuine damper on the growth and practices, scholarly and artistic, of junior faculty. I could go on. And I know dozens of colleagues around the country who have their own far worse "Greatest Hits" battle scars.

Yet while I understand the utility of detailing and parsing such indignities, it seems less compelling than what I experience in the classroom with my students as we, together, try to confront the havoc wreaked by structural stigma, discrimination, and privilege. So I find myself wanting to reflect on my own challenges and breakthroughs with the limits of my understanding and behavior. I also want to write about the interplay between the creative process and the process of developing selves, between pedagogy and the spiritual questions that arise while trying to build community and criticality through diversity in the classroom. Our classrooms are not separate from our institutions, of course. But they are perhaps the place where we as teachers have the greatest say in what might go right and what might go terribly wrong in how our students experience the learning and growth that is ostensibly a major reason for them being in our presence.

As I assemble a collection of classroom anecdotes, I worry about reducing any of my students to a single subjectivity, and an overly reductive reading at that. I feel this concern even as I endeavor to open up a space where social inequality can be meaningfully examined and dismantled through art. So I hope to delve into the dissonance that can emerge amid discrimination, miscomprehension, or the sheer silence in our schools, along with the corresponding courage that so many of our students manifest in shaping and being their unique selves. In doing so, I suggest that diversity might be experienced not simply as disparate divergences but also as a series of interconnected convergences.

ONE, AN OTHER

Over the past fifteen years, I have taught studio art as an adjunct art professor at both a large public university and a private commercial design school, and have also twice served as a visiting assistant professor at small private liberal arts colleges. My photo courses have generally been designed to teach photographic methodologies and the creative process, not any specific overarching thematic content. Yet even in an introductory photography course where cultural and political diversity may not seem to be explicit themes or subjects, such issues will inevitably surface. Diversity is present in our conversations because diversity is present in our cultures and interactions. This diversity is dynamic, debated, and generative—a source of creative exchange and shared learning. Concerns pertaining to diversity are, in the end, about power, and we are everywhere presented with opportunities to abuse, contest, reshape, and share power. The photography classroom is no exception. Whose attitudes, resources, and priorities prevail? I have found that the in-class art critique is an invaluable space for exploring such questions.

Invariably, young people who are in the process of making art are also in the process of naming, discovering, adjusting, and making themselves anew. They do such acts of creation in relationship to their peers, their communities, and the broader world. Whether conceived as being in, of, for, against or as the world, students and their art must eventually contend with the political. This is true even when the political may not appear to be a primary motive, narrative, or material. As art critic and philosopher Boris Groys (2010) has noted, "Art and politics are connected in at least one fundamental respect: both are areas in which a struggle for recognition is being waged" (96). Art and politics are means to test our legibility, vitality, and viability—to ourselves, with one another, and in relation to institutions. One of the things a critical art classroom can do is help us to discern these concerns and our values, our impression of ourselves and that which makes us who we are.

I am thinking of we and selves in the most plural sense, an understanding that might be as polymorphic as it is collective. In his lithe and supple scholarship, ethnic studies professor Michael Hames-García (2011) asserts that identity is complex and relational, and always forged by what he calls multiplicity:

No one in U.S. society (or anywhere in the modern world, for that matter) ever exists without class, ethnicity, gender, or sexuality, and so forth, even if someone's class, ethnicity, gender or sexuality might be ambiguous, confusing, blurry and multiple, or might vary across different contexts and locations. . . . As a result, . . . social identities, within the context of the self, expand one another and mutually constitute each other's meanings. In other words, the subjective experience of any social identity always depends fundamentally on relations to other social identities (6).

It is vital for educators to nurture conversations that are mindful of these multiplicities that shape our students' lives. Sometimes we may approach such issues frontally and consistently in our curricula. Other times we may listen for the faint echoes or loud insistence of urgency in students' body language and comments. Frequently the exchanges first happen outside the classroom or creative arts lab—during office hours or advisement, over e-mail, in the hallway, or at departmental exhibition openings. Always, we must work to respond with sensitivity, candor, humility, and open-mindedness when students present these issues in their work and in the school context. Students crave so much more than approval. They seek connection, recognition, challenges, know-how, understanding, and the freedom to create. I fail them when I do not meet their needs for meaningful engagement and support.

Different students may need various kinds of backing. Some of my students get stopped en route to class by campus security and police who question them about their reason for being on campus. Some students are not welcome to bring their queer lovers home to meet family over holiday meals. Some students are made to feel particularly vulnerable because of their size, gender, age, or color and are extravigilant in their daily movements, especially when walking alone or at night. Some students cannot afford to buy books or film for homework assignments, let alone airline tickets for fun or "exotic" spring break vacations.

Such conditions of inequity are driven by differences in power and privilege, their abuses, and the ways in which social inequality is systematically reinforced and made to seem normal. Indeed some of my students can feel debilitated under the pressures of animosity and stigma. In addition to the usual questions regarding letters of recommendation and job prospects, or the weekly readings and art projects, my advisement sessions are filled with students of color strategizing against prejudice and loneliness, immigrants and international students grappling with the quirks of American culture and the complexities of multilingual learning, and folks transitioning and embracing their gender, questioning and asserting their sexuality, wrestling with class in all its precarity and exile, or privilege and betrayal. These are not merely matters of misperception or isolated occurrences. They are painfully real differences of lived experience and freedom in the world. How we conceive and enact our collective responses to these inequities will determine to what extent injustice will perniciously persist into the future, or steadily evolve into structures, understanding, and commitments that are emancipatory and shared. Part of my job is to support students as they cope with these forces while sculpting their own sense of self.

British curator Susan Bright (2010) has observed that "the author of a self-portrait is always presenting an impossible image, as he or she can never mimetically represent the physical reality that other people see. The 'self' therefore is always in some respects also an 'other'" (8). Bright's ideas may be helpful in thinking about the stories we tell ourselves about ourselves, and the stories we tell one another about others. To teach art is to work in the space that is created between one (self) and one another (group), thereby revealing: within one, an other. The significance we perceive, feel, and believe is often very real to us. But it may not always be in alignment with the perceptions, feelings, and beliefs of those with whom we share the world. In my introductory photography courses, I like to scrutinize these ideas with students by giving a self-portrait assignment that asks them to deepen their consideration of who they are and how they are each perceived by others.

Here is an abbreviated abstract of the assignment: "Create three self-portraits. You will present three prints based on the following guidelines: At least one print must involve photographing your own self/body. A second image must address (counter?) a misperception that people have of you. A third image must reveal something about you that people do not usually see." In addition to exposing notions of the self, the assignment is intended to accelerate and deepen the process of building our community of critical image-makers. It aims to do so by inviting us to reveal to one another more about our experiences, aspirations, limitations, and insights.

LISTENING TO OUR BODIES

The first part of the assignment asks students to make an image using their body. Few students use this assignment to share nude self-portraits. They mostly photograph themselves in portrait or repose, in the mirror or casting shadows, in abstract compositions of limbs akimbo or in unflattering and silly send-ups in their domestic interiors. The body is a primary object in these images and sometimes the subject, yet the sense of self usually gets revealed through incidental personal items like fashion preferences or posters on walls. Some students, however, do use the assignment as a way to deal directly with challenging issues related to their bodies and sense of self: eating disorders, body image and self-esteem, scars, abuse, medical history, desire, and sexuality. In her essay "Uncanny Likeness: Photographers Photographing Themselves," Bright (2010) reminds us, "The body is still commonly used as a political vehicle in much self-portraiture, and artists often use their own bodies as a ready-to-hand model to express abstract or non-narrative concepts. The human body's relationship to space, land, history, age, race, religion, sexuality and gender is often explored in visceral ways" (20).

A few years ago, one of my students made work for this assignment that not only featured his body but also did so in a way that incorporated explicit homoerotic codes. A fifth-year senior and confidently out white gay man, he put up images in reference to *BUTT magazine* (2013), which bills itself as "the pocket-size magazine by, for and about homosexuals." During his critique, he provocatively asked if anyone had heard of the publication. I was the only person in the room to raise a hand. Only a few months prior, the publication had featured the posterior of my friend and long-standing dance floor *compadre* from the Los Angeles house music scene. I did not reveal any of this during the class critique a few months later because it didn't seem particularly pertinent. When my student asked if anyone knew of the cultural reference he was making in his work, I just answered honestly to the question at hand. Yet I was also subtly outing myself and signaling something both to the artist whose work we were discussing and to the larger class with whom I was trying to open up a space beyond the dangers of individualism and isolation.

After his query, the student went on to explain that *BUTT* features interviews, homoerotic photography, and a sex-positive editorial approach. He wanted to locate his work in direct conversation with this sensibility, and he did so by creating photographs that featured his own body, including aroused genitalia and sexual acts. In general, the class was neither particularly titillated nor offended by his work. But they did engage in a lively discussion about heteronormativity; the body and sex as sacred and quotidian; the imagined lines between erotica, pornography, and art; and whether the work could expand the existing vocabulary of *BUTT* or merely parrot it.

After this critique had ended, and as the class atomized for our ten-minute break, another student in the course approached me for the first time. A woman of color, she discreetly told me that the conversation had made her feel like students could be themselves in the classroom, that it was "a safe space" where they could be honest and seen. A few weeks later I received word from Student Services that she had stopped attending all her other courses. It became crucial for me to hold these various pieces of information in synergy while maximizing the context of my class to sustain connection with her throughout the rest of the semester. What had made her so proactive in some areas of her studies and so absent in others? How best to support someone in his or her learning process, particularly when it entails the delicate dance of trying to remain enrolled in times of crisis? Where our bodies are matters.

How our bodies act and feel in class also provides crucial clues. I find that when people are actively gesturing or when everyone starts talking at once in response to a question or image, it is usually a sign that we are on to something. Our critiques—or crits—can begin to feel less like a staid college classroom exercise and more like people playing and discovering together. Middle-class codes of propriety, common and so often unexamined on university campuses, can give way to a more dynamic space of honest exchange. But this exchange requires constant calibration, a sense of when to nudge, when to push, when to pause. This is especially true when someone has had the dedication to create a new artwork and the courage to put it on display in front of peers. That vulnerability can hold possibilities, but also perils.

Over the course of a crit, I might wonder whether my voice sounds open and encouraging as I ask the artist or group to rethink an assumption, or do I seem sharp, condescending, impatient, dismissive, disinterested? And how do I respond when students challenge *my* assumptions and neglect? My students can be invaluable in crafting a more inclusive classroom dynamic, especially if I take the time to ask for and then heed their input. Last year one of my students asked for "a less top-down style of conversation" during crits. He felt like I was doing too much talking and he let me know so in front of others, yet in a way that was proactive and productive while also being respectful. In my desire to introduce lots of new photo-specific vocabulary and embody an enthusiasm for discussing visual ideas, I had taken up too much space. I had slipped into what I call my blahblahdor mode—too much speaking, not enough asking, waiting, and listening. My intentions and actions had fallen out of registration with my students' needs and experience.

REDIRECTING MISPERCEPTIONS

Crits can reveal images that defy and expand expectations. The second part of the self-portrait assignment asks students to address misperceptions. As Susan Bright (2010) reminds us, "Any representation of the self is a subjective rendering by the author. When we look at a photographic self-portrait we do not see an individual or a visual depiction of an inner existential being, but rather a display of 'self-regard, self-preservation, self-revelation and self-creation' open to any interpretation imposed upon it by each individual viewer" (9).

My students are asked to consider what is inherent, interpreted, constructed, confining. These questions then drive us to critically position ourselves in relationship to the misinterpretations that we face from others. This notion of self vis-à-vis how others interpret us can be especially tricky with photographs. When does the (photographic) use of one's body constitute a self-portrait? A self? Does the open-endedness of interpretation erode or preclude self-certainty? Is a sense of self ever not under development? Is this an opportunity for creativity and discovery, or does it produce an endless state of paralyzing self-consciousness? These questions can help us delve deeper into Bright's ideas of self-creation and self-revelation, especially amid the struggles for self-regard and self-preservation that occur in the face of discriminatory social forces. The images that students create in this part of the assignment have sometimes pushed the class to tussle with constructions of selves that are counterposed to racist or sexist ideas—malevolent misperceptions that can leave our real-world selves feeling compromised and diminished.

One of my students dove headlong into this thicket and created a composited triptych that tackled stereotypes that she repeatedly confronted as a Black woman. She costumed and photographed herself spotlit against a rich, infinite, dark backdrop, posing as the hoochie mama, earthen sage, and hip-hop thugette stereotypes that she aimed to lampoon and critique. As one of a small number of Black students at a private design school, she regularly experienced racist misunderstanding, disregard, and disrespect. So she was proactive, consistently creating photographic interventions in her work and in public installations throughout the school that made Black people more present via representations of various ages, incomes, skin tones, and sensibilities. Her strategies of self-care also included knowing how to make friends, finding darkroom buddies, developing allies, establishing a sense of vital if incomplete community beyond the classroom, and crafting independent studies with me that could support her focus on issues that were not being addressed in her other courses.

During the critique of her work, she framed the intentions of her project and opened up the floor for comments. Initially there was considerable silence. I have encountered this situation many times. The silence is often tinged with an edge of awkwardness, even anxiety. Normative cultures and those in power are not usually comfortable being called to account. Artists who are interested in instigating such conversations have to learn to navigate the subsequent turbulence. But they should not have to do so alone. Sometimes a collective resistance is hostile, sometimes more passive. Other times there is a desire to engage but a fear of either misspeaking or outright laying bare one's prejudices despite efforts to remain masked. But usually there is at least one classmate who is willing to wade in, whether through debate or in solidarity. Part of my role as an instructor is to help cultivate an environment where these kinds of exchanges can occur with civility *and* criticality. It is important to support artists in their inquiry, without allowing the ensuing critique to isolate or exacerbate. In the case of this project, the triptych in concert with the other two images for the assignment added up to a body of work strong enough to pull people out of their initial silence and into a cautious but healthy debate about race and racism, gender and sexism, and the limiting assumptions that were all too alive at the school.

When working on the self-portrait assignment, another student created photographs that hinted at what it means to be a bookish introvert in Los Angeles's hybridly brown working- and lower-middle-class suburbs. His work employed a wry sense of humor and a devastatingly effective ability to critique in multiple directions simultaneously. His images made fun of himself as a parodied protagonist seemingly unworthy of the lead role. The pictures also took subtle jabs at his more cocksure and therefore less reflexive neighbors and former high school classmates, all the while challenging viewers' potential misperceptions about conformity and suburban sanctity. The work he began for this assignment then ended up leading to a larger, multiyear study of suburban vignettes that used satire, melancholy, and staged tableaux photography to confront the slippages between archetypes and stereotypes. He prodded at simultaneous nodes of race, class, gender, geography, age, and domesticity, looking to construct scenes of suburban life that might reveal larger social fissures. The result was a body of work that is at turns subtle, haunting, and hilarious as it messes with our perceptions.

NO LONGER UNSEEN

The third part of the assignment focuses on the aspects of our selves that may not be seen at all. Our group process of discernment features difficulties not unlike the challenges that the student artists themselves take on when seeking to make a compelling self-portrait. As Bright (2010) notes, "For many, the self is difficult to represent and may be captured through a depiction of the face or the body, through a performance or a location, or purely as a theoretical concept ripe for sabotage. It is all pervasive but also elusive, hidden, collaborative, duplicitous, camouflaged, constructed, disguised, discursive and fleeting, always present but impossible to pin down" (21). When we critique the self-portraits, the images and the artist are both present in the room. This leads to a process that has multiple trajectories in which we try to question that which is extant and that which is not readily apparent. There is a special potential for immediacy in the mutual learning rhythms of an art classroom. But it requires us to be invested in one another's work and present in a dialogic process. The critique sessions for the self-portrait assignment can help to make this abundantly clear, particularly at the levels of politics and interpersonal exchange. Crits also give us the opportunity to consider things that we had previously assumed, ignored, avoided, or neglected.

Once during the self-portrait assignment, a student put up handsome black-and-white prints featuring stark lighting, wide tonal ranges, and elegant, almost dancelike poses of herself. But the images also felt somehow measured, a smidge forlorn. They included artisan blankets and decorative stylings that could be read as ethnic signifiers within a spaciously appointed upper-middle-class glass-and-wood interior. In critiquing the photographs, the artist's peers spoke almost exclusively about the formal elements of the work, how it looked, its use of pose, composition, and shadow. Into this nearly exclusive conversation about form, I asked, "Is anything else going on in these images? How would you characterize the figure? What is her relationship to the place her body inhabits? Any other aspects?" Despite some initial quiet, people did begin to tease out a sense that the figure appeared to be familiar with the domestic space she occupied. They also began to put their finger on a shifting quality of both comfort and unsettledness in the work. I offered that while I try not to make assumptions about people, or how they self-identify, I might read the blanket in the image as being from Latin America, and that in relationship to the light-brown-skinned woman in the picture (and classroom), this could raise additional questions regarding what else the work might be trying to say.

At that point, the artist then spoke about her mother being Mexican and the close relationship they have with one another and their family home. Her comments were unrushed, almost reflective, but she intimated how different her experience is back home in Southern California compared to the college campus where our class was being conducted, in Portland, Oregon (Portland is the whitest major city in the United States [Hannah-Jones 2013]). Then she asked me, "Are you Latino?" I responded that I am, my mother being from Panamá and my father a white American. "I couldn't tell," she said, no doubt referencing my light skin and her perceptions of me. Her work, her courage, and our exchange opened up a space where race and its signifiers could be discussed—in the classroom, through our bodies and perceptions, in the ways we shape our living and learning spaces, and with the artworks we create.

WHEN WE WORK

In recent semesters, while preparing the guide sheet for the self-portrait assignment, I have chosen to include the following insights from meditation teacher Christina Feldman's "Long Journey to a Bow" (2008):

The conceit of self (*mana* in Pali) is said to be the last of the great obstacles to full awakening. Conceit is an ingenious creature, at times masquerading as humility, empathy, or virtue. Conceit manifests in the feelings of being better than, worse than, and equal to another. Within these three dimensions of conceit are held the whole tormented world of comparing, evaluating, and judging that afflicts our hearts. Jealousy, resentment, fear, and low self-esteem spring from this deeply embedded pattern. Conceit perpetuates the dualities of "self" and "other"—the schisms that are the root of the enormous alienation and suffering in our world. Our commitment to awakening asks us to explore honestly the ways in which conceit manifests in our lives and to find the way to its end.

I have been thinking a lot about my own conceit—of self, toward others— and how detrimental my conceit is to successful teaching, equitable community building, dynamic art making, and free living. Yet I am both comforted and invigorated in knowing that this sojourn with self is never truly solitary. My sense of self may not even be necessary, at least not in its most narrow, brittle, defensive, and conceited forms. It is more important that I work to recognize patterns, relations, associations, repercussions, and productive deviations in my attitudes and actions. What matters is contributing to a fellowship that is brave and flexible enough to fly even as it may be repeatedly flustered. In considering his journey of consciousness with regard to multiplicity and political commitments, Hames-García (2011) notes, "True solidarity with others can never leave me unaltered because my complicity in the victimization of others always has implications for how I live and how I understand my life. Whether in coming to see myself as a queer person of color or as normal, I am transformed deeply and irrevocably" (36).

I attempt to teach into and from this prospect of collective transformation. How might we come to see ourselves fully implicated and illuminated in the lives of others, without solely being self-absorbed? How might this shape our sense of mutability, accountability, and possibility? One of the things I am currently trying to practice when looking at art is a deepening of engagement that is activated and accompanied by a suspension of judgment. How to sit more openly with the work, the silences, the disagreements, the misperceptions, the diversity, and the mystery that manifest every day in the shared space of the classroom, which is to say, the world? Perhaps with nuance, patience, and elasticity? Buddhist scholar Dzogchen Ponlop Rinpoche (2006) notes, "Through our analysis, we begin to develop a more subtle understanding. We begin to see how we cling to the self as permanent when it is impermanent, singular when it is multiple, and independent when it relies on causes and conditions. In this way, we discover that our original assumptions do not reflect reality" (238).

Soon after I began to write this essay, I started teaching at a large, private university in New York City. I work with graduate students who are expressly interested in the synergies between art and politics, and the formation of new notions of work, self, context, and community. I facilitate a class that explores how we envision and shape the fields in which a creative practice might blossom. During my first semester of teaching this course, my language became less than inclusive. One of my students is an immigrant whose family fled civil war. She is inspired by a love for young people and she has an interest in photography, underground politics, and rich veins of humor. She has also trained in popular education strategies and community organizing. In one of our early gatherings, she keyed in on the limits of my language and the laziness of my thinking. She asked if everyone, including me, could say, "When *we* work . . ." instead of "When *you* work . . ." She was reminding me not to speak at her and the students as if I were so distant, elevated, or distinct. She was also giving me the gift of seeing myself not just as a teacher, and certainly not simply as the (only, singular) teacher, but also as a fellow artist, one who makes art as part of a working process of learning and discovery just as "students" do.

This shift from *you* to *we* is what can make me more open and connected. This entails not a denial of diversity and discrimination but, rather, a fuller turning into them. I hope to embrace such exposures always, and I wish for no less from the colleagues and institutions that would claim or disregard me. Together we may all need to learn how to let go of our selves occasionally in order to discover a less limited and prejudiced sense of who we might truly and expansively be.

6 ◆ THE PROFESSOR, HER COLLEAGUE, AND HER STUDENT

Two Race-Related Stories

SARAH WILLIE-LEBRETON

Others fail to see us for who we are . . . , or repress us because of who they think we are . . . [All of this and more shapes] the way we look at and constitute ourselves.

—Craig Calhoun

In the late 1990s, I had begun a job at a highly selective small liberal arts college as an assistant professor; it was the third time I was beginning a job as a tenure track assistant professor in the course of five years. At that moment, I compared the situation to two failed starter-marriages: I had chosen inappropriate partners for what I expected would be lifelong employment. The metaphor, however, was not appropriate: employment with the same organization, even in a field with a stable reputation like academia, was waning for most employees. These days, American adults will hold between ten and fifteen jobs over their lifetimes (U.S. Bureau of Labor Statistics 2011). And, although I could quickly identify my own peculiarities and those of the colleges I had left, it's important to remember Marx's

(1852) famous insight: while we make choices, they are rarely accomplished under conditions of our own making. That particular moment—the 1990s in the United States—was an interesting one in which to be coming of academic age.

With the transition from the Reagan-Bush years to the Clinton administration, a space had opened for the voices of progressives in public discussions. In higher education, fellowship opportunities for graduate students of color offered hope that some of the nation's colleges and universities might begin to recruit and retain faculty of color in more than single-digit numbers. Simultaneously, *multiculturalism* had become the watchword of the day and most colleges and universities embraced its rhetoric, named it in mission statements, and began slowly to add a woman in science here, a man or woman of color in the humanities or social sciences there. The fear expressed by conservatives in the 1980s and early 1990s that colleges and universities were being taken over by fire-breathing radicals had not materialized, even as many of the nation's most prestigious public and private universities admitted more racially and economically diverse student bodies than ever before in the country's history (Duster 1991).

Those faculty who did identify with groups that were once unwelcome on elite, historically white college campuses had the strange experience of being tacitly accused of changing the culture, while, for most of our careers, there had been so few of us that any change had resulted more from the changed attitudes of majority faculty and staff members and sometimes a transformed and more diverse student body than from our presence.[1] I have observed that it is sometimes easier to accuse outsiders of disrupting our families than it is to have uncomfortable conversations about diversity within one's own family. In this way, college campuses have been similar to families.

When I began college in the early 1980s, affirmative action had been explained to me as a way that a variety of institutions' members might begin to mitigate their own propensity for excluding those unlike themselves. By the 1990s, when I was entering the job market, it felt to me as if affirmative action had become a race card that privileged whites had played and then forfeited it. What do I mean? Affirmative action had also benefited white women, perhaps more than the women and men who are African American, Native American, and Latino that it was also charged with targeting.

Indeed, I would argue that the successes of affirmative action for women and people of color were beginning to expose the fundamental unfairness of many American organizations, not only of education and school admission but also of work, health care, and pay and across a spectrum that was wider than race and gender and included religion, ethnicity, class, sexual orientation, and national origin.[2] This forfeiture meant that, as affirmative action was succeeding for white, affluent, straight, Protestant women, white liberals were no longer willing to defend affirmative action as a racial equalizer. The debate about affirmative action changed from one about a leveling of the playing field and the deficits of all-white organizations to one that assumed the playing field had been leveled and that focused on the deficits of racial minorities.

I began my career at the moment of this public debate, and the burdens the debate placed on me, others like me, and our allies were substantial enough that I was ready to leave higher education just as I crossed the finish line of graduate school. Other things were happening, however, that gave me more degrees of freedom than was given to some of my fellow academics entering the job market at the same time. First, many colleges and universities were ensuring that they had at least one course on race in the United States, a topic about which I had already had the chance to teach as a graduate student. Other schools were making sure that they had at least two classes on African Americans, a topic that I had never studied systemically but was assumed to know something about (and in which I quickly and systematically schooled myself) because of my heritage; and still others were anxious to ensure that the students of color on their campuses had one or two faculty to whom they could turn. There was a second wave of attention to these issues as hundreds of students on college and university campuses participated in marches to protest financial investments at the expense of black Africans living under apartheid in South Africa.

I had the benefit of parents with jobs and incomes in academia and the arts, an appreciation for higher education, and the opportunity (denied for many years to African Americans) to live in a zip code with an outstanding public school system. After a successful high school experience, I was well positioned to attend a selective college or university (which I did) and, again well positioned after a successful experience there, to attend a high-ranking graduate or professional school (which I did). My family's class status and work ethic and my parents' occupations allowed me, and my two siblings, to attend college, and to imagine professional careers. Although we left college having worked during it, our parents shouldered our substantial undergraduate debt, because they were willing *and able* to do so. With a parent in academia, and advisers among the faculty at my college, I learned that scholarships and stipends were available for graduate study and was counseled to apply for them; I won several, allowing me to choose which graduate school I attended. I went into the social sciences, which itself had more job possibilities for graduates than did the humanities. And having attended predominantly white schools and grown up in mostly white neighborhoods, save for one important semester spent at an HBCU (historically black college or university) when I was twenty, I had had a great deal of practice at navigating the white campus setting with ease, if not always comfort.

Even with all these aspects of my history that favored success in the elite and predominantly white campus context, when one is about to begin one's third job in five years and is already exhausted by institutional racism and sexism, one ought to be anxious about the experience working out or at least be ready with a plan B. I was indeed anxious and hopeful that this third position would be one that would work out, one where I would be granted tenure, be promoted, and have a long and fruitful career. I was not ready with a plan B.

In the balance of this essay, I share two experiences that were part of my professional coming of age. Each occurred outside the classroom. One was with a student and administrator, another with a co-worker and senior colleagues. The time spent in navigation activities outside the classroom is as fundamental to professional success as that inside the classroom.

THE STORIES

I call the stories that I share in this essay "race related" because race rises to the surface in my memory. They are also gender related, class related, age related, and marital status related and probably related in other ways that I have not considered. I call them stories only to highlight the extent to which they reflect my perspective rather than the perspectives of my interlocutors. The stories are also defined by the moment in which we interacted, with all the social forces that worked upon us, some of which I have already described. Social theorist Craig Calhoun (1995) helps me to honor these significant memories, when my racial and gender identities felt so salient and the stakes so high, with his observation that "we have been led by our theories often to underestimate the struggle involved in forging identities, the tension inherent in the fact that we all have multiple, incomplete, and/or fragmented identities [and] the politics implied by the differential public standing of various identities or identity-claims, and the possibilities for our salient constructions of identities to change in the context of powerfully meaningful, emotionally significant events" (218).

Of course, I remember the multiple identities of my interlocutors as well. Reassembling and re-membering these moments has led me to reach increasingly complex understandings of what and how much we can and cannot change. Most of all, I have been led to interpret my own behavior, that of the persons I saw as antagonists, and the situations in which we found ourselves, with the aid of sociological lenses that do for social life what the Hubble telescope does for space—making many things clearer, sometimes more painful or frightening in their starkness, and occasionally more beautiful.

A Story about a Colleague

It is the fall of 1998, and in this memory my interlocutor and I occupy interstitial positions. I am, among other things, a woman of color without tenure but with a doctorate and on the tenure track. He is, among other things, a white man on a continuing appointment who has not yet completed his doctorate and is not on the tenure track.

As I remember the faculty in the department, I was the only untenured, tenure-track woman as well as the only untenured, tenure-track person of color in the department. At the same time, ours was among the most diverse and, I perceived, friendliest departments on campus to women and persons of color. There were eight tenured and tenure-track members of the department, four men and four women: one white male with tenure and one without who had just come onto the tenure track, one Latino and one Latin American, both with tenure, three white women with tenure (two were serving the college outside the department in administrative posts), and me. There were also two faculty who were visiting and not on the tenure track, one white male and one white female.

Each year, the student body was becoming more diverse, a plan that the dean of admissions was overseeing at the charge of the president. The college had made an explicit effort to admit more American students of color over the half dozen years leading up to this moment, but particularly with the class that entered in the fall of 1996. The result of the effort had been a significant increase in the numbers of students of color. In 1995, for example, 78 percent of the entering class identified as white or European American. The very next year, only 58 percent of the entering class identified as white or European American. Within that class, the class of 2000, the percentage of American students of color had more than doubled compared with the class of 1999. Although the change involved only *one-fifth of one-quarter* of the student body, the increase of students of color was experienced by almost everyone as dramatic.

In any predominantly white or predominantly male organization, as Daphne Patai (1991) has argued, women and people of color stand out and, when they speak, sound louder than others, since their presence—especially in certain arenas—is often new and unusual. Patai's observations confirm those of Rosabeth Moss Kanter (1977), whose research shows that attention is disproportionately drawn to those who appear different, particularly in positions where people like them have not been before, in part, paradoxically, because their numbers are small. As if the dramatic increase in their numbers was not enough to draw attention to the students of color in the class of 2000, a couple of members of the admissions staff admitted to "taking a few risks," as they tentatively made their way toward discovering what attributes were likely to create a class with good chemistry full of students who would find their footing at the college and be academically and extracurricularly successful by senior year, if not before. In this process, they admitted a handful of minority students who they were not absolutely sure would have a successful experience but who had shown intellectual passion, creativity, commitment, and drive during their high school careers despite attending public schools without advanced placement courses, or with quantitative test scores that were below the median. The acknowledgment to faculty, however, that "a few risks had been taken," together with some of the new students of color's suffering challenges on their first tests in large lecture classes during their first semester, combined with the over-all increase in the numbers of students of color to create a tempting liquor. The brew was circulated among faculty like an illicit flask at a football game. Happily, not everyone was intoxicated by it, but the effect was, nonethe-less, devastating to the reputation of many of these students, the rest of the class, and some of the faculty, whose faith was temporarily shaken in the admissions department. *The class of 2000* became a euphemism for several other phrases, two of which were treated as synonyms: *lack of preparation* and *students of color.*

So back to the particular conversation that inspires this story. I was in the departmental office with my colleague, David (I'm using pseudonyms); the administrative assistant was also present, working at her desk. The AA iden-tifies as white and female. David identifies as white and male. As I remem-ber it, we were talking about students we had in common. He mentioned his disappointment with a student whom he said with a knowing look was "class of 2000." We had been mirroring each other in genial conversation up to this point. But then I hesitated and did not respond verbally. David met my silence with a sigh and continued, "I'm just looking forward to the day when the college admits students based on ability again." I didn't know whether he was baiting me or speaking authentically, but I guessed the latter.

"The college never stopped admitting students based on ability," I coun-tered. (My defensiveness, the AA later tells me, showed. I didn't know if she was trying to be helpful, to chastise me, or to warn me.) I continued, saying that I was sorry he had missed the faculty meeting where the dean of admis-sions went over the numbers—how there is very little difference between classes in terms of grade point averages and test scores.

"That's not how it seems to me," David responded. I was quiet. He was quiet. We were at a standoff. He shrugged and exited the room.

On the train ride home, I mulled over our interaction, thinking of all the things I might have said, wished I'd said. I realized I could have answered, "The college has never admitted students based only on ability," but the more I thought about our conversation, I imagined the comment was as much about me as about his student, that it was not made thoughtlessly to just any member of the department who happened to be at the copy machine, but to me in particular. David's comment could be read, though

I have no way of knowing his intention, as what he thought of affirmative action for faculty, indeed what he thought of affirmative action for me. We had sparred over my first year and a half about issues having to do with race and racism. He had approached me several times with a piece of candy or a compliment about my clothes or pleasant demeanor after one of these arguments. David regularly called attention to characteristics of mine that were feminine, reminding me of my (informally subordinate) status as female and by association, his (informally superordinate) status as male. I'm no psychologist, but I began to suspect that his treatment of me with the politeness and flirtation that he would treat any (culturally normative and straight) woman was assurance to any witness, including himself, that he was not racist.

These difficult-to-name, and what I think of as subcutaneous, interactions are so frequent that they are now called microaggressions (Sue et al. 2007). Because these interactions repeat themselves with different people in different hallways and classrooms, the offending party is multiple and ghostly, offending with impunity. And the offended party, as Iris Marion Young (1990) observes, often begins to feel crazy.

I wanted to share this interaction and others with co-workers but I was unclear about who would be the safest choice, so I waited a few months and shared the story with senior colleagues in a panel presentation at a regional professional meeting. My off-campus senior colleagues acknowledged the awkwardness of the situation, validated my reality, and offered a range of responses and advice that gave me courage. At the same time, they reminded me that I was not anonymous and urged caution and prudence before getting tenure.

A Story about a Student

This is the story as I remember it. Peter (also a pseudonym) was a European American male and had come to my office hours angry about having received a lower grade on his paper than he felt he deserved (perhaps a B instead of an A). A brilliant young man, he had written about Durkheim's concept of the social fact. He wanted to go over the paper sentence by sentence. We began to do so. He did a much better job of telling me what he meant in my office hours than I thought he had done in the paper. He was upset with my interpretation of his writing, and he began to rock slightly in his chair and gesture with his hands. Spittle flew from his mouth as his voice rose, and I sensed that neither of us was going to come away from this meeting satisfied. He insisted he had done a good job of communicating his thesis. I countered that I disagreed for all the reasons to which I had alluded in the margins. At an impasse, I reminded Peter that the college had vested us with different roles and responsibilities: his to write a paper and mine to grade it. In such roles, he was not the final arbiter of whether he communicated something well to me. I checked my watch and realized I had spent thirty-five minutes with him. Other students were waiting outside the door. I brought the session to a close and invited him to return the next week to continue our conversation.

The next day, when I did not have office hours, Peter knocked at my door. I invited him in. He was contrite. He told me that he had bipolar disorder. His manic depression, he said, might undermine his ability to complete the work in the course. He told me that his father was coming to pick him up at the college later in the day. He apologized for what he called an outburst the previous day. I told him that I was glad to have some context for our previous interaction, and that I hoped he felt better. I released him from in-class responsibilities for leading discussions. Since it was my perception that Peter had consistently dominated class discussion, my action was motivated as much by my desire to engage other students as it was by empathy.

Four months later, at the end of summer recess, I was preparing my fall syllabi when I received a call from the provost. She asked to see me in her office to talk about Peter, who, she tells me, brought a serious complaint against me to her at the close of the spring semester. I agreed to meet with her immediately, anxiety having quickened my pulse as I made my way to her office with all deliberate speed. In her office, the provost told me that Peter had initially followed up with my department chair, asking if she was willing to read the paper that, he argued, I had failed to understand and to which I had assigned an inappropriate grade. Apparently, he told her that he felt I was not competent to grade the paper. The chair encouraged him to consult with me and then, as I understand it, volunteered to have a meeting with the three of us but said that she would not read the paper without my knowledge and did not have the authority to overturn a grade I had given. He then went to the provost, also a member of my department, and asked her to read the paper. I learned from her that he felt that I was not competent to grade the paper. She repeated what the chair had said, clarifying that she could not herself change, or force a colleague to change, a grade. He then told her that his primary concern was not, after all, with the grade but had been with the dynamic of the class, which had felt to him to be racially unsafe for white males. The provost reported to me that Peter had told her he was forbidden from challenging the arguments of a certain author because the author was black and he is white.

I was stunned. Although I denied that he was forbidden from disagreeing with any author we read—indeed, such an idea was preposterous for the learning goals I have for my students—I encouraged the provost to speak with other members of the class to discern whether this was also their perception. I spent ninety minutes with her, talking about my challenges with that class, my sense of my own limitations and strengths as a teacher, my challenges with that student, and the degrees of freedom that I do and do not have to teach certain classes in particular ways. As someone who is black and female, I am fully aware of the stereotype that holds that it is unlikely someone with my characteristics would excel at understanding or teaching what is most theoretical and abstract in the discipline. In my second year at the college, and hired to teach about race, (in a small department, everyone does a bit of everything and our resident theoretician was on leave), my teaching this subject may also have been seen by colleagues and students as overreaching. In other words, teaching certain subjects is a privilege that also reveals one's right to do so; teaching others is a requirement that low status requires.

It is true that I had put social theory from the mid-1800s written by European men in conversation with social theory from the late 1900s written by European American and African American women. I thought that the concepts might be seen and understood in greater relief across time and space, and that this would be a way to appreciate the applicability of classical social theory in a racially tense moment in the country and on campus. The attacks on Anita Hill at Clarence Thomas's confirmation hearings, the beating of Rodney King and the acquittal of his police aggressors, the O. J. Simpson trial, and President Clinton's "end of welfare as we know it" that had particularly negative ramifications for poor people, women, people of color and children were all in the immediate rear view mirror.

By the end of my conversation with the provost, I felt as though I had learned about becoming a better teacher, about defending myself from slander, and about taking the time for genuine exchange with a superior. Among many insights, what I was most grateful for was her appreciation that this was an empirical example of the "black tax," the toll levied on black faculty to justify their teaching and their intelligence, in other words, the payment for time that must be paid to educate colleagues about the racism experienced and the challenges faced.

I have never forgotten the time that the provost took with me and the space she gave me to acknowledge not only structural inequalities that would continue to rise up to test me but also the space to acknowledge my own learning curve. Had the provost been unsympathetic to the situation of marginalized faculty, had she been unfamiliar with the concept of a tax on minorities, had she not seen her role as mentor, the outcome might have been very different. Likewise, however, if I had been so defensive about my teaching or refused to acknowledge that that class in particular had been tense and difficult, the outcome might have been very different. Our interview came to an end, and I was relieved at her interpretation; it actually gave me the space to consider my own pedagogical choices. Although I returned to my office, I did so only to retrieve my belongings and head for home. I was deeply shaken and I wondered about all the unseen and unknown elements that might come up in my case for tenure.

CONSEQUENCES AND RECOMMENDATIONS

While either of these situations could have happened to any of my colleagues regardless of race or gender, and no doubt did to several people, the import of each was going to be more consequential for me and any other female faculty member, faculty member of color, or female faculty member of color. What makes the outcome of these two stories positive for me (and there are, of course, dozens of other stories) is that I happened upon the best place to complain about the first situation (a professional meeting) and I received the kind of advice that was career saving. In the second case, I had a provost who was educated about these issues and compassionate and clear about the challenges I faced but who also created the space to help me grow into greater maturity. Of course, there were plenty of other situations that neither I nor my colleagues handled with as much grace or fortitude, but having senior members of the professorate and the administration available to guide, suggest, mentor, and advise was crucial in my being able to look back on these experiences as parables rather than as horror stories.

ADVICE FORWARD

In the larger picture, many of us will be tapped as mentors and will listen to the stories of younger or newer colleagues. Some of us will share identity characteristics with them; some of us will not. But over the years now of seeking my own advice and listening to the stories of colleagues more junior to me, I'm struck by the complexity of the stories. Any of us can and do blurt out racist, sexist, heterosexist, and classist comments—they are ubiquitous in the larger culture and thus easily accessible to most of us in tense situations. More often, the behavior that is so perplexing and the missteps we each make are, as the psychoanalysts like to say, overdetermined. There are many things that lead to bad behavior or inappropriate assumptions— the continued structural inequalities that are understood as individual choices; the foot-in-mouth moments when stereotypical maxims roll off the tongue; the colleagues, students and co-workers who, for a range of reasons, are more sensitive to them; and the genuine anxiety and confusion of living with more difference without learning how to respect others, apologize, actively become more sensitive ourselves, and ask for do-overs.

I have decided to be less worried about faulting others on the occasional misstep—in part because I, too, am guilty of those—and to focus more on nurturing a community among students, faculty, and staff in which anyone can turn to anyone else with the expectation that we're willing to work at undermining our assumptions, naming structural inequality, challenging stereotypes, relying on evidence, and strategizing success.

I have long resented the idea that outsiders must work twice as hard as anyone else to achieve recognition or success. I now see that observation less as an injunction and more as an admission (sometimes a resentment and sometimes a celebration) that a tremendous amount of emotional energy is and will be spent navigating these ubiquitous moments. One important step toward eliminating them is the acknowledgment by persons in authority that they exist, and not just as moments but as aspects fundamental to the structures that historically white colleges and universities were created to be. A second important step is ensuring that persons from diverse backgrounds are in those positions of authority. If these two things become common, the American college and university campus will transform into a place of wholeness and integrity.

NOTES

I would like to thank Howard Taylor, who invited me to present a version of this essay at a session of the Eastern Sociological Society Meetings in 1999 along with copresenters Charles Willie and Howard Winant and discussant Margaret Andersen.

1 One of the colleges where I taught was just beginning to hire women in substantial numbers when I arrived. A searing experience was enduring a browbeating by the wife of a senior colleague who—during a party at the home of another single, straight female colleague—followed me into the bathroom, locked the door, and spent a quarter of an hour bemoaning the loss of community at the hands of "all these young women PhDs." Social change is not only an abstract concept but also has ramifications for our daily lives. The changes that my colleague's spouse experienced produced both rage and anxiety, and that evening I was her target (or the only person who would listen).

2 The story about affirmative action and Asian Americans is an important one, complicated by whether individuals, and the groups with which they identify, arrived before or after the immigration reform of 1965, and depending on how many generations have been in the United States.

7 ◆ CHALLENGING OPPRESSION IN MODERATION?

Student Feedback in Diversity Courses

ANITA CHIKKATUR

It's a gray and cloudy Sunday during the winter term of my first year as a tenure-track professor and I'm meeting with a student in my office. While I do not usually meet with students on weekends, this student is struggling with whether she should stay at Carleton College. I feel particularly invested in her well-being, as she is one of the few African American students in my class. We discuss a wide range of topics for two hours. She uses frequently the term *students of color* as a self-descriptor, which I note with interest, because in the two classes she has taken with me, she has spoken several times about how she resents the fact that she is referred to as a student of color by the institution. She tells me about an incident that happened during her first week at the college. When she told a senior that she was from Chicago, the senior replied, "Oh, isn't that the ghetto?" I express surprise and sympathy, and give her a few suggestions about what she could have said in response. The student tells me that it was her first week here and she did not know what she could have said in response. I nod. She then tells me about a summer job experience where her co-worker kept calling her by the wrong name—the name of a Black person who had worked there the previous summer. The co-worker had asked her, "Well, what should I call you?" We both laugh at the absurdity of the question. She asks me whether I had similar experiences in college, whether I had felt like I did not quite belong. I tell her about how my cohort at another small liberal arts college was very diverse, both racially and socioeconomically, and about how my undergraduate institution was not prepared to welcome and educate all my classmates. When she leaves, I wonder if our discussion was useful for the student, who was struggling with depression, which she said was only made worse by being at Carleton. Later, I also wonder if I had said anything that I should not have said—something that might be construed as critical of the institution and whether that would have negative repercussions for me as a junior faculty member. I later find out that the student has taken an indefinite leave of absence from the college.

THE ISSUE

Envisioning the classroom as a zone of encounter, this essay is a critical reflection on teaching courses on racial and gender diversity in education at a predominantly White undergraduate institution. College classrooms are an important space where students encounter difference, not only in the curriculum of courses that focus on race and other forms of difference but also often in the very bodies of their non-White instructors who teach such courses. I started this essay retelling the story of an encounter with a student outside the classroom because it speaks to the negotiations I feel I have to make in my role as a junior faculty member and to my commitments as a faculty member of color. These negotiations and commitments inform how I approach teaching classes about issues of difference and diversity on a campus with a predominantly White and economically privileged student body.

In my meeting with the student, I believed that it was important to share some of the difficulties I had faced as a student at a similar college and the cultural differences I had to decode and navigate. Listening to the struggles of students of color at my current place of employment often leaves me feeling frustrated at the slow pace at which institutions seem to change. Although more than a decade has passed since I graduated from college, conversations with my students demonstrate that the dominant discourse about difference and diversity has not changed much. It seems like bodies of color are still wanted, but the challenges these bodies might pose to the institution and changes these bodies might demand from the institution still are not always acknowledged, and certainly not welcomed.

My interest in teaching and researching how racial differences, in particular, organize educational experiences in the United States stems primarily from my experiences as a student of color at a liberal arts college, the conversations I had with my peers of color there about race, and the classes that I took in sociology and educational studies. When I started my teaching career at a similar institution, I hoped to be a part of the effort to interrupt and transform the dominant discourse about how and why differences matter. In my classes, I wanted students to explore how to interrupt harmful discourses about racialized students, parents, and communities and to imagine and develop more equitable classrooms, schools, and societies.

Writing about anti-oppressive education, Kumashiro (2002) argues that such education has to disrupt "our commonsense view of the world," rather than merely affirming or repeating what we already know (63). However, encountering such disruptive information can be painful and uncomfortable. As Leonardo and Porter (2010) posit, "Critical race pedagogy is inherently risky, uncomfortable, and fundamentally unsafe . . . particularly for whites" (139). While this pain and discomfort might eventually motivate students to work toward building a more equitable society, the short-term effects might include negative evaluations of the particular course or instructor. There is evidence based on "empirical studies examining instructor race and student ratings [that] minority faculty receive significantly lower evaluations than their white colleagues," regardless of the specific course material (Merritt 2008, 236). Given that I am at an institution that places a high premium on student evaluations of faculty in the promotion and tenure process, attempting to teach in a way that might lead students into a crisis as a minority faculty member is a risky proposition.

This essay is not about my heroic efforts to challenge my students' ideas about the status quo despite the risks. Rather, I argue that the seemingly positive student feedback in my courses speaks to how I might be moderating my responses to students to ensure that they feel comfortable in my classes. The absence of explicit student resistance to having their worldviews challenged leaves me wondering if I am succeeding at all in interrupting their discourses and beliefs about diversity and difference or about privilege and disadvantage.

WEARING A MASK?

During a discussion with a friend who is also a tenure-track professor at a small liberal arts college, she talks about hanging out with a few of the other newly hired female faculty and she jokes about how they are all essentially the same person—women in their late twenties with certain ways of speaking, teaching, and dressing. We talk about whether this is what happens when one of the criteria for getting hired at such colleges is whether you are a fit for the institution. We discuss how this notion of fit only ends up replicating, rather than radically altering, the composition of the faculty at such places. Sure, our skins might be of a different hue, our names might be harder to pronounce, and our childhood memories might include conversations in languages other than English, but at the end of the day, we fit because we are comfortable with and use White, middle-class ways of speaking, dressing, and being. I am reminded of what Ladson-Billings (1996) wrote about her experiences as an African American female faculty member: "Must I be doubly gracious and accommodating so as not to appear embittered and militant? Do they want me to wear a mask so they will not have to?" (84). And it seems like my answer to her questions is yes. Yes, I must be and apparently have been doubly gracious and accommodating. Through my undergraduate experiences at a small, elite liberal arts college, I learned and became comfortable with White, middle-class behaviors and linguistic styles. I have learned to mask my anger and outrage at the racist, sexist, and heterosexist comments made by colleagues and students. I have learned instead to express that anger and outrage only in conversations I have with a few trusted friends.

INSTITUTIONAL CONTEXT

I currently teach at a small liberal arts college with approximately two thousand students, located in a rural town in the Midwest. On a personal level, my experiences have been fairly positive—I have found my colleagues to be supportive, the students to be invested in and dedicated to their studies. There is also, however, an undercurrent of unease as I go through the daily motions of preparing for class, meeting with students, teaching, and grading.

The students at the college are privileged, particularly in terms of their socioeconomic backgrounds. For example, according to data available on the college website, 74 percent of the students in the class of 2014 come from families who make more than one hundred thousand dollars a year. In comparison, only 26 percent of American families have annual incomes of more than one hundred thousand dollars (U.S. Census Bureau 2008); at all four-year colleges and universities, 37 percent of students have parents who make more than one hundred thousand dollars ("This Year's Freshmen at 4-Year Colleges" 2010). Approximately 22 percent of the students identified as African American, Asian American, Latino/a, Native American, or "two or more races" in 2012. Given the overall demographics of the United States, this number seems proportionate. According to U.S. census data, as of 2008, almost 75 percent of Americans identified as White. However, the shift in demographics occurring largely because of immigration over the past few decades is reflected differently in the population of the nation's young people. As of 2006, for example, about 62 percent of Americans between the ages of eighteen and twenty-five identified as White; 14 percent identified as African American, 18 percent as Latino, and 5 percent as Asian American.

Data on the racial demographics of the faculty at my institution were harder to locate than similar data on students. According to the 2010 Higher Education Research Institute (HERI) faculty survey, 82 percent of faculty who took the survey identified as White/Caucasian.[1] From 2001 to 2010, seven African American faculty, nine Latino/a faculty, and twenty-two Asian faculty were hired—approximately 36 percent of the total faculty members who were hired during this period. There is no information about whether those hired were U.S.-born domestic racial minorities or were educated primarily outside the United States. While diversity among faculty needs to be conceptualized in broad and multiple ways, and not just limited to race, the experiences of immigrants racialized as "Black" or "Asian" and their racialized politics might be different from U.S.-born racial minorities (Pierre 2004). At the very least, experiencing racial discrimination at the age of seven or seventeen is different from experiencing it at the age of twenty-two or thirty. My own understanding of the nation's racial landscape, the particular commitments I have developed to communities of color, and even the fact that I strongly identify as a woman of color stem largely from racialized experiences I had as a teenager living in New York City and as an undergraduate at an institution with a predominantly White student body.

These numbers provide some information about the particular context in which I teach courses about race, gender, socioeconomic class, and sexuality in education. While there are many ways in which the college supports all faculty, through formal mentoring programs, a learning and teaching center, and generous material and personnel resources for teaching and research, some faculty of color (and women faculty) still feel less supported and welcomed at the institution than do their White (and male) counterparts. These experiences and feelings were brought to the attention of the wider campus through the results of two surveys conducted around the time I started working there.

A campus climate survey, conducted in spring 2008, revealed that differences in racial and gender identities, socioeconomic status, and religious beliefs were perceived, understood, and navigated by members of the campus community in different ways, depending on membership in various identity-based communities. Race was found to be the second-most-common reason indicated by students, faculty, and staff survey respondents as the source of harassment they have experienced on campus. An analysis of the survey results, for example, suggested that more than half the respondents of color who said that they have been harassed attributed this harassment to their racial identities, compared with only 5 percent of White respondents.

The results of the 2007 HERI faculty survey also revealed differences in the experiences of White faculty and faculty of color at the college.[2] For example, while 80 percent of the White faculty thought that the statement "faculty respect each other" was very descriptive of the college, only 45 percent of faculty of color did. Similarly, while 95 percent of White faculty respondents believed that faculty of color were treated fairly at the college, 68 percent of faculty of color respondents believed that. Not surprisingly, then, more faculty of color indicated that they had experienced subtle discrimination (38 percent) than did White faculty (20 percent). While 40 percent of White faculty respondents in 2007 were extensively or somewhat stressed about the review and promotion process, 68 percent of faculty of color respondents felt stressed about the process. The 2010 HERI survey found similar results, except that in 2010, approximately 64 percent of the faculty of color respondents thought the statement "faculty respect each other" was very descriptive of the college, up from the 45 percent in 2007.

The results of the campus climate and the 2007 HERI surveys were made available to the campus community during my first term at Carleton College. Along with the stories that friends who worked at similar institutions had shared with me, these results influenced how I understood and evaluated the context in which I was going to be teaching courses about race, gender, sexuality, and education and the students' reactions to me and my courses.

EMBODIED DIFFERENCE

I decide to give some general feedback to students in my Introduction to Educational Studies class about their first essays and I tell them that they have the option of revising their essays. I discuss what it means to provide evidence for their assertions, discuss citation conventions, and urge them to read over and revise their essays before they hand them in. During my office hours following that class meeting, a student comes to meet with me. As soon as she sits down, she tells me, "You must not have been clear with your instructions for the essay, since you had to tell us all that in class." Her statement puzzles me but I ask her if she wanted to talk specifically about her paper. We discuss her paper for a while and eventually I understand that she is not happy with her grade, B+. I tell her that I do not give out As for essays that meet the requirements. Her paper was good, I tell her, but it did not exceed the requirements. Later, I wonder if this student—a White female from a socioeconomically privileged background—would have made similar comments to my colleague in the department, a White man in his fifties.

Being a younger, female faculty of color sometimes means that I am not automatically afforded the respect that an older White, male professor usually is. While I have not had any student directly challenge or question my qualifications (as some of my colleagues of color have), there have been more indirect ways in which my qualifications and authority have been questioned. This potential lack of respect becomes even more pertinent because I teach courses where we investigate how identities and differences matter, and how they usually matter in negative ways for bodies marked by differences—racial, gendered, sexual, class, or ability. While I emphasize in my classes that we are all marked by race, gender, sexuality, class, and ability—we all have an accent, to paraphrase Minow (1990)—the particular ways in which my body gets marked as "different" by students has consequences for how they understand what I am trying to do in classes. For those of us who teach about issues of diversity and difference, our classes always entail risks. These risks, however, might be greater for those of us whose bodies get read as being "different" because we do not look like we are a part of the dominant community. As Ravitch (2005) notes:

> For instructors of color, or instructors who are gay, lesbian, bisexual, and transgender, who are immigrants and/or who have disabilities, teaching provocative material . . . brings with it particular challenges and vulnerabilities. This increased vulnerability is caused in part because these instructors are not just teaching the material as their White, heterosexual, nondisabled counterparts do, but, rather, they are living the realities of oppression and marginalization that are the focus of their course material and discussions. Therefore, the ways in which students react, resist, or resent the course content and structure are aimed at them not only . . . professionally but personally (7).

Female faculty and faculty of color might face challenges to their authority, expertise, and qualifications, regardless of the field in which they teach (Merritt 2008). Being a faculty of color who teaches about racism and racial privilege, however, means that challenges to one's authority stem not only from stereotypes of who looks like an expert or a professor but also from students' discomfort and pain about having to recognize, name, and acknowledge their privileges.

(NOT) CHALLENGING OPPRESSION

"I found both [ethnographies] to be really jarring to my own personal experiences. I think that this feature was one of the best parts of the course: it alerted me to my own complacency, privilege, and ignorance of certain subordinated groups." A student wrote this on the end-of-the-term course evaluation form for my Multicultural Education course. It stood out to me because this was the only time a student wrote explicitly about having his or her "commonsense" view of the world being challenged (Kumashiro 2002). In contrast, most of the positive comments were about how "comfortable" I made students feel and how I was able to listen to all perspectives and make the classroom a space where different perspectives could be heard.

In most of my classes, we spend some time at the beginning of the term discussing what it means to have a class where everyone feels that they can and should participate. I share with them some guidelines for discussion: for example, speak from your experience rather than generalizing experiences to others, listen closely to others, and engage in friendly disagreement—challenge ideas, not people. I tell my students (and firmly believe) that each of them has a role to play in class and that everyone's contributions are important. However, I have had a difficult time finding the balance between ensuring that students feel comfortable enough to engage in class discussions and pushing them to challenge their assumptions and un- or under-informed beliefs. As Kumashiro puts it, anti-oppressive education involves "teaching and learning . . . that 'what is normal' and 'who we are' are really social constructs maintained only through the Othering, marginalization, or silencing of other possible worlds and selves . . . constantly learning, in other words, about our own complicity with oppression" (57). If that is the goal, then I have serious doubts about the extent to which my classes involve anti-oppressive education if only one out of more than a hundred students I have taught mentioned how their complacency was challenged by my course.

Kumashiro notes that there are serious, ethical questions to consider when our teaching might lead students to crisis. While that might be part of my hesitation to challenge students' views and beliefs, I have to admit that at least part of my tentativeness arises from my awareness of the importance of student evaluations in tenure and promotion decisions. The one time I did challenge a student, and the reaction to that challenge, illustrates why I was and have remained cautious in how willing I am to push students out of their comfort zone.

It's one of the final class sessions of my Race, Immigration, and Urban Schools course. We had spent eight weeks discussing the experiences of various immigrant groups in K–12 schools. We had read authors who challenged us, or so I thought, to be careful about attributing student achievement or failure solely to individual effort. We are discussing what practices and policies schools could implement to better support immigrant students. A student raises her hand and says, "Well, there's only so much we can do, though, right? If a student just doesn't try?" I can barely contain my frustration at that remark. I reply in an exasperated tone that a recent guest speaker—the head of a local organization that works with Latino high school students—had noted that every student can and should be helped. The student replies that the organization has the luck of being located in a town with two colleges and therefore has many resources to draw on that other schools would not. I counter by noting that all the ethnographies we read were about high schools in urban areas and that it would be hard to find an urban area without a college or a university. Two weeks later, I see this comment on a student's course evaluation and assume that he or she was referring to this discussion in class: "[Anita] is not very good at hiding her personal ideas when in disagreement with a student's opinions, and can come off a bit harsh when portraying this; a bit of a shocker because in all other ways, she is a very excellent and understanding professor."

At liberal arts institutions, where teaching tends to be valued as much as research and scholarship in tenure and promotion decisions, cordial relationships with students matter. Many times, being "cordial" becomes about being the same. It becomes about "fitting" students' (and colleagues') notions of being a good teacher. It becomes, as Ahmed (2012) notes, about who is "the kind of person you could take down to the pub" (39). As noted earlier, these notions of "fit" do not always allow for the kind of teaching where faculty members feel free to take the risk of offending a student by challenging their "commonsense" views of the world. They do not help students or faculty colleagues understand that "excellent" teaching can include disagreement with students' opinions or the incorporation of the professor's ideas and experiences.

Notwithstanding my guideline for classroom participation that encourages friendly disagreement, I have received very little training in graduate school or elsewhere on how to engage students effectively in conversations where their (and my) assumptions can be challenged and perhaps changed. My exasperation with the student's comment in the vignette above could not be considered necessarily effective or productive, even if it had not led to a comment about how I was "a bit harsh." I did not attempt, for example, to probe further into what the student meant by her comment. Perhaps the student was right to complain that all I did, at that moment, was shut down a conversation. At the same time, I have to admit that I am frustrated by having to counter constantly such comments about students of color or immigrant students. What Moll and González (1994) have said about language minority children captures well this frustration: "[We] . . . lament that we have to spend so much of our careers documenting competence, when it should simply be assumed, suggesting that 'language minority' students have the intellectual capabilities of any other children, when it should simply be acknowledged" (454). Similarly, I feel the need to include course material that refutes dominant theories about the shortcomings of racial or linguistic minority children as a reason for why they might not succeed in schools, rather than assuming that my students will know that such students are as capable as students from racial and linguistic majority children.

Additionally, as a member of groups that have been traditionally and continue to be marginalized in the academy and in society, I have to contend with students who might question whether my curricular and pedagogical choices are "balanced" (a few students in their course evaluations of my Multicultural Education and Race, Immigration, and Urban Schools courses indicated that they wanted a more "balanced" perspective on the issues). I am also expected to "hide [my] personal ideas." At the same time that some students questioned whether my curriculum is "biased," another student noted that I should be "more radical" in class. I am left wondering if either type of comment would be made with equal frequency if an older, White male professor were teaching the course.

RECOMMENDATIONS

If multicultural education courses often make students, particularly White students, uncomfortable (Delgado Bernal and Villalpando 2005; Leonardo and Porter 2010), and faculty of color are more likely to teach such courses, what can be done to support faculty who want to structure their classes in ways that challenge students and that lead students to be uncomfortable and perhaps even angry?[3] Stanley (2006) suggests that faculty of color should talk to campus administrators about "whether working to incorporate diversity and social justice issues in courses and curricula will place them at risk in regard to promotion and tenure, merit, or reappointment" (726). Given that junior faculty, both White and of color, often feel constrained in how frank a discussion they can have about the promotion and review process with senior colleagues, it might be better for senior colleagues to initiate such discussions.

Further, what about the training and support that faculty need in order to provide students with the kinds of emotional support that they might need if faculty are to challenge substantially what students believe to be true about the world and themselves? One way to address this question is to ensure that development programs for new faculty include explicit discussions about how social identities matter in our classrooms, for students and for faculty. Senior faculty of color, as well as women faculty and LGBT faculty, could be asked to speak about their experiences in the classroom and offer suggestions about how they negotiated their social identities in classrooms and on campus. Senior faculty members who incorporate issues of diversity and social justice could speak about how that affected their review and promotion process.

Since presenting this essay in its initial form at the Anthropological Meetings in 2010, I have undergone a formal third-year review. As part of that review, students were solicited for letters that evaluate my teaching. To explore systemic biases in the review process, colleges and universities should undertake an audit of the tenure files of faculty who have already been tenured. (I suggest that the audit should be done on already tenured faculty files because institutions might be reluctant, for legal reasons, to conduct such an audit on faculty who are not yet tenured.) This way schools could investigate for themselves privately whether faculty of color (or LGBT faculty or women faculty, particularly in science, technology, engineering and medical, or STEM, fields) were more likely to be described as "biased," "indoctrinating," or "didactic" by students or by senior colleagues than were White, straight, and male faculty. Some institutions might include classroom observations of junior faculty as part of the review process. In my case, while students did not use such terms in their evaluations of my teaching, my faculty colleagues who observed my classes expressed concern about whether I was "indoctrinating" my students. The results of such an audit could either assure junior faculty of color (and faculty from other marginalized groups) that there is no systemic bias in the review and tenure processes, possibly reducing some of the stress that they feel about these processes, or expose systemic biases that the institution could work to mitigate.

Of course, arguing that the institution needs to do something might just be a way for me to shift the focus and not take responsibility for what I do in my own classroom. There are plenty of examples of faculty of color who effectively challenge students' worldviews and work toward changing the inequities in our educational system and society, despite the risks to their jobs or careers. Perhaps I need to keep reminding myself, as hooks (1990) has pointed out, that being on the margins allows one to stay aware of who is being included and who is not in institutional (and other) spaces. I will keep reminding myself that discomfort can be a place of learning, not only for my students, but also for me.

NOTES

1 These data are made available to Carleton faculty and staff on the website of the college's Office of Institutional Research and Assessment.

2 The HERI survey is conducted in multiple institutions across the nation. In this chapter, I discuss the Carleton-specific data. In the survey results, the responses were attributed to "White" respondents and "Other" respondents. The director of institutional research and assessment at the college explained that because of small sample sizes, all respondents who chose categories of racial and ethnic identities other than White were grouped together. I have decided to use the term *faculty of color* rather than *Other faculty*.

3 In the 2007 HERI survey, for example, 9 percent of the White faculty respondents at Carleton College indicated that they have taught an ethnic studies course, while 36 percent of faculty of color respondents indicated that they had taught such a course. Similarly, only 21 percent of White faculty respondents but 54 percent of the faculty of color respondents indicated that they had research or writing assignments in class that focused on racial or ethnic minorities.

PART II WITNESSING
PROTEST

8 ◆ THE (S)PACES OF ACADEMIC WORK

Disability, Access, and Higher Education

KRISTIN LINDGREN

Twenty years ago, in my first year of teaching at the liberal arts college where I still work, my department chair called me into her office to apologize for placing a particular first-year student in my class. The student, she explained, was deaf, and she had to put him *somewhere*. I imagine my newbie status determined his placement in my class. I was puzzled that she felt the need to apologize, but at the time I wasn't angered by her apology. I met with the student, whose clear understanding and explanation of the accommodations he needed made me feel I was up to the task. I wasn't yet familiar either with basic disability accommodations or with the concept of universal design, which aims to create a classroom that is accessible to all learning styles and abilities; however, it quickly became apparent that "accommodating" Peter created a richer learning environment for all of us. Because he absorbed information by reading lips, other students learned to face him when they spoke rather than mumbling into their notebooks. All of us began to articulate our ideas more clearly and to take our time in doing so. Every so often, I asked a student to recap the conversation, initially to ensure that Peter wasn't missing anything but finally as a way for all of us to learn how to revisit and deepen our discussion. In this class, I learned peda-gogical strategies that have served me well ever since, and even though I had been teaching college and high school students for several years, I became far more reflective and creative about the set of practices we call teaching and learning. I'm lucky that the *somewhere* Peter was put happened to be my classroom.

Why is disability so reluctantly embraced as a form of diversity that enriches our classrooms and our campus community? Conversations about disability in the academy often focus on the legal and financial implications of admitting disabled students or hiring disabled faculty and staff rather than on the knowledge and new perspectives they might contribute. Most of my colleagues value biodiversity in the realms of plant and animal life and the natural world. They also value cultural diversity and worry about the disappearance of cultural traditions and minority languages. However, both inside and outside the academy, little value is placed on human diversity in the form of bodies and minds that differ from what we conceive of as normative. The daily lives of most disabled people require inventiveness, creative interdependence, and artful navigation of the built environment. People with disabilities are not simply objects of study but also producers of knowledge, art, and culture. The idea that variability in human form and function might give rise to creativity and new knowledge, and thus might be worth preserving, is viewed at best as eccentric. (In the case of people whose primary language is a sign language, bodily difference has produced significant cultural and linguistic diversity. Indeed, Deaf people often consider themselves to be culturally different rather than disabled. Thus *deafness*, as in "to suffer from deafness," and *deaf*, as in "to be deaf," are usually not capitalized but the latter in "Deaf people" and "Deaf culture" often is, signaling that deafness might be understood not only as incomplete or burdensome but also as a gift, complete with its own culture and language.)

As Sarah Willie-LeBreton points out in the Introduction, the rhetoric of diversity has been enthusiastically embraced in higher education. Citing Lennard J. Davis, she notes that the call for diversity is no longer a challenge to dominant modes of thinking; it has in some sense been co-opted by the voice of the institution. Davis (2013) argues that "*normal* is being decommissioned as a discursive organizer. . . . *Diverse* serves as the new normalizing term. Another way of putting this . . . is that *diversity* is the new *normality*" (1). Yet, he continues, diversity in its current conception is built on the exclusion of disability: "While diversity is the regnant ideology, the older concept of normal still holds sway, but only when it comes to disability" (6). Disability, in other words, remains the abject other of diversity. Colleges and universities routinely proclaim and advertise the diversity of their student "body," but some forms of difference are more highly valued than others. Much work remains to be done in building institutions that embrace diversity in all its dimensions, but disability, in many cases, is not even at the table. Too often, disability continues to be viewed through frameworks of pathology and abnormalcy rather than those of identity and human diversity.

The cultural history of disability has been marked by eugenics, charity, institutionalization, underemployment, and the valorization of medical procedures and elusive cures over systems of support that enable disabled people to lead rich, interdependent lives. Disability rights activists have long contested these approaches and in recent years have gained considerable ground. K–12 education has been transformed by the Americans with Disabilities Act (ADA) and the ADA Amendments Act; Section 504 of the Rehabilitation Act; and especially the Individuals with Disabilities Education Act (IDEA), which requires that schools provide eligible students with a "free appropriate public education" in the "least restrictive environment," that they create an individualized education plan (IEP) for each student, and that they prepare students for "further education, employment, and independent living" (For the full text of IDEA, see U.S. Department of Education n.d.). As a result of this legislation, students now in college attended K–12 schools in which students with and without documented disabilities have learned together in the same classroom. To be sure, the practices of mainstreaming and IEPs still leave much to be desired and often fall short of the ideal of full inclusion. For some, mainstreaming has potentially negative effects: Deaf schools have historically been the site of Deaf cultural life and the development and transmission of sign languages, and thus their gradual disappearance is a loss. Nonetheless, most of my students are at home with disability in a way that their parents' generation—which includes me, and many of my colleagues—is not. They are much more likely to have friends with disabilities and to have grown up with disabled siblings or neighbors. And students with physical and mental disabilities are entering college in record numbers. (According to one report, "Students with disabilities represented nearly 11 percent of all postsecondary students in 2008.") In 2008, students with disabilities were similar to their peers without disabilities with regard to age, race, and the schools they attended. (See U.S. Government Accountability Office [2009].)

Yet disabled students pursuing postsecondary education still face considerable challenges. A report sponsored by the Institute for Higher Education Policy concluded:

> In higher education there is no legal guarantee of a "free appropriate public education," no individual education plan (IEP), no significant parental involvement, no publicly-provided assessments, and no "modifications" to the curriculum that change it in any "fundamental" or "substantial" way. Students with disabilities in K–12 have a structured process provided for them to lead to successful outcomes. In higher education, the student is protected against discrimination and provided an equal opportunity, but there is no process aimed at achieving success (Steele and Wolanin 2004, viii).

Broad systems of support have been slow to develop in higher education in part because the pervasive rhetoric of diversity has only recently, and reluctantly, begun to include disability. I doubt that many faculty and administrators could explain why it might be a generative and important practice, as opposed to simply a legal mandate, to include disabled students, faculty, and staff in our academic communities. (The Association for Higher Education and Disability [AHEAD] has been a leader in changing this culture and building support for students with disabilities.)

Most institutions understand what they need to do in order to be in compliance with the ADA clauses requiring access to physical spaces, though some have been schooled in compliance by federal lawsuits or settlement agreements.[1] Often noncompliance results from a failure to imagine disabled people as part of our communities. In one such instance, the college where I teach renovated an older dormitory, and in so doing triggered the ADA clause that requires the construction of a wheelchair-accessible dormitory room and bathroom. Finally, we had a fully accessible dorm room, but no ramp to gain access to the building. The college's position, for many years, was that they would build a ramp if and when a student who uses a wheelchair enrolled. Meanwhile, students who led admissions tours told me of their considerable embarrassment when they had to explain to prospective students touring the campus by wheelchair that an accessible room existed, but they couldn't visit it because they couldn't get into the building. Many years ago, at a committee meeting with a provost, a feminist scholar committed to gender equity whom I admired, I raised the issue of the rampless building. The provost politely explained that we couldn't "have everything"; for instance, she continued, the college lacks its own swimming pool. In the case of the pool, a student must get on the shuttle bus and travel five minutes to our partner campus to swim. In the case of the ramp, a student who uses a wheelchair could not, until recently, live in any campus building at a college where 98 percent of students and over 60 percent of faculty live on campus.[2] Frankly, I was astounded that our progressive provost saw no connection between providing equal access to students, faculty, and staff of different genders, races, and socioeconomic backgrounds and access to those with disabilities. She is hardly alone.

Focusing on access to higher education for one subordinated group at a time denies the powerful connections between these groups as well as the intersectional nature of embodied identities. Examining one axis of intersection, Steele and Wolanin (2004) found:

> Students with disabilities generally have lower incomes than their peers without disabilities. . . . In addition, it is expensive for low-income students with disabilities to meet the special needs associated with daily life and academic life. . . . Students with disabilities also generally need more time for self-care, daily living, and academic tasks than their peers without disabilities. This results in students with disabilities taking twice as long to complete their degrees as their peers without disabilities. The longer time that students with disabilities need to complete their studies increases their costs and the financial barriers they face. (ix)

Many institutions are now working to improve access to higher education for low-income students, but *low income* is often treated as a category that doesn't intersect with race, gender, sexuality, or disability.

While it is crucial to enable physical access to the academic, residential, and social spaces on campus, altering the built environment addresses only one dimension of access. Moreover, the very notion of *compliance* is a legalistic one that suggests responding to the letter of the law rather than willingly and creatively envisioning flexible spaces and practices to accommodate a variety of bodies and minds. Providing access can mean making information available in multiple modes; hiring American Sign Language interpreters familiar with academic discourse; using technology creatively; providing texts in large print, braille, and alternative formats; and so on. Once we begin to imagine what access might look like, the possibilities seem endless, the concept elusive and protean. I like to think that providing access involves more than checking off a list of practical accommodations, though these practical matters are incredibly important. Access also involves a way of thinking about the world that challenges us to imagine how another body, another mind, experiences it.

If disability is the abject other of diversity, mental disability is the abject other of disability. The barriers for those with mental disabilities, broadly defined, can be considerably greater than the barriers for those with disabilities that are primarily physical. In her important study *Mad at School: Rhetorics of Mental Disability and Academic Life*, Margaret Price (2011) addresses the seeming paradox of mental disability in the academy, a space that privileges rationality, logic, and coherence. She employs *mental disability* as a capacious term that includes people with psychiatric disabilities, people on the autism spectrum, people with cognitive impairments, and those experiencing the brain fog that accompanies some chronic illnesses. Price calls attention to who is excluded and to the consequences of that exclusion both for those without full access to academic life and for those who lose the opportunity to work alongside people representing a wide variation of minds. She asks us to rethink radically the work we aim to accomplish in the academy and who can and should participate in this work.

Access demands temporal as well as spatial accommodations. The temporal dimension of access is often overlooked in an academic culture built on norms of productivity. The only standard disability accommodation I can think of that recognizes this dimension is untimed testing, in which a student performs the same task as every other student but is given more time in which to do it. The temporal aspects of access, however, are not limited to "extra" time. Disabled students, faculty, or staff may experience differences in pace and stamina, either in general or in relation to particular cognitive or physical tasks. They may also experience interruptions in teaching and learning related to medical or disability issues, unusual sleep-wake schedules, rhythms of high and low productivity. The structure of academic life is built around semesters, trimesters, or quarters in which even a missed week or two, for either teacher or student, significantly affects the rhythm and sequence of work. While some colleges and universities encourage students to take a set number of credit hours, those usually translate into a set number of courses. A course load for a full-time student is typically three to five courses taken simultaneously; a course load for a full-time faculty member has a far more dramatic range, from one course each semester to four courses each semester, depending on the status of the faculty member, his or her additional responsibilities, and the type of institution. Some people who live with illness or disability cannot manage four or more courses a semester. Most graduate and many undergraduate curricula include three-hour seminars that require both physical and mental stamina. The tenure "clock" typically runs for seven years and sometimes competes with a woman's biological "clock." An academic career follows a temporal arc, and any significant deviation from this arc—except an unusually rapid pace of productivity—raises questions at each stage of evaluation, at the point of hiring, the granting of tenure, and further promotions.

For me, and for many others who live with chronic illnesses that affect their stamina, the most significant barrier to full participation in academic life is the pace at which a faculty member, and indeed most everyone in the modern workplace, is expected to move and work. The physical *spaces* of academic work are accessible to me, but the *pace* of academic life is not. I do all the things other academics do: I teach, write, serve on committees, do administrative work, organize and attend conferences. But I cannot do all these things at the same time, and I cannot do them at the same pace as my nondisabled colleagues. Thus, I have worked part time for most of my career. I am fortunate to have taught at the same college for many years and to have worked with many extraordinary students and colleagues. I love what I do. At the same time, I am troubled by the inequities of part-time labor and by the necessity of being underemployed to avoid being unemployed or overemployed.

I have chosen not to apply for full-time or tenure-line jobs because I cannot yet envision a workplace in which I could operate at my own pace. My concerns about being able to perform a conventionally defined academic job begin with the marathon day required of a job candidate visiting a campus. I imagine myself on the phone scheduling a campus interview at another institution: "Could we start my interview day at about noon? Could we do it all in one building so I don't have to walk long distances? I'd love to meet some students, but maybe I could skip dinner with the whole department? And by the way, if my visit falls on one of those days, weeks, or months when I'm feeling great, you can ignore everything I just said." Somehow I don't think I'd get too far in this search. At the college where I teach, I recently I served on a search committee that required an overworked administrative assistant to find a different three-hour time slot every week in which several busy people, including the provost, could meet. The first time she called me into her office to ask about available time slots, I told her I could clear everything from my schedule on Monday, Wednesday, and Friday afternoons. She replied that the provost was only available on Tuesday or Thursday mornings from eight to ten. I told her I couldn't be there until eleven. She looked at me as if to say, "Are you crazy? Do you really think your schedule is more important than the provost's?" I explained that I have a chronic illness that affects my stamina and sleep schedule. I was in luck; she has a cousin with a similar illness, and she immediately understood my limitations. We brainstormed together about how I could participate as fully as possible in the meeting without being physically present for it.

If everyone were as understanding as this person, perhaps it would be possible to navigate academic culture more easily. But because there is no systemic accommodation in place for people like me, doing my job requires that I negotiate with many individual people—administrative assistants, registrars, department chairs, provosts—to make sure that I can both perform well and take care of my health. This in itself can be exhausting.

In some respects, academic work is more flexible than most careers. After I became ill nearly two decades ago, I was gradually able to return to teaching and writing. If I had been a waitress, or a dancer, or a trial lawyer, my career would have been over. But the vision that many nonacademics have of the leisurely academic life—teaching a few hours a week, reading novels the rest of the time, spending summers at the beach—belies the reality. Academic life is far more demanding than this popular image suggests, and a full load of teaching, research, and service requires both physical and mental stamina. The "life of the mind" implies the absence, or irrelevance, of the body. But of course our bodies not only enable us to work—the brain is, after all, a body part—they also shape the work that we do.

Within the disability community, many use the term *crip time* to signify a flexible approach to temporal demands. (*Crip* shortens the word *crippled* and reappropriates it as an honorable identity.) As Alison Kafer (2013) explains, "Crip time is flex time not just expanded but exploded; it requires reimagining our notions of what can and should happen in time. . . . Rather than bend disabled bodies and minds to meet the clock, crip time bends the clock to meet disabled bodies and minds" (27).

For academics whose work lives have been altered by parenthood, disability, illness, caregiving, or other life events, current practice is generally a time-limited "leave" (for example, maternity, medical, or family leave) rather than a flexible restructuring of how, when, and at what pace work gets done. The institutional cultures we inhabit place a premium on certain rhythms of productivity, thus making it difficult to envision other ones. Colleagues, even those I don't know well, sometimes come to my office, close the door tightly, and ask my advice about how to manage disability at work. Few have considered that in a flexible institutional environment, living with disability might give them tools that enrich their teaching, research, and mentoring.

People with disabilities—whether students, faculty, or staff—have a great deal to contribute to academic life. But enabling our full participation requires creatively rethinking how academic jobs, conferences, classrooms, and academic culture more generally can accommodate bodies and minds that move, think, and communicate in different ways and at different paces. How, then, might we rethink both the spaces and paces of academic work? I offer three places to begin.

First, we can construct flexibly configured jobs. Shared positions and dignified, stable part-time positions with benefits would enable academics who can't work sixty hours a week to enter the profession and to remain in it if they became disabled. Our profession loses many talented people with disabilities because there are so few positions that are configured in a flexible way. I know many academics who live with some form of chronic illness: diabetes, multiple sclerosis, lupus, heart disease, chronic fatigue syndrome. Those who were well established in their careers before they became ill are sometimes able to negotiate a reduced course load or other accommodations; others must relinquish their jobs. Those of us who became ill early in our careers often don't even apply for tenure-line positions. Wouldn't all of us—not just those of us with disabilities—benefit from more flexibility in the configuration of academic jobs? How might we adapt models of job sharing and part-time work common in other professions to ours? Why does this sound like an unreachable, utopian ideal?

Second, we can rethink academic conferences. By design, conferences pack a lot of academic work, socializing, and networking into a few days. This is a viable model for some people, but not for others. Traveling takes a lot of energy, and the long days of conferences are stimulating but also exhausting. I love small conferences where most events take place in the same building or adjacent ones, where there's a convenient lounge to rest in without retreating to my hotel room, where I can take time out without feeling as if I'm missing everything, where events are planned to allow time for real conversation and collaboration. A recent conference at the University of Delaware titled "Disability Disclosure in/and Higher Education," organized by Stephanie Kerschbaum and Margaret Price (2013), was sponsored by the University's Center for the Study of Diversity and modeled a variety of approaches to access, including generous time for Q&A, longer breaks between sessions, and a quiet room for resting during the conference. Bringing in speakers via Skype is becoming a more common practice at conferences, one that enables participation by those who can't travel for a variety of reasons, including finances, logistics, and disability. Posting conference papers and conversations online improves access too. People with disabilities are often the first to use new digital resources and technologies, resources that then become more widely used by others.

Third, we can train teachers in universal instructional design, which offers us ways of making our classrooms more welcoming to students and faculty with a variety of learning and teaching styles. As many have pointed out, accessibility and universal design are always aspirational, never fully achieved. Price (2011) writes, "Universal design sets as its ideal a learning environment that is accessible to all learning styles, abilities, and personalities, but acknowledges that such efforts must always be partial and engaged in a process of continual revision" (87). Yet pedagogical practices ranging from a statement on the syllabus inviting students to discuss their learning styles to carefully and flexibly paced course readings contribute to a more inclusive classroom. When all students are offered a variety of modes through which to engage with course material, discussion, and assessment, students with disabilities are less often singled out for special accommodations, and everyone benefits. (In fact, one of Price's chapters is titled "Ways to Move: Presence, Participation, and Resistance in Kairotic Space," and it offers an excellent discussion of universal design and a wealth of practical suggestions for redesigning the classroom.)

Thinking about how to make the academy more inclusive takes me back to the deaf student I taught twenty years ago, the first time I consciously made room for disability in my classroom. During that year, I was gradually developing the chronic illness with which I still live, and which reshaped the course of my career. I consider Peter to be one of my mentors—though neither of us was aware of it at the time—in navigating academic life with a disability. Learning how to make room for deafness in my classroom, I had no idea that I would soon need to learn to advocate for disability accommodations for myself. That's the thing about disability: while some people have been "doing disability" their whole lives, many of us encounter it midstream, and there's a steep learning curve. As many scholars and activists have pointed out, disability is an identity category that is mutable, and most of us will inhabit at some point in our lives. Looking back, I realize that the responsibility for educating Peter's teachers, deans, and fellow students about access was placed almost entirely on him. He was treated as an anomaly, a problem to be solved, and I can only imagine the energy it cost him to educate us, one at a time, day after day. We need to bring conversations about disability, access, and higher education into the open and into every sector of the academy so that no single student, faculty, or staff member is tasked with educating their community. We need to cultivate collaboration among faculty members teaching disability studies, staff members charged with providing disability accommodations, and administrators invested in including disability in conversations about diversity. Collectively, we can build a flexible teaching and learning environment that values and welcomes the contributions of people with disabilities.

NOTES

1 The Department of Justice and a liberal arts college reached a settlement agreement that requires the college to address each of the areas identified in the suit: "The agreement results from a compliance review in which the Department [of Justice] found

barriers to access in existing facilities and elements such as doors, restrooms, seating, signage, and interior and exterior circulation routes. It addresses a wide variety of services and facilities, including administrative buildings, housing, access between facilities, parking, directional signage and emergency preparedness" (U.S. Department of Justice 2007).

2 http://www.haverford.edu/admission/files/Haverford-College-Viewbook.pdf.

9 ◆ QUEER AFFECTS/ QUEER ACCESS

ANNA WARD

Given the institutional locations I have held over the years, I cannot speak to what it feels like to be a queer faculty member and educator at avowedly conservative institutions and the degree of hostility, insecurity, and perhaps downright terror that must entail. I can, however, speak to having one's lived experience of an institution feel off-message. The stakes are quite high for institutions that pride themselves on an image of diversity and inclusivity, so high that failures to live up to these ideals are defined as necessarily exterior to the institution ("that's not who we are") or are reframed as coming *from* whoever has expressed a grievance towards the institution.

Institutionalization in the form of gender studies and LGBT programs, resource centers, anti-discrimination policies, and a few high-profile LGBT administrators can provide a certain kind of cover for insidious and deeply entrenched heteronormativity, even in putatively progressive institutions. Indeed, sitting in faculty-wide meetings over the years, "queer" seems like the least apt descriptor as the same tired dynamics play out, with senior, straight-identified male colleagues talking the longest and loudest, and certainly the most often, and where the socializing among colleagues is skewed towards networks of spouses and children, which *could* include LGBT faculty but largely do not.

The queerness of these institutions is more driven by the students than we would like to admit, with a smattering of queer faculty and staff "microclimates" as Martha Ackelsberg et al. (2009) have termed them. Drawing from the meaning of "microclimate" in ecology as "the atmospheric conditions affecting an individual or a small group of organisms, esp. when they differ from the climate of the rest of the community," Ackelsberg et al. argue that understanding how microclimates operate in academia is critically important in evaluating the support for and retention of faculty from underrepresented groups (100). In colleges and universities, a microclimate is "a small, relatively self-contained environment within which a faculty member operates. It could be a department, a committee, an interdisciplinary program, a reading group, or a purely social configuration" (84). Ackelsberg et al. demonstrate how faculty from underrepresented groups "may experience different conditions than the majority faculty in any given institution," and that microclimates are often at the heart of whether those conditions are positive, tolerable, or intolerable.

The move to incorporate faculty from underrepresented groups or marginal positionalities creates a complicated dynamic for faculty members and the micro/macroclimate in which they are embedded. For the program, department, and larger institution, if you identify as one of these faculty, you represent the double-edged sword of diversity. On one hand, the institution benefits from your presence with respect to diversity as public relations, a gesture towards inclusivity and "cutting-edge" teaching and scholarship; on the other hand, you are often viewed as imposing a certain stress on the institutional climate when you embody the very diversity you were hired to represent. For the faculty member, the diversity as public relations position feels tokenizing and it can often lead to demands for time and energy that are exhausting and difficult to refuse, particularly for junior and adjunct faculty members.

The more you embody the difference you are called on to represent, however, the more you experience cues to minimize it; if you cannot minimize your difference or refuse to, you run the risk of becoming that difference absolutely. This latter dynamic becomes particularly troubling when your scholarly specialization is viewed as mapping on to your identity or positionality; becoming difference absolutely, or being reduced to it, also becomes a way to delegitimize your expertise and/or your perspective on relevant issues affecting the institution. Queer faculty members whose primary specialization is queer studies may find that it is through their teaching and research that they continue to experience both overt hostility and/or microaggressions from other faculty members. Working in "'marginal' and/or 'cutting-edge' specialties in their disciplines" (Ackelsberg 2009, 100), queer faculty doing queer work may find that what they *do* becomes a convenient target for tensions over who they are and who they are seen to represent in the institution. I'll never forget my first week working at Swarthmore when a professor from another department knocked on my office door to introduce himself. After the briefest of welcomes, he pointed to the course flyer on my door and remarked, "I noticed the flyer on your door as I was walking by. I guess Swarthmore will let people teach anything now."

Thinking in terms of micro/macroclimates may be a helpful way to understand the complex maneuvering that faculty from underrepresented or marginalized groups must engage in as we move through institutions, often occupying spaces that can feel radically askew from one another. The classroom itself can function as its own microclimate, and in some cases, the space of the classroom can feel more amenable to queer faculty members than spaces beyond it. Queer faculty and queer students can experience parallel frustrations with the heteronormativity of particular microclimates and the institutional macroclimate. This is particularly true in regard to the *content* of one's teaching and research. Due to the relatively self-selecting nature of enrollment, the students that enroll in my courses on queer studies tend to be there because they value the framework and welcome its inclusion in the curriculum; it is often the case that the inclusion of queer content into the curriculum is, in part, a response to student demand. Thus, in a strange fashion, the microclimate of the classroom can become the one that feels most welcoming to marginalized specialties within a discipline or field, or within the wider culture of the institution, or at the very least, the microclimate within which we have the most agency. To position the space of the classroom as a potentially amenable space to queer work does not mean, however, that it is altogether clear *how* queerness enters the classroom and how the space of the classroom informs and is informed by the larger institutional context.

In addition to institutional dynamics, the question that many scholars and educators have asked is whether and how queer makes a difference in the classroom. This question is particularly relevant given that fundamental to queer is the repudiation of stable referents that might properly fix someone as queer in the first place. Mary Bryson and Suzanne de Castell ask, "What difference does it make—*being queer* in the classroom? What does that mean, anyway—*being* queer? How does it matter—with whom, or how, we re/construct sexual and affectional relations" (1993, 271)? If queer does not attach to any specific sexual and/or affectional relations, but is rather posited as constituting an exterior to whatever is positioned as normal, as some queer scholars have argued, then how does one do queer within institutions that are largely in service to the project of normal? Connie Monson and Jacqueline Rhodes sum up the dilemma, "If we, as somewhat complicitous, somewhat radical, always desirous, always lacking 'literacy workers' (teachers/scholars/tutors/students) seek ourselves to articulate positionality, we move toward an understanding of a performative, *queer* pedagogy that does not rely on a false personal for its critical energy" (2004, 88). Pamela Caughie (1994) has productively pressed this question in her work on "passing" in relation to pedagogy, re-working our common associations with the term:

> Passing takes many forms, from the strategic adoption of a culturally empowered identity to the disempowering mimicry of a threatening difference. But all passing is marked by the double bind that opens a discrepancy between what one professes to be and how one is actually positioned in a society, institution, discourse, or classroom. The passer must always run the risk of self-betrayal in any particular performance. Thus, the double bind cannot be resolved only theoretically, but must be confronted performatively as well through a performative pedagogy that seeks to enact rather than endorse certain positions. (78)

Drawing on Bryson and de Castell, as well as Caughie's work, Monson and Rhodes argue that, "[A] queer pedagogy invites us to strain against and yet celebrate our double binds—to risk 'self-betrayal' in our im/perfect praxis, our fictive and temporary stability, our momentary selves" (2004, 90). The "double-bind," and the straining that goes along with, is a dynamic that I sense most queer professors experience on some level.

At no time in my career as a teacher has the call to "strain against and yet celebrate our double binds—to risk 'self-betrayal' in our im/perfect praxis, our fictive and temporary stability, our momentary selves" felt more pressing. At the moment, I am just a handful of class sessions into a course I have never taught before, a course entitled Queering Disability. Offered through the Program for the Study of Women and Gender at Smith

College, the course is aimed at second-year students and beyond, requiring our introductory course, Introduction to the Study of Women and Gender, as a prerequisite. Due to the prerequisite and other course content students are likely to encounter at Smith, students are coming in with a fairly good grounding in feminist theory, LGBT studies, and a bit of queer theory; however, most of the students have never taken a course in disability studies and have little to no background in the field. Given this, I structured the course in such a way that the first few weeks of class would introduce them to foundational texts in the field of disability studies before the course transitioned to a more specific focus on texts taking up dis/ability in relation to gender and sexuality. The course weaves academic texts with memoir, poetry, and performance, though the focus remains largely on disability studies as an academic field of knowledge production.

Laboring over a syllabus largely structured around disability studies immediately brings an unavoidable contradiction to the fore as academia is perhaps one of the most glaring institutional sites of ableism, so much so that to do disability studies within it feels uncomfortable, if not downright ridiculous. Is that why there is so very little of it across the curriculum? Does taking disability studies seriously necessarily call into question the project of the academy itself and our complicity in it? In short, yes. Noting this is nothing new, but it has helped me articulate for myself why queerness so often feels similarly out of step within academic institutions yet so trapped within it. Designing this course put pressure on my nondisabled privilege, as I expected it would, but I did not anticipate the extent to which it would exert pressure on who and what travels as queer, particularly as that positionality is refracted in and through the lens of dis/ability.

Affect is the realm within which I find queer studies and disability studies colliding in the most thrilling fashion, and which comes to bear the most on the debates and controversies that have indelibly marked the liberal arts institutions with which I have come to be affiliated, but which are by no means limited to these sites. In the past five years, I have witnessed campuses wrenched apart by issues of sexual assault, mental health services, racism, fraternity culture, vandalism, the inclusion of trans students, fossil fuel divestment, and two high-profile incidents of students objecting to the awarding of an honorary degree and an honorary speaker invitation for commencement. While each of these issues brings its own complexities, I am consistently struck by how quickly these controversies become focused on the perceived impropriety of student responses to them. As Elizabeth Ellsworth notes, "In schools, rational deliberation, reflection, and consideration of all viewpoints has become a vehicle for regulating conflict and the power to speak" (1989, 301). Civility and critical thinking become the new buzzwords by which to chastise and infantilize student objections to conditions of inequality and the violence of normalization. Before students are to be heard at all, their demands must be rerouted through institutionalized channels. Student responses are framed as disturbing the macroclimate of the institution itself, tarnishing a symbolic community and creating disease within it.

Sara Ahmed's work (2010) on affect is particularly useful in this regard. Grounded in phenomenology, Ahmed's work interrogates how certain affects *stick* to marginalized positionalities. In *The Promise of Happiness*, Ahmed calls for "suspending the belief that happiness is a good thing" (13) in order to understand how happiness becomes a normalizing requirement imposed on marginalized communities in order to stem critique. She argues, "The demand for happiness is increasingly articulated as a demand to return to social ideals, as if what explains the crisis of happiness is not the failure of these ideals but our failure to follow them" (7). How this demand is imposed, according to Ahmed, is by burdening marginalized subjects with the responsibility for the happiness of the privileged. The "killjoy" critique that Ahmed has become known for, "feminist killjoys" in particular, is "the idea that there is a necessary and inevitable relationship of dependence between one person's happiness and the happiness of others" and that killjoys prevent the happiness of others by calling out instances of sexism or refusing to be made happy by relations of inequality. "Happiness," Ahmed argues, "becomes the expected 'default position' for those who are oppressed, such that it comes to define the sphere of neutrality" (66). To register unease, discomfort, unhappiness, sadness, or anger is to be cast out from the realm of neutrality, objectivity, and rationality.

One of the aspects I have always appreciated about the fields of feminist studies, critical race studies, and certainly queer studies as a field, is the relentless insistence on interrogating how reason and emotion are falsely construed as antithetical, how some affective responses get stuck to some identities and/or communities and not others, how some affective responses come to be codified as positive and others negative, and how affective responses are regulated across time and space. There is an intensity to students' needs; I can feel frustration, sadness, disappointment, and rage radiating from them as they move through institutional spaces they have come to understand as being set against them. At times, I find this intensity overwhelming and can understand the desire to contain it, manage it, ease it, particularly on the part of administration and staff who are perhaps more directly implicated in campus life and student wellbeing than faculty may be. Nonetheless, the move to create quickly "teachable moments" is understood by students for what they usually are—attempts to change the conversation. These conversations may be no less important, but they are distinctly *different* conversations. We do not give students enough credit, in this respect, as I think many of them are well aware of the dangers of institutionalization, particularly the kind of institutionalization that can seem like progress. Roderick A. Ferguson's work provides a useful interrogation of the dangers of "the will to institutionalization" and "the academy's transformation of minority cultures and differences into objects of institutional knowledge" (2012, 214), a transformation of which my field of gender studies must be understood as an integral part. This "will to institutionalization" extends beyond just field formations, but also includes our insistence that the very systems that are the sites of conflict be the arbiters of how that conflict unfolds.

What would change if we slowed down the process of trying to contain student responses to events on campus or reroute these responses into institutional channels? What would we risk by letting students risk their selves in this way? There is a mistaken assumption that being emotional or passionate—publicly—is easy. That always strikes me as a presumption that comes from tremendous privilege. For students from marginalized backgrounds, communities, and positionalities, emotionality is a liability, a liability from which many students have worked very hard to distance themselves in order to have access to these institutions. The students I encounter in my classrooms are quite familiar with the politics of respectability and the high costs of deviating from a presentation of self that only displays the *right* emotions at the *right* times to the *right* degree. K. Hyoejin Yoon provocatively interrogates how the field of critical pedagogy can perpetuate this dynamic, even if unintentionally:

The discourse of critical pedagogy achieves its cultural currency, not solely through its reliance on rationalism, but also through an unacknowledged reliance on *pathos*. Appeals to *pathos* play a crucial role in shaping teaching identity. Such appeals persuade the teacher or speaker to internalize a particular ethos, a self-image of oneself who, according to Aristotle, "looks right" and is thought "to entertain the right feelings," a speaker in whose "good sense, good moral and goodwill" we trust—the noble character of the "transformative intellectual" or "teacher-intellectual" (2005, 718).

Catherine Fox takes up Yoon's argument and builds upon it, arguing that the "binary logic in which 'others' (uncritical students, 'bad teachers,' inauthentic daughters of the transformative intellectual) are constructed over and against the 'nobility' of the transformative intellectual" significantly impacts and limits how debates unfold across campuses (2006, 246). Faculty members from underrepresented groups feel this constraint no less than do students. Very often, I find myself in a trap familiar to many faculty members from marginalized positionalities: the trap of having my perspective interpreted as the product of an emotional, and, therefore irrational, grievance. These are the dynamics by which we become, as Ahmed suggests, "constrained even by the categories we love" in the institutions within which we work (4). More and more, I feel less and less like a "transformative teacher-intellectual" than I do simply a teacher transformed by the demand to perform a certain kind of critical distance and rationality.

Designing a course and being in a classroom that is, in part, dedicated to interrogating critically how fields of knowledge production create and maintain categories of normality and abnormality with respect to rationality, cognitive processing, learning, emotion, social interaction, relationality, and desire, just to name a few, has brought this into sharp relief. Most instructors who have written about queer pedagogy write about queerness in relation to how courses unfold: being in the classroom and the dynamic that emerges between the instructor and students, between students and students, and even within students themselves. Less attention is paid to before being in the classroom: course design, our most private aspirations, or our most serious sources of dread. Over the course of my career, I have often thought carefully about how I take up space in the classroom, how I perform my body in front of the class, and how my body is read. When lecturing on gender presentation, for example, I am aware of how much my students take in about my presence in the classroom and how much the content of the lecture boomerangs off my own embodied and aesthetic performance of gender, sexuality, race, class, and ability. Teaching now at the intersection of "queer" and "disability" has pushed me towards new considerations of how I teach and the difference that queer difference makes. The enactment of queer studies, the *how* of it, is often over-determined by the attempt to render it legible as a legitimate field of knowledge production. This is enacted through a certain amount of oft-noted obfuscation. I do not think my experience designing the Queering Disability course will change *what* I teach, necessarily—I remain committed to providing students a thorough grounding in the field of queer studies and doing so directly through the texts that are often-cited in the field, rather than having students only read interpretations of that work. Those texts tend to be dense, theoretically complex, and difficult. Besides what I teach, I can begin to alter how I teach, moving differently, being aware of my performance, and becoming more mindful of how even performing one subdominant identity, queerness, is also always simultaneously being read through my performance of a dominant identity, *able-bodied*.

The class could just as easily be called Cripping Queer, in that many of the texts specifically address the ableism of LGBT studies, queer studies, and queer cultures. I feel less authorized, however, to deploy "crip" in this fashion, particularly to stake a claim to the term in the title of a class. Indeed, I felt a need to position myself as nondisabled on the first day of class. My explicit decision to interrogate my own positionality as the instructor (of a class centered on disabilities) who does not identify as a person with a disability seemed in line with the good feminist practice in which I was trained, namely, of recognizing one's positionality, owning it and naming it. I wanted to make sure that the many students in the room who do identify as people with disabilities understood that I was not claiming authority to speak on their behalf or their experiences. On the other hand, I am at the front of the class and they are not; that fact alone necessarily authorizes me to speak with the full weight of institutional privilege that trails behind a professor and becomes the background of the classroom, a background against which everything else that happens in that space is so often juxtaposed. This is further reinforced by the sheer size of the class; as a 200-level course, there is no enrollment cap, and I currently have fifty-two students enrolled. In a class this large, the usual tactics I employ to deemphasize the traditional framework of me as bearer of knowledge with students as recipients become difficult. The classroom space fans out auditorium-style with fixed seats facing forward with me positioned at the front, a spatial configuration that reinforces the giver-receiver model of education.

One of my tasks at the front of this room is to find ways to disrupt certain enactments of ability from sliding too easily into queerness and vice versa. Part of that task is to resist the urge to rob queer theory of its moments of irrationality, its rage, its wallowing, its shame, its mean-spiritedness, its randomness, its non-sense, and its trenchant need to remain illegible; to let queer theory's *in*accessibility also be a site of tremendous accessibility in its insistence on merging enactments of academic language with unabashed or barely-muted fervor and total disregard for academic protocols. Caughie highlights the importance of risk, or even pedagogy *as* risk, in her work, highlighting not only the risks we ask our students to take, but also those we as teachers take. Some of us are more authorized to take risks than others; certainly, being white and able to deemphasize my working-class background offers me more room to maneuver than my colleagues who are positioned differently. Keeping in mind the degree to which each of us can take on these risks, we would benefit from pushing ourselves as far as we can safely go, "to keep asking what we are doing with diversity" (Ahmed, 2012, 17) when we find ourselves called upon to *be* diversity.

Quite a few scholars have written about their experiences as openly queer faculty in rather conservative institutions and/or departments, often reflecting on the burdens that come with being "the only one." I am fortunate to have had associations with institutions and programs more likely to be associated *with* rather than against queerness, namely the Gender and Sexuality Studies Program at Swarthmore College and, currently, the Program for the Study of Women and Gender at Smith College. Both institutions—small liberal arts colleges that actively cultivate a reputation for open-mindedness and inclusivity—have sizeable and active queer student communities and a number of openly LGBT and queer faculty and staff.

While the degree to which these institutions live up to their ideal is the subject of debate and should continue to be so, I do not want to discount how powerful even *the expectation of inclusivity* is for queer faculty members, particularly junior and adjunct faculty members such as myself. In addition, I have never experienced overt hostility from students for being open about my sexuality or for my gender presentation that often announces my queerness even when I do not.

At the same time, thinking through the Queering Disability course, with the intense debates that have erupted on college campuses as the unavoidable backdrop, has pushed me to think carefully about affect in the classroom and take more risks with respect to my performance of competency, expertise, and self-management. We have become so accustomed to performing in these ways that it is easy to forget how much work goes into making it seem like it comes naturally. To make classrooms, and the institutional sites within which they are located, both more accessible *and* queer, also means to risk losing control of the affective terms of engagement and not knowing, in advance, where that will get us.

My sincere hope is that it will look a bit like what Ferguson imagined it could be, performing "a different type of will to institutionality, one that searches for interpretative and institutional practices that will more likely protect and incite a dynamism around the meanings of minority culture and difference, a will to institutionality that honors that feeling that 'this world is not enough'" (232).

10 ◆ GEOGRAPHIES OF DIFFERENCE

From Unity to Solidarity

BETTY G. SASAKI

> Beloved community is formed not by the eradication of difference but by its affirmation, by each of us claiming the identities and cultural legacies that shape who we are and how we live in the world.
>
> —bell hooks

During the fall semester of the 2012–2013 academic year, as part of Colby College's bicentennial celebration, bell hooks was invited to speak on campus. Addressing a packed house, hooks spoke to the notion of community as a process that requires of its members the commitment and courage to end domination so that we can connect. In the face of interlocking privilege systems (patriarchy, capitalism, racism, imperialism) that hold domination in place, she exhorted us to go to the edge together to understand how privilege works in our lives so that we can move forward. Specifically, hooks encouraged us to challenge the logic of domination by cultivating a "beloved community," a community whose members ask themselves and each other what makes bonding possible across difference. A fundamental part of that inquiry will manifest as conflict, which, as hooks reminded us, is an inevitable part of any love relation. How we deal with conflict, however, is filled with possibility, a crucial first step being a willingness to decolonize ourselves and, by extension, our institutions, through rigorous and honest self-evaluation.

hooks's challenge to us is as urgent as it is daunting—urgent because without intentional strategies to negotiate our differences in relationship to one another, our communities remain fractured, and daunting because conflict, from an institutional perspective, is often considered a sign of failed community. This contradiction—the need for and resistance to community conflict—is one of the underlying causes of what the editor of this volume terms "academic-induced neurosis." It is a result of the difficult, often crazy-making process of trying to make sense of one's experiences in academic institutions whose practices, policies, and discourses are fraught with contradiction and ambivalence. Negotiating such institutional fault lines and cracks can be especially intimidating and potentially harmful to subdominant, multicultural community members, many of whom are actively recruited for the diversity they promise to bring to the institution, but whose *differences*, ironically, make them more vulnerable to catching a bad case of academic neurosis. As a biracial (Asian-White) woman from a working-class background who teaches Spanish at a private liberal arts college in New England, I have grappled with academic neurosis both directly and indirectly over the past two decades. The ongoing project of trying to make sense of these experiences for myself, my colleagues, and my students is at the heart of this essay and informs its broad objective to formulate a practical response to how we as educators and citizens move closer to hooks's notion of beloved community. Implicit in that inquiry are the questions raised by the ongoing labor described in the title of this collection, *Transforming the Academy*: How do we nurture relationships across difference? Whose experiences count among diverse social groups? What is the place of multiculturalism in community, and how do we interpret diverse experiences in relation to community policies, practices, and values? To begin to answer these questions, I want first to examine some of the mechanisms and contradictory messages used and invoked by my institution to simultaneously suppress and promote *difference*.

CONSENSUS, UNITY, AND IDEAL COMMUNITY

In her critique of an ideal of community as an antidote to oppression, Iris Marion Young (1986) points out that "the desire for community relies on the same desire for social wholeness and identification that underlies racism and ethnic chauvinism, on the one hand, and political sectarianism, on the other" (1–2). Social wholeness as a tenet of ideal community is fraught because it suggests a kind of harmonious correspondence among different groups, which is both seductive and dangerous to the extent that it denies difference between subjects. An uncomplicated understanding of social wholeness easily conflates wholeness with harmony, and harmony with fairness, the result of which is the failure to consider critically the social structures, practices, and policies by which such "wholeness" is achieved.

In the more specific context of a small liberal arts college committed to diversifying its historically White, heterosexual, upper-middle-class, Christian, able-bodied majority, the desire for social wholeness informs its understanding of multiculturalism as a kind of invitation to historically marginalized groups to join an already established community. The failure to acknowledge the dominant culture as one of the many cultures at play can reduce the gesture of inclusion to little more than an invitation to join "a game after the rules and standards have already been set, and having to prove oneself according to those rules and standards" (Young 1990, 164). Thus the operations of such unexamined diversifying enterprises end up reinforcing the very binaries (center-margin, oppressor-oppressed, and so forth) and exclusionary practices it purportedly seeks to interrupt, while the desire to uphold an ideal of social wholeness ironically ends up masking that subordination of difference.

At my institution, one of the most effective strategies for promoting the ideal of social wholeness and harmony as common community values is through a discourse of consensus. By a *discourse of consensus* I mean a repertoire of sanctioned narratives, from captions in the college's marketing guide books to websites about campus life to admissions literature to conduct codes and policies, which communicate widely held views about Colby as a unified, just, and inclusive community. (I refer to Young's definition of such discourses as "a system of stories and expert knowledge diffused through the society, which convey widely accepted generalizations about how society operates . . . , as well as the social norms and cultural values to which most of the people appeal when discussing their social and political problems and proposed solutions" [2001, 685].) Precisely because this idealized view of community is disseminated through multiple, sanctioned venues, it is not only accepted but also embraced as an essential part of the college's institutional identity. Moreover, the insistence on a seamless correspondence and a sense of shared unity among all the members of the community lends such a discourse a totalizing function that denies difference—not only different categories of social identity, but also the diversity of experiences among constituents and their different, sometimes critical, perspective of ideal community.

Given that consensus discourse not only promotes a totalizing sense of unity that denies difference but also masks this denial, what happens when community members try to unmask those contradictions? What might we learn from these acts of resistance and dissent? What do we stand to lose by ignoring or quelling those dissenting voices? By examining some recent personal experiences that I have had as a citizen of my imperfect academic community, these are some of the questions I want to explore. In the process, I hope to clarify some of the institutional challenges to the development of an alternative model of community, one in which dissent is understood not as an obstacle to but rather as an imperative for the creation of greater institutional justice for all its members.

CONFLICT AND DISSENT

Uncovering the contradictions of an unexamined notion of ideal community is a first step toward productively addressing its limitations and short-comings as a viable model for a just and democratic society. This process of uncovering and unlearning buried (and often unconscious) assumptions is what hooks (1995) and others refer to as decolonizing ourselves, our pedagogies, and our institutional practices. (For further discussions on the pedagogy, research methodology, and institutional practice of decolonization, see also Freire 2000; Mohanty 1994; Mostern 1994; and Pérez 1999.) Unsurprisingly, but no less dismaying, there is a great deal of institutional resistance even to admitting, let alone examining, organizational and structural incongruences that foster inequity and injustice among different members of the community. In its response to dissenting voices of some of its members, the institution's anxious efforts to maintain the illusion of unified community do more to sever connection than to secure it. If, however, we take up Chandra Mohanty's call to create "public cultures of dissent," where issues of inequity, marginalization, and oppression can be discussed in the context of institutional structures and practices, we not only recover connection but, more important, also open up the possibility to redefine and even reenvision it.

Returning to Colby's bicentennial, I want to examine a series of events that took place around February 27, 2013, the official "birthday" celebration for the college. The first of these events, which occurred on the birthday itself, included a student speech contest called If I Were President of Colby for a Day, and the convocation speech, given by the president himself, which was unexpectedly followed by a group of student activists. Juxtaposed, these two events, officially scheduled as they were, essentially bookended the day, literally and figuratively emphasizing the containment and order so valued as attributes of unified community. In contrast, the student actions at the center of each example were motivated by a desire to open up oppositional public space and, by extension, the possibility of reimagining community. Following this discussion, I will examine the varied institutional responses to these actions. In the process, I will discuss how accepted mechanisms of control and containment serve to protect the dominant construction of unified community.

On February 27, 2013, four months after bell hooks's visit, Colby celebrated the two hundredth anniversary of its founding, to the day, by canceling classes and organizing a series of celebratory events. The student speech contest took place shortly after lunch in the Page Commons Room, the large public auditorium in the student center. The room was filled with students, faculty, and administrators, including the president, who was seated front and center with other senior staff members. Spirits ran high among the audience as each contestant spoke—some seriously, some satirically, some in parody. It was, however, when Hernando (I have used pseudonyms for members of the Colby community), the ultimate winner of the contest and the only contestant of color, delivered his speech that a riveted silence filled the auditorium. Unlike his peers, Hernando walked past the podium to the edge of the stage. Promising to put everything back as he moved flower arrangements and vases, he cleared a space for himself where he sat facing the president and gave his speech, a five-minute spoken-word poem, which he literally spoke *to* the president rather than *about* him or *instead of* him.

> If I could be *you* for a day,
> I'm sorry to say
> that I just can't stay
> *normal*, I just can't do
> what *you* do.
> No, I just can't help it.
> I must go out of my way
> and do what I do.
> Personally, I would
> Change things up a bit.

These opening lines (italics added), directly addressing the president, immediately call him into relationship with the speaker even as the rest of the speech critiques him for being out of relationship with his community. Thus Hernando models for the president the very thing he wants from him: connection. At the same time, by insisting that he "just can't stay / normal," Hernando resists the dominant discourse of consensus, insisting, instead, on connection across differences. In much the same way that Hernando distinguishes himself from the institutional "normal," he also breaks with the grammatical norm of probability. By postponing the conditional tense called for in a counterfactual if-clause (If I could be you, I *couldn't / would not be able* to stay normal) and detouring into the present tense (I just *can't* stay normal), Hernando moves beyond speculating about what could be and describes what is. Rather than tarry in the hypothetical realm of improbability, he turns toward the lived experiences of his everyday life, suggesting (albeit indirectly) that any vision for future change must be built on an honest, uncompromising view of the present.

> I have to ask
> Do you see what I see?
> I see a campus too scared to talk,

a campus too scared to act,
an administration too busy to care,
a faculty that's understaffed,
which just ain't fair,
a student body that's perfectly content
with mediocrity.
As a group and as a whole,
we see no issue
    with the lack of discussion,
    no issue
    with the silenced minority.
    As a group and as a whole,
    we'd rather stay blind
    to the subtle and not so subtle
    microaggressions
that happen all the time.

Even as Hernando invites the president to see the campus through his eyes, what is most striking and powerful in this section is Hernando's refusal to lay individual blame on the president. On the contrary, as he describes what he sees—a campus, an administration, a faculty, a student body—he simultaneously distinguishes the various campus constituencies and holds them together in relationship, just as he holds them responsible as a community for its injustices. The repeated invocation of "As a group and as a whole" underscores the sense of *shared responsibility* for the injustices that "happen all the time" and suggests that such injustices are not random individual acts but rather pervasive and systemic. Unwittingly, but nonetheless poignantly, Hernando invokes Young's view that we all bear responsibility for structural injustices because we contribute to the processes that produce unjust outcomes. Young's (2011) model of social responsibility invokes social connection rather than blame and liability, because "our responsibility derives from belonging together . . . , participating [together] in the diverse institutional processes that produce structural injustice" (105).

At the same time, Hernando's appeal to the president acknowledges that, while we may all bear responsibility for such structural injustices as members of a community, we are not all the same, nor do we all have equal power.

Implicit in this acknowledgment is the question that bell hooks asked us to ponder four months earlier: What makes bonding possible across difference? To answer that question, Hernando very consciously changes his verbal strategy by using the conditional (I *would*), a move that emphasizes what *isn't* by expressing a contrary-to-fact situation:

> Sir, if I were you
> I would explore this campus
> I would implore this campus
> With my ears,
> With my arms stretched wide.
> I would travel around all day
> To hear what others have to say
> Every nook and every cranny
> I would inquire:
> What do you think?
> What've I done wrong?
> What've I done right?
> What should I change?
> What should I ask of others
> To do after I'm gone?

Most compelling about this section (and subsequent passages) is the extended metaphor of citizenship and, specifically, leadership as travel, as exploration, as the movement necessary to traverse difference. By the same token, the questions he would ask of his fellow community members if he were their leader are posed with "ears and arms stretched wide," from a position of openness, curiosity, and humility—his whole body in this subjunctive fantasy (or model) invites discussion, disagreement, even dissent. In contrast to a model of ideal community whose unity is protected by policies and practices that quell oppositional viewpoints, Hernando reimagines it as a space of exchange, dialogue, and critique. In his vision of community, inclusion is not confused with sameness but rather is aimed toward the possibility of greater equality. Thus, Hernando closes his speech in an inclusive declaration:

You ask, "What would *I* do?"

. . .

If I could do anything,
Well, that's a simple answer:
I would turn this mic around
And ask *them* for the answer.

Except for the president and his fellow administrators, who politely smiled and applauded, the rest of the audience immediately leapt to its feet with thunderous applause and cheers of affirmation. Hernando calmly got to his feet and put all the flower arrangements and vases back in their places at the edge of the stage. Despite the gesture of a "return to normal," there was, in that moment, a sense of no return to what was. A faculty member next to me leaned over and whispered, "That made me cry!" And I understood because hadn't I, too, been moved to tears? Hadn't we all been transported to a space of possibility by the complete sincerity and candor of Hernando's message and the utter forthrightness and courage with which he delivered it? In many ways, Hernando not only had identified the hypocrisy of institutional leadership in claiming community while remaining largely apart from it but also had directly engaged the leadership. And, in that act of engagement, rather than demonize the president, he humanized him, not just for himself but for all of us. I was both struck and heartened by the crowd's enthusiastic reaction to Hernando's speech because it seemed to bring us together despite our differences, and in that tenuous moment of connection, it seemed that we shared something close to hope.

In contrast to the student speech contest, the convocation address was a solemn affair that took place in the college chapel, a space most often reserved for the college's most important events. As a student choir sang, the president, accompanied by an entourage of administrators, trustees, and faculty marshals, dressed in full academic regalia, marched up the central aisle to the front of the chapel. There, he spoke to a packed house for about forty minutes, summarizing the rich history of Colby's achievements—academic, political, and social. Speaking to the college's history of activism, the president proudly listed a number of political movements that had affected the college through the centuries—abolition, the world wars, civil rights—concluding with "It's a good bet

Colby students today will be eager to bring new issues to the attention of faculty and administrators." In his reflections on the role our work plays, as an educational institution, in advancing the common good, the president insisted that "we must continue to teach students to care about the world they share with others and attempt to instill in them a sense of obligation to others and the desire to make a difference." And, as he contemplated the challenges we face as we move forward, the president observed that "our greatest risk . . . is complacency. . . . We must not give in to complacency." After he finished, and with the audience still applauding, the student body vice president, Afham Afsa, dressed in suit and tie, unexpectedly approached the podium to speak. Before he could take the mic, however, he was physically blocked by a member of the president's entourage, who put herself between Afham and the podium, while covering the mic with her hand. The audience watched while Afham spoke quietly to her until the administrator, with a look of chagrin, reluctantly moved aside. At that point, Afham returned to his seat, and four other students, representing a coalition of different interests, took the podium. Describing themselves as "a growing group of students comprised of all races, nationalities, identities, and dreams," they posited their vision for change, focusing on a variety of issues that ranged from the "still serious issues of racism, classism, sexism, and homophobia" to the rising cost of tuition to living wages for all campus employees. The first student who spoke began by stating clearly why she chose to act: "I love Colby tremendously. I respect Colby, and I'm so proud of all we have accomplished. But it's because of that love that I'm committed to making it the best place it can be for every one of us." (Colby Bicentennial 2013) These students spoke calmly and respectfully for about ten minutes, during which time the president, his entourage, and about 70 percent of the audience walked out of the chapel. Watching people leave, I recognized many of the same faces I had seen so joyfully celebrating Hernando's critical message during the student speech contest. Where just a few hours earlier, I had felt the power of our combined desire to work together across our differences, here I witnessed a surprising dissolution of that bond. Once again, I was perplexed. What was it about this instance of institutional critique that compelled people, literally, to turn away? Whether in agreement or not with the students' message, couldn't we agree that, in their action, they had just fulfilled the president's expectation that Colby students today carry on the legacy of civic engagement by "bring[ing] new issues to the attention of faculty and administrators"? Had they not just expressed "a desire to make a difference" and lived up to the president's mandate to "not give in to complacency"?

In the days that followed, the fallout from the student action at the presidential speech was intense and heated. Postings on The Civil Discourse, the student-centered Listserv, were contentious, many students voicing outrage at their activist peers for disrupting the president's address and disrespecting the bicentennial celebration. Others validated the issues that the protesters had raised but insisted that raising them at the convocation was inappropriate. *The wrong place and the wrong time* became a catch phrase for many who appreciated the message but not the medium. As one campus life administrator stated when interviewed for *the Colby Echo* (March 6, 2013), "The environment and the way [the protest] took place didn't allow for discussion. . . . So I regret that I don't think the intended outcome, of inspiring a better Colby, was reached."

In that same issue of the student paper, a full-page open letter from James King (also a pseudonym), a professor in the Department of Government, to Afham Afsa, was also published. I mention this letter not to single out an individual but rather because I believe that the outrage expressed in the letter represents the attitude of many community members—students, faculty, and administrators. This faculty member begins his letter, a scathing indictment of the student vice president, whom he holds responsible for the events at the convocation, by stating explicitly, "Your actions made me angry." The rest of the letter goes on to express his indignation at the student protest, which he perceives to be an egregious act of disrespect: "You and your friends slighted the president by presuming that your friends' speeches were somehow equal to his. . . . Indeed, you insulted all of us in the audience by claiming for yourselves the special privilege of speaking out, though uninvited, while expecting the rest of us to listen to you politely." At the same time as the speaker erroneously assumes authority to speak for the rest of *us*, the *victimized* community, he, even more problematically, understands the act of "speaking out" to be a special privilege, one that requires an invitation if it is to be considered at all. By speaking out of turn, the students have disrupted a hierarchical order, which the speaker unquestioningly holds as a natural dimension of his social reality. The inability to recognize social and political relationships outside that hierarchy is what makes it so difficult for him and other community members to understand and appreciate the importance of activism and dissent. Thus, the speaker attributes to the students an expectation that they did not hold, that "the rest of us . . . listen to you politely." The fact that the activists continued to speak, despite most of the audience walking out of the chapel, both disproves that claim and suggests that the goal of dissent is not always to engender discussion. According to Young (2001), activists believe that "activities of protest, boycott, and disruption are most appropriate for getting citizens to think seriously about what until then they may have found normal and acceptable" (675). Thus, the assumption here that the students anticipated a courteous reception from the crowd, like the campus life administrator's assumption that discussion was necessary for a "successful" outcome, doesn't see that the disruption itself might be the goal. This misunderstanding of activism divests not only the students' action but also, and more harmfully, the students themselves of political and social value to the community. Thus even as the student activists challenge the notion of an ideal and unified community, their critical perspective is not only undervalued; it is also often discredited and excluded from public discussions about institutional processes.

Although a group of faculty wrote a collective response to King's letter, expressing their outrage that a Colby professor would "use his authority and stature as a bully pulpit against a student member of the community,"(Abe et al. 2013) there was no response from either the leadership of the college or other faculty members. The sniping, and often hurtful, exchanges between students on The Civil Discourse continued for a couple of weeks, but there was no broader institutional engagement of either the student action or the issues they raised. This issue, like so many other contentious issues on campus, lost its momentum as it came up against the seeming inertia of a large part of the community, leaving me with three urgent questions: Why is it that, on a broader institutional level, nothing more happened in response to this painful and divisive situation? Who is responsible for that lack of action? And, looking forward, how can we, as a community, envision productive, healthy ways to respond to these cases of institutional malaise?

RESPONSIBILITY AND SOLIDARITY

To begin to answer the first question, I'd like to go back to my earlier question about why so many people felt compelled to leave the chapel when the student activists took the podium after the president's address. Whereas the community seemed to come together after Hernando's speech, it seemed all too easily to break apart after the student activists spoke. Comparing the two speech events, I would hazard that the honesty, astuteness, and power of Hernando's criticism of the president were contained, and hence diffused, by the fact that the speech contest was a sanctioned event of the bicentennial celebration. The legitimacy of the event thus ensured, on both a physical and a psychological level, that the speech contest constituted a "safe" space. In a sense, institutional permission was given to express dissent publicly within the well-defined rules of a speech contest that invited playful, even affectionate, critiques of the president. In the "safe" space of the planned event, the sense of unified community, while momentarily disturbed, remained intact.[1]

In contrast to the collective joy generated by Hernando's speech, the student action at the presidential address generated collective fear. The unexpected and unsanctioned nature of this act along with its insertion into the solemn, sacred space of the bicentennial convocation constituted a clear threat to the cohesion and unity of ideal community. Whereas Hernando, in his critique of the president, turned toward him to speak, the president not only turned away from the student activists—he walked out on them. To the extent that our humanity is rooted in our ability to be in relationship to others, walking away, in this context, was also a dehumanizing act. The fear of being dehumanized or of being identified as one of the dehumanized is, at least, a partial answer to the question of why the community seemed to shatter and to become paralyzed in the aftermath of the convocation protest. Judith Butler (2004) astutely identifies how this fear of being dehumanized works to suppress opposition and resistance: "Dissent is quelled, in part, through threatening the speaking subject with uninhabitable identification. Because it would be heinous to identify as treasonous, as a collaborator, one fails to speak or speaks in throttled ways, in order to sidestep the terrorizing identification that threatens to take hold" (xix). A climate in which, to borrow Professor King's term, "speaking out" can lead to being branded and shamed as a traitor, and where dominant community norms oppose and devalue disruptive political behavior, many citizens "decline to engage in or support such actions for fear of being thought uncivil and unreasonable" (Young 2002, 48).

As we think about moving forward, the question of responsibility is central to envisioning a more just and democratic community. I believe that Young's social connection model of responsibility provides an excellent framework for reconceptualizing a community that, more than for social wholeness, strives for justice across different social locations and positions of greater and lesser political power. The idea of *connection* is the basis for Young's (2011) conception of responsibility because it finds that "all those who contribute by their actions to structural processes with some unjust outcomes share responsibility for the injustice" (96). In a model that distributes responsibility to all community members across their differences, responsibility itself becomes one of the valuable bonds that brings us together, even as, at times, it requires us to dissent from widely held public opinion.

In contrast to the liability model of responsibility, which focuses on a single agent to blame for an injustice in our institutions, the social connection model asserts that "we have the responsibility to try *to speak out* against [institutions] with the intention of mobilizing others to oppose them" (93). It is ironic, but instructive, that in Young's view of social responsibility, speaking out is posited as a political imperative, while, in King's view, such speaking out constitutes a crime. To criminalize those who speak out not only delegitimizes dissent as a viable mode of political participation but also dangerously limits what can and cannot be talked about within the public domain. In contrast, by recognizing dissent as a necessary activity to creating a more just society, the social connection model encourages citizens to turn toward one another across their differences even when that engagement is conflicted. It is here that I think hooks's concept of "beloved community" resonates with Young's social connection model of responsibility to provide us with some fundamental conceptual tools for moving forward. If we take seriously hooks's assertion that a central challenge to building beloved community is not about eradicating or avoiding conflict but rather about being able to resolve conflict, we need to reexamine the value of conflict in our community so that we don't simply shut down dissent and dehumanize dissenters. If there had been an opportunity for a public discussion about how to resolve the conflict ensuing the bicentennial protest, I am sure there would have been many productive ideas and just as many moments of conflict. But without a conception of community that welcomes conflict, or a language or discourse to name it and talk about it, there is nothing to resolve.

Because public discourses of blame oversimplify, Young stresses the importance of developing a "rhetoric of responsibility" based on a notion of solidarity as a relationship between diverse community constituents who decide to act with and for one another.

> People who understand themselves in solidarity with close and distant others aim to work together to improve the state of well-being of themselves and/or others. . . . Rather than take existing social structures and relations as what they are, as given, they take them as *possibilities*—*perhaps* things can be improved. This active stance opens to a future that can be made, but is risky and uncertain. Solidarity, inspired and tempered by the perhaps, is thus a call to responsibility (120).

In stark contrast to the discourse of consensus, Young's rhetoric of responsibility proposes a relational model that lets in not only difference but also the many contingencies that arise around it. Rather than reactively striving to maintain existing social structures, citizens in solidarity actively move into the future in all its uncertainty. They do not see difference, disagreement, or conflict as threats to unity but rather as integral and necessary to a democratic process that works to eliminate injustice. From this perspective, struggle with a commitment to justice in community is, to answer hooks's question, what makes bonding possible across difference. Struggle, however, can be meaningful, productive, and *bonding* only if we, in our difference, turn toward one another. Thus, it is not just a question of creating more public spaces for debate and difference but also one of creating "public cultures of dissent," where issues of injustice, privilege, and conflict can be "debated in terms of our pedagogies and institutionalized practices" (Mohanty 1994, 162). Such cultures of dissent not only invite activism but also value it as an indispensable part of the process of decolonization and, by extension, of the democratic process. It is not that activism replaces other, more institutionally sanctioned, forms of political engagement but rather that it lets us conceive the exchanges and communications in community "as far more rowdy, disorderly, and decentered" (Young 2001, 688). Deliberation and reasonable discourse are not only aspects of democracy; they are how administrators and boards, and sometimes even faculty members, like for colleges to work. But Young argues for the value of activism as an equally important mode of communication because "participants [activists] articulate reasonable appeals to justice and also expose the sources and consequences of structural inequalities in law, the hegemonic terms of discourse, and the environment of everyday practice" (688).

RECOMMENDATIONS FOR REIMAGINING THE PAST

In the spirit of Young's (2001) vision that we "try together to alter the social processes that we understand produce injustices, and *perhaps* we will have some successes" (120), I want to reflect on what we can do differently by reimagining the bicentennial protest for the possibilities that such reimagining offers us. Thus, I ask what if, as the activists took the podium, the president had stayed? If, instead of turning away, he had been willing to listen, even if he expressed his disagreement, and, by his example, he encouraged others to do the same, how might this have played out differently? Viewed through this lens of possibility, might such a response have illuminated the *rightness* of the claim that the action took place at "the *wrong* place, *wrong* time"? It's easy to imagine that the hostile and shaming responses that followed might never have emerged, but perhaps it's more realistic to imagine that in their emergence, the entire exchange would have been different. Different constituents of the community may not have felt so dramatically disregarded, unseen, chastised, unwelcome. And if no one felt unseen, chastised, and unwelcome, would there have been more of an opportunity to participate in debate about how we as community define justice and injustice? Could we, perhaps, have imagined that debate as ongoing, a process of struggle and engagement that, as such, might have taken many forms—from community forums to classroom discussions, from workshops on pedagogy to some on how higher education administration works? Could we, perhaps, understand these multiple efforts less as a short-term solution to a conflict to be resolved immediately and more as a long-term process committed to cultural and political change? And, if we could get to a place like this, what if we also embraced Hernando's vision of a citizenry that travels the geographies of its differences, that explores its community, and that implores its members "to hear what others have to say" more than for approval or consensus? We might find in that exploration, in the plenitude of our difference(s), that the ground of our engagement is with one another such that our differences bind us in solidarity.

NOTES

1 I want to clarify that even as the institutional legitimacy of the speech contest as an official bicentennial event diffuses audience discomfort, Hernando's speech was, nevertheless, a meaningful critical action to the extent that his unconventional delivery moved the audience to a sense of shared possibility. In this sense, his speech exemplifies the kind of ideology critique that, in Young's (2001) view, is necessary to unmask the unjust power relations that are often accepted in institutional modes of communication: "The activist believes it is important to continue to challenge the discourses and the deliberative processes that rely on them and often he must do so by non-discursive means—pictures, songs, poetic imagery . . . performed in rowdy and even playful ways aimed not an commanding assent but disturbing complacency" (687).

11 ◆ *LA PROMESA*

Working with Latina and Latino Students in an Elite Liberal Arts College

AURORA CAMACHO de SCHMIDT

The end of the spring of 2013 will not be easily forgotten at Swarthmore College. A significant number of students were unhappy, and their unhappiness erupted in a variety of ways: demonstrations, visits to college officers and the board of managers, gatherings with faculty and administrators, and an impromptu Collection. In a college founded by Quakers, a Collection is an open assembly in which the speech of those present acquires a special value. The gathering seeks to communicate at a deep level. Quakers still hold these meetings as worship. In the secular culture of the college, however, Collection remains an important form of gathering; each member of the assembly is equally empowered to speak. All present are charged with an obligation to listen deeply, because something very important is being discerned.

In May, as students were getting ready for examinations, one of the most interesting Collections ever took place in the Scott Amphitheater, a large and beautiful outdoor space reserved for special moments, such as graduation. Tension on campus was high. Students believed they needed to be heard. A group of them had spent the previous night writing a statement that included proposals and demands. The assembly was the culmination of two months of previous efforts to speak up. Walking into the terraced space among majestic trees in the spring afternoon, students, faculty, and administrators were apprehensive. The assembly started solemnly, with an explanation by religious adviser Barbara Thomas (I have used pseudonyms for members of the Swarthmore community) of the purpose of the gathering: to share openly and respectfully whatever anybody present wished to say. Soon students took the mobile microphone, and the sharing began. They spoke about what hurt them and what needed to change. Occasionally responding to each other, they were always respectful. For me as a listener, the absence of any intervention by staff or faculty marked the meeting as extraordinary, since there had been no previous agreement to cede the arena to students alone. The silence of those in power offered students all the space for their own free communication, to each other and to the professors and college administrators, including college president Rachel Dice. Many of us took heart from that silence.

At last Collection, the annual penultimate gathering before graduation ceremonies, Augustus Maximilian Alpes, the senior who had been elected to speak by the graduating class, recognized the enormity of the stress many students had suffered. He ended, however, on a bright and hopeful note: "I leave on Sunday knowing that although it has been a rough couple of months and most of us are exhausted, physically, emotionally, and mentally, I find comfort in thinking that even from the biggest of our mistakes, something beautiful is emerging and growing, and we will be on our way to healing. Not yet, not now, but soon."

I will return to May 2013, when problems connected with race, gender, class, and the college's response to sexual assault, as President Dice recognized in her commencement address, overwhelmed the capacity of the college community to contain or resolve them through the usual channels. The impulse of this essay is the desire to express how I see, after twenty-one years at Swarthmore College, what is at stake for Latino students and for a college still in the process of desegregation. I love and respect many aspects of the college's unique combination of academic breadth and depth, and its openness to the world. As a scholar, however, I am also a critic, and I know the college will be unable to make good on the promise it has made to students of color until we who constitute it are ready to embrace deep change, and, as Augustus Maximilian Alpes said, "commit to it so much that we are willing to live in the tension that comes with the territory." Not an easy task.

UNDER A NEW MANDATE

I came to Swarthmore in the early 1990s, just after a new president, Abe Flowers, had launched a plan to diversify the student body within the restrictions and expectations set by affirmative action guidelines. (For the Supreme Court's landmark decision of 1978, see *Regents of the University of California v. Bakke.*) In his 1992 inaugural speech, "A New Mandate for American Higher Education," President Flowers promised to make Swarthmore College an inclusive community, committed to the promise of a top-quality liberal arts education open to all and especially to students traditionally absent at elite institutions. Rachel Dice, at the start of her presidency in 2009, reiterated that promise.

President Flowers's beautiful text does not consider the stretching—both painful and immensely enriching—required of any institution that embraces diversity, the full extent of which is never predictable. During the first fifth of Flowers's eighteen-year administration, Latino students were a very small minority, and the college adapted fairly well to a different admissions policy. Some faculty discussions brought up the question of how to teach students whose preparation might be below the college's norm, but in general professors accepted their new leader's proposal.

I arrived as a visiting professor at an environment that included one Latin American full professor and two untenured Latino faculty members, all male. Of the two Latinos, one was never tenured, the other one left as a full professor. I am a citizen of Mexico, where I was born, raised, and educated as an undergraduate. I was far from a typical new assistant professor, even after my position became tenure track. I had been away from the field for thirteen years and I was nearly fifty years old. Although I had received a doctorate in literature, it had not been with the purpose of becoming a professor. For many years, I worked on social justice issues in the nonprofit sector, especially with the American Friends Service Committee (AFSC). As the director of the AFSC's newly created Mexico-U.S. Border Program, I became involved in the politics of the Latino (especially Chicano) and immigrant communities. I did not know much about higher education. All I wanted was a chance to teach and write about the literature I love, not only in its aesthetic power but also in its rootedness in Latin American societies and their painful transformations.

I was extremely ambitious, but not in the usual career-building way. It is possible that this atypical and possibly inauspicious beginning was the basis of a strong identification with the marginality that Latino students experience. Many years later, I realize that my age, politics, and way of understanding my profession made it easier for many Latino students to trust me, and perhaps concomitantly more difficult for some colleagues to see me as their true peer. The complicated experience of rejection and disapproval, new in my life, opened an opportunity to empathize with many members of the college community early on, and to value with gratitude the support and friendship I found among many colleagues.

It was my great fortune to have joined the faculty when President Flowers announced his intention to open a wide door to many more students of color. Undoubtedly my involvement with Latina and Latino students, whose numbers have grown fast and constantly over the past two decades, was one of the best gifts life gave me in these intense twenty-one years of work, even when I taught, advised, and befriended students of every description.

I have enjoyed immensely teaching Spanish and literature to Latina and Latino students. Most of my literature courses deal with works that are intimately connected with popular struggles in Latin America, and I have found that many students are hungry for knowledge about the culture and history of the region from where their parents came. Perhaps the effect of studying the violence of Latin America in its literature can result in cathartic liberation for some of them. The attention I have given to the social and political dimensions of texts under discussion, and the interdisciplinary approach I have used, have been key elements of my connection to Latinos and Latinas at the college. I am honored to be considered their ally, and in their friendship I find great joy and support, as well as the validation of my work.

LONG-DISTANCE RUNNERS

I will never forget the loneliness of two Latino students from Texas in 1992. Nothing had prepared them for the cumulative effect of different kinds of academic challenges, different foods, a different geographical climate, and perhaps most especially different ways of human interaction. They felt they were in a foreign country, and I could relate to that feeling very well. A critical mass of Latino students elevates the quality of life for every member of this group. (In a more recent case, the class of 2018 is composed of roughly one in eight Latinos and Latinas in the total student population.) Having each other is extremely important for social and academic success at an elite college. Naturally, Latinos and Latinas befriend members of all other groups, but when they face a wall, they often need to sort things out with one of their peers who "have been there."

Today, the large majority of Latino students on campus often feel empowered by each other. Together, they can be critical of the college and identify ways in which many aspects of their experience could be better. Even as some feel the estrangement of being in a foreign place, most of them develop survival strategies. Most of them have overall good experiences and relate enthusiastically to most of their courses and professors. Many take advantage of special programs the college offers to all its students, such as peer tutoring and faculty mentorships. While we need more solid research on the long-term outcomes of the education of Latinos and Latinas in elite colleges, we know that at Swarthmore many of them graduate successfully every year and go on to pursue fruitful graduate studies and careers.

Swarthmore College admits Latino and Latina students who graduated at the top of their high school class and have demonstrated academic passion and a clear capacity to work hard. Like typical Swarthmore students, they are bright, eager to do well in a variety of fields, creative, and resilient. In general, their SAT scores are close to Swarthmore's median, but it is important to remember that SATs measure aptitude, not achievement. Many Latino and Latina students are the first in their families to go to college and come from low-income backgrounds. Since minority and poor students are disproportionately concentrated in public high schools without the benefit that financial resources afford, such as access to advanced placement classes, college counseling, and optimal student-teacher ratios (Fletcher and Tienda 2011), it is easy to imagine that a considerable proportion of Latinos and Latinas attended schools that were unable to articulate high expectations of them. On the other hand, students who complained about their faulty high school preparation in their conversations with me frequently mentioned their parents' diligent involvement in their education, a well-known predictor of success.

Sophistication in social and political understanding is the most salient single quality of many of the Latinos and Latinas I have known at the college. They understand they are pioneers in a process of social transformation as they are crossing lines that only some years ago would have been insurmountable obstacles for their education. They are passionate about standing up for each other, and they participate in student groups where political action is essential. They expect to develop these assets academically, and not only outside the classroom, in the margins, yet few courses offer them those opportunities. Some of the most visible activists among Latinos and Latinas at Swarthmore are the children of immigrants and refugees whose lives were marked by political violence and economic deprivation in Latin America. It is no surprise that their children should have a keen awareness of the importance of protecting civil rights and engaging in community action in a way that is integrated in their education.

Long-distance runners are experts in perseverance and endurance. By the time low-income students arrive at an elite college, they have already covered a long metaphorical distance in their short lives, and they have acquired unique social and cultural capital, often as a result of struggle. They come as neither needy receptors nor exotic representatives of difference but as fellow students with particular experiences able both to give and to receive. That cultural capital is available to the institutions that welcome them, but those institutions need to be set up at the right radio wave frequency. Some of the greatest frustration for students of color is to know that there is often only one channel of communication in the classroom or the institution as a whole. Frequently the normative culture of college communities, like this one, is unprepared to see them for who they are, to hear their voices, or to receive their gifts. But receiving the cultural gift Latino students bring to the college is also a vital part of the tacit promise made upon admission, and an integral element in the students' development. They wish to leave their mark in the institution that graduates them.

THE DIFFICULTIES

In 1994, three other Latin American/Latino faculty, one lecturer, and I asked Latino students how they felt they were doing at Swarthmore College. Their answers pointed to a strong sense of anxiety in the classroom. Many of them felt the professors directed their teaching to only the strongest students. One of them asked what the point was of admitting students who had no way of surviving. Another one said that nothing in his previous experience had prepared him for this style of academic work, even when he was one of the best students in his high school. If a good number of students are still anxious now about the high academic expectation at the college, many aspects of what made those years so difficult have changed. There are formal and informal networks of support, and many, if not most, faculty see the presence of Latino students as an asset to their classrooms.

Around the same time, I had an academic advisee in tears in my office. Her professor had written on the back of her exam words that conveyed that he should not have to teach a student like her. Another student told me that her adviser had suggested transferring to a less demanding college when she spoke about her difficulties. I can't imagine anyone doing this now. Nor can I imagine hearing again what a young faculty member told me: "Many of these [minority] students should have never been admitted." (For a thorough treatment of the relation between race and achievement in elite higher education institutions, see Massey et al. 2006)

In their study of the racial atmosphere for Latino and Latina college students, Yosso et al. (2009, 663) borrow Chester Pierce's (1969) now famous concept of *microaggressions* to refer to the many "subtle, innocuous, preconscious, or unconscious degradations, and putdowns" the students in their study experienced. Using critical race theory (CRT), the team of four researchers found that over time, microaggressions cause mental, emotional, and physical stress.[1] Instances of aggression, micro and otherwise, are not unknown at Swarthmore. Some years ago, a Puerto Rican student was speaking Spanish with a friend as she walked behind a group of young white men. One of the men turned around and asked her to leave, saying loudly, "Go back to where you came from!" She replied, "I belong right here, where I am." The incident caused an uproar, and the faculty formally considered how to react to hate speech on campus. After a series of discussions, we agreed that hate speech could not be banned. We figured that at least out in the open, racial aggression could be unmasked for what it is.

Even more recently, a student who had just been upbraided by her professor came to my office, still shaken by the experience. She had failed to turn in an application form on time but had called the intended recipient to say she had just sent it by special delivery. Before she had the opportunity to explain herself, she told me, as soon as she went to see her professor, that professor started yelling at her. The student remarked, "Nobody has ever talked to me like that!" As a Dominican student from New York, she felt wounded by what she understood to be a racial incident.

Unquestionably, the majority of the faculty, staff, and student body of the college would disapprove of these occurrences, especially when a member of the institution had exercised undue power over someone who was his or her racial other. While the college has no clear, visible, and effective institutional ways of redressing these assaults, the public affirmation of the victim's personal worth and the condemnation of the action go a long way to restoring peace. Two years ago, after offensive writings on the sidewalks with chalk appeared on campus directed against Queer students, President Dice called for a gathering of the community in an open space. It was a sunny day, and community members were asked to wear white shirts to symbolize unity and solidarity with those who had been directly insulted. The speeches, the large number of participants, and the ambiance of the gathering gave everyone hope that nothing like that would happen again.

There is another way in which racial, class, and gender boundaries are subtly reestablished: lack of engagement with those who are different. In our classrooms, as an example, students often sit together with those they know. For all students, the reasons for this may be fear or discomfort. But when we are admitting students who have never had the opportunity to engage with those who are different from them—and may be experiencing that lack of engagement with those whom they don't know very differently—the job ahead requires a new level of sensitivity on the part of everyone to undo what can quickly become another hidden form of marginalization.

LATINOS/LATINAS VERSUS LATIN AMERICANS

Born and raised in Mexico, I had never intended to immigrate to the United States. My marriage to a U.S. citizen required me to leave my country, although at the time neither my husband nor I thought that we would always live here. Our rootedness in Mexico, however, has always remained strong. Thus, my identification as a Latina came later as a political choice and as part of my work with the American Friends Service Committee before I joined the academic world. Most of my students saw me as a Latin American, but they knew that I identified strongly with them.

Unlike many Latinas, I was a young adult when I first arrived in this country. I had attended a bilingual private independent school, where I learned English, and a private university. My family had enjoyed a good life in Mexico at a time of economic expansion following World War II. Mexico City was an exciting place to live, a window into world culture and the extraordinary power of Mexican art. I did not know it then, but I had experienced the exhilarating change of the early sixties that followed the Cuban Revolution, the end of Vatican Council II, the beginnings of liberation theology, and the early development of the New Left student movement. Meeting my husband was a result of a naive, but sincere, wish on the part of students from Harvard University and Universidad Iberoamericana, our respective schools, to spend a summer working together in a Mexico City slum when my future husband and I were both nineteen. (We would marry several years later.) This background marked me as a non-Latina but also as a Latin American with at least a strong predisposition to celebrate and support the formation of the largest minority in the United States as it asserts its presence, its great diversity and commonalities, its needs, and its powerful transforming potential.

For Latino students, the distinction between Latinos and Latin Americans is important. They proudly know, like Chicana writer Gloria Anzaldúa (1999), that they are involved in the creation of a new culture:

I am cultureless because, as a feminist, I challenge the collective cultural/religious male-derived beliefs of Indo-Hispanics and Anglos; yet I am cultured because I am participating in the creation of yet another culture, a new story to explain the world and our participation in it, a new value system with images and symbols that connect us to each other and to the planet. Soy un amasamiento, I am an act of kneading, of uniting, and joining that not only has produced both a creature of darkness and a creature of light, but also a creature that questions the definitions of light and dark and gives them new meanings.

In addition to identifying with a new culture in the process of shaping itself, Latino students may consciously try to separate themselves from Latin Americans for reasons of class at the college. Until very recently, no foreign student received financial aid, a policy that meant that Latin American students admitted at Swarthmore came mostly from affluent families. At a gathering in the Intercultural Center in the mid-1990s, a young woman of Dominican origin asked a Latin American student, "What do I, born and raised in the Bronx, have to do with you? How is our life experience similar?" At times, some animosity has developed between Latino and Latin American students, but each generation of students has grappled with this difference and resolved it productively by acknowledging and accepting their separate trajectories and looking for common ground. I have witnessed collaboration and deep friendship among members of both groups.

A good part of the student irritation that surfaced in the spring of 2013 pointed to the curriculum. For years, students had been asking the college to create an interdisciplinary program in Latino studies. When the Latin American Studies Program was willing to change its name to Latin American and Latino Studies Program, students did not think that the change of name was good enough. They were seriously interested in courses in the social sciences that addressed Latino history, public policy, education, and social and cultural traditions and in courses in the humanities on the literature, religion, music, and art that are part of the Latino experience in the United States. They see that as their world, and they want to know it deeply. And they yearned to have their fellow students be able to take such courses as well.

While students do not think that their Latin American professors are incapable of teaching a Latino studies curriculum, they long to recognize themselves in members of the faculty. The only Latino full professor had left the college. And the only Latino dean had also left by the spring of 2012. In informal conversations and formal communications with college officials, students have expressed the great desire to have more Latino faculty at least since the late nineties.[2]

THE SPRING OF 2013

The pervasive student discontent that erupted in April this year is rooted in both old and new problems. Some can be found in any institution of higher education, including excellent ones, and some are peculiarly ours. What many women saw as the college's lack of an adequate response to sexual assault on campus came to a head. At the same time, Latino students experienced the cumulative effect of inadequate answers to their curricular demands and the irritation caused by their perceived marginality. Students who did not identify as Latino, Queer, or female, however, joined in solidarity in frustration over curricular shortcomings, which I have mentioned above, and disrespect from fellow students, which I will mention below. I had never seen either so much pain or so much anger shared by so many of our students.

Two incidents are particularly significant for me: Until 2002, the Intercultural Center (IC) housed only four groups: ENLACE (Latino/a student organization), the Native American Student Association (NASA), the Swarthmore Asian Organization (SAO) and the Swarthmore Queer Union (SQU). Now it also encompasses DESHI (South Asian student organization), MULTI (multiracial students), COLORS (queer students of color), the Queer-Straight Alliance (QSA), and the Class Awareness Month (CAM) committee (http://www.swarthmore.edu/student-life/intercultural-center/student-groups.xml). In the spring of 2013, members of those groups experienced the aberrant aggression of anonymous perpetrators who urinated on the door of the IC on repeated occasions. Anger in these groups flared, and the difficulty in identifying the perpetrators increased the students' frustration and sense of abandonment by college authorities that many students were already feeling. Here was a cowardly act of hate speech without words, what Chester Pierce might call a kinetic aggression.

Just before her graduation, one of my Latina students came to see me. "When all is said and done," she told me, referring to the recent crisis, "Swarthmore College is an elite institution. If it has to choose whom to support, it will support its elite students, not its students of color." This is a student leader, a maverick, an achiever in many areas, including academics, yet someone who confesses to being close to leaving at the end of her first year. Her reaction in

May 2013 reveals she expected more from the college as a response to student discontent. This student saw the college's lack of clear policies and procedures in the cases of sexual assault and its ensuing unresponsiveness to victims as directly connected to the way the demands of Latino students and those of other students of color and Queer groups had been ignored.

A first-year Latino student rose to speak at the Collection with which I began this essay. He pointed to his difficulties in meeting the academic expectations of the college, sharing the conditions in his high school where there were no laboratories, no college counselors, no advanced mathematics courses, and few academic resources to equip him "to survive in a place like this." Later that week, the associate dean for academic affairs asked faculty to consider leniency with term paper deadlines, since so many students had been involved in the spring crisis, taking their responsibilities to each other and to the college very seriously with conversations and planning day after day and late into the night. When this student asked one of his professors for an extension, she called his request "simply ridiculous." A difficult exchange ensued in front of the class. The student apologized for raising his voice and left the class in tears.

Latina and Latino students at Swarthmore College have experienced a sense of exclusion that causes real sorrow, what Freud called *melancholia*. It is kind of symbolic violence, to use Pierre Bourdieu's phrase, causing feelings of internalized inadequacy. There are, on the other side, invaluable sources of support for students at the college: fellow students, staff, and faculty, who act as real allies and sources of constant affirmation and who share and comfort when students have painful experiences. They know that Latinas and Latinos and other people defined by their difference from *the norm* are in the midst of a struggle to undo the power of prejudice. They support that struggle, and many of the faculty actively teach the realities of social subordination in the United States and the world at large, in a variety of disciplines at a very high level of intellectual complexity. Equally important in the academic arena are Swarthmore's interdisciplinary programs, some of which are centrally concerned with excluded populations. They fulfill a radically important role in providing an intellectual arena where the ideologies of white supremacy are unmasked. Many faculty and administrators have embarked on major efforts to address the issues that produced the student discontent in the spring of 2013.

As a whole, the allies of all students at Swarthmore College are the source of a unique form of liberal arts education. Together they provide a space of freedom in explorations; discoveries; the framing of great questions; the birth of passionate devotions to the sciences, the humanities, the arts, and athletics; and the making of lifetime friendships and alliances.

OUR HOPE FOR THE FUTURE: RECOMMENDATIONS

Ideologues of the right like Dinesh D'Souza (1991), William Bennett (1994), and David Wilezol (in Bennett 2013) mordantly criticize liberal arts education in the United States, while other scholars eagerly want to save the treasure of an education that covers all possible human knowledge, including race and sexual difference, and invites learners to search, guided by mentors and professors in small groups. Among the latter are Columbia University professor Andrew Delbanco (2012), and Victor Ferrall (2012), a lawyer and former president of Beloit College in Wisconsin. It is imperative that we inject the issue of how racism is experienced on campus into this discussion, going beyond the vision that William Bowen and Derek Bok, former presidents of Princeton and Harvard, respectively, presented in their famous book, *The Shape of the River* (2000).

Beyond the clichés of identity politics, a discussion of the place of race and ethnicity in higher education and especially in liberal arts elite institutions has the potential to be intellectually rich in its profound practical implications. Such a discussion could benefit every student, every professor, and perhaps every member of the staff in any college. Below I list some of the most valuable things Swarthmore College has done, some it might consider adding, and a few suggestions for all liberal arts colleges and universities:

1. *Mentorships.* The college currently has two formal programs for students and one for faculty. Of the ones for students, one is funded from within and another is funded from outside. They are well established and, for the most part, very successful. Student scholars are paired with a mentor, who assumes responsibility for guiding them and alerting them to summer learning opportunities, such as internships and community

service. One of the programs is for students with demonstrated financial need; the other was historically for students of color and is now for any student considering a career in the professorate who is committed to increasing the representation of diversity among students. The mentoring program for faculty is for all tenure-track faculty and continuing full-time faculty who are not on the tenure track. Mentoring students and junior faculty requires time, so the college needs to recognize the practice as a significant investment on the part of faculty mentors. One of the programs allows staff to serve as mentors to students as well. Educator David Alberto Quijada writes about a professor in graduate school and the difference she made for him as a Chicano student far from home: "By engaging my commitments to social justice, this professor transformed my relationship to research, practice, and theory, by reconstituting 'education, as a site of liberation'" (262). Quijada adds that mentoring brings into positive crisis power relations between faculty and students, making them partners in addressing marginalization in academia. Increasingly, such programs are open to all students, reminding everyone that we each need mentoring for different things and at different times in our lives and that mentoring is not the same as remedial tutoring.

2. *Validation of Latina and Latino Cultural Capital in Experiential Learning.* Ideally, this goal would be achieved through courses that include components requiring students to work in the community. This requires a great investment of time on the part of faculty. Centers that coordinate community-based service learning courses or community service involvement are ideal sites for the development of such courses. A Latina student who graduated from Swarthmore in 2008 founded Club Despertar, a program to help the children of farmworkers from Mexico, who live in a nearby town, with their homework. Many colleges and universities find themselves with Latin American and Latino populations nearby who already offer a cultural richness to the area. A greater sense of mutuality might be achieved if students worked on issues that are important to these peoples, and this is another place where Latino and Latina students who are interested could act as initial cultural brokers.

3. *An Academic Program That Reflects the Interests, Needs, and Experiences of*

Latina and Latino Students. Although the administration has welcomed the idea of a Latino and Latina studies program, Swarthmore and other colleges will have to prioritize its importance. That means turning to faculty today who are equipped to teach on these subjects, and turning to other colleges and universities that have successfully created programs already. Williams College, for example describes its Latina/o Studies program as involving "collective work and scholarly collaboration; a commitment to uniting theory and practice; and an interdisciplinary focus" (see Williams College [2015]). That seems an excellent environment for the flourishing of the critical race theory tenets as described by University of California–Los Angeles sociologist of education Daniel Solórzano (1997), which include a challenge to dominant ideology and an understanding of race and racism as endemic to U.S. society. Students are challenging the integrity of the college's present curricular plan and their demands need to be taken seriously; this challenge is present in many campuses nationwide. Such a program would offer interdisciplinary courses that cross boundaries; stand in tension with other courses; and consider the instability and plurality of cultures, texts, and histories.

4. *A New Effort to Diversify the Faculty.* Just after the dawn of the new century, the faculty at Swarthmore unanimously adopted a resolution to increase the number of faculty of color for the second time since the civil rights movement. While the efforts have not been insignificant here or elsewhere, most colleges, including our own, have not met the targets they once proposed. Since the late nineties, Latina and Latino students have made this a central demand in their conversations with faculty and administrators at Swarthmore. Leadership will make the difference, and that leadership often includes discovering how other colleges and universities have moved this curricular priority forward. It also includes reaching out to graduate programs that train large numbers of doctorates of color.

5. *Religious Advisers and Counselors in Psychological Services that Recognize the Needs of Latina and Latino Students.* I am grateful for the special outreach work done in every one of the religious groups that meet on campus and the counselors who identify with and are trained to serve Latinos and Latinas. Still, there is a need to implement culturally rel-

evant liturgies and celebrations, involving students in their preparation, as a way of expressing the rich traditions from their countries of origin.

6. *New Goals in Spanish-Language Teaching.* Latina and Latino students in higher education have a complex relation with the Spanish language. Many of them are excellent speakers, but even those who have not abandoned oral Spanish often have difficulties writing and reading, unless they have taken the time to study Spanish in high school. For Latina and Latino students to own the Spanish language on their own terms seems important to many linguists, who question the standard set by Spanish departments all over the United States.[3] Spanish is a key to their culture and history. They should not have to feel anxiety because other, non-Latino students speak, read, and write with standard grammar. While many campuses are now adding Spanish courses for heritage speakers, if I had my way, I would instead call such a course *"Español para Latina/os."* Energized and exciting, it might even become a requirement for Latino studies, and a prerequisite for study abroad and for doing advanced work in the social sciences and humanities.

7. *Creation of an Interdisciplinary Minor Requirement for Everyone at the College.* Among the demands that students shared with the administration during the spring of 2013 was the creation of an ethnic studies program. Underlying the students' demand is the sense that they want to be known and understood at the very least by their peers, and that basic literacy requires the study of "the centrality of race" in U.S. society. While the faculty committees that govern the creation of curricular changes could not immediately envision from where the funding for such a program would come or how it would be staffed, there are currently several programs and classes that address issues of racial and ethnic difference, social inequality, racism, prejudice and xenophobia, and the rich cultural traditions that make up the United States' history. Can we imagine a curriculum in which every student either graduates with an interdisciplinary minor or takes at least a couple of those classes that challenge the boundaries of disciplines and promote the kinds of knowledge the student protesters' crave? This venture might also have the unintended consequence of decentering some of our students' identification with pre-professional curricular pathways and perhaps acquaint them with knowledge-in-the-making and with a world that

includes counter-hegemonic histories, cultures, and ways of being.

8. *Recognition of Faculty Investment in Service to Students.* Mentorships, the preparation of service-learning courses or other courses relevant to the needs of Latino and Latina students, the fostering of cultural celebrations, and the act of being present in the community currently receive little to no recognition when faculty are evaluated for promotion and tenure, at Swarthmore and other places. Sometimes older peers warn young faculty not to dissipate their energy in such endeavors. But much of what gives Swarthmore—and frankly each college or university—its special character that lives on in the minds of its alumni comes from the alliances established between students and their professors, and the payoffs for both are inestimable. The burden of expectation placed on minority faculty could be eased by increasing the number of faculty who identify as persons of color, by increasing the number of faculty members of all backgrounds who are willing to serve as mentors, formal or informal, and by insisting that colleges and universities recognize those contributions as part of faculty evaluations.

CONCLUSION

I am newly retired as I finish this essay, full of overwhelming gratitude for my time at Swarthmore College and proud of the students and their capacity to express themselves. "Something beautiful is emerging and growing," said our last Collection speaker of 2013, even as he warned us of the difficulties of the past and those still ahead. Most top-quality educational institutions are, in the twenty-first century, proud of their student diversity and advertise it in their websites and recruiting materials. We all need to recognize that accepting difference is not a seamless process but the first step in an arduous journey of dialogue, accommodation, and mutual discovery. To embrace fully Latina and Latino students at this college and others—to respect their dignity, to welcome them and receive their immense wealth in cultural and social capital, to get to know them and celebrate who they are, to guide them and work side by side with them, to help open wide possibilities for their development in a liberal arts setting—is a most important task for educators committed to social justice. It is the only way of keeping the brave promise that previous presidents, faculty and staff made many years ago, and to which we continue to be bound, each time we open our doors to a new young person.

NOTES

1 For them, the particular values and practices of critical race theory "present a unique approach to existing modes of scholarship in higher education because they explicitly focus on how the social construct of race shapes university structures, practices, and discourses from the perspectives of those injured by and fighting against institutional racism" (Yosso et al. 2009, 663).

2 The lack of identification between Latino students and Latin American professors is part of an interesting study of Spanish departments conducted at Stanford University and other institutions of higher education in 2003. See Valdés et al. 2003.

3 UCLA San Diego emerita professor Ana Celia Zentella, a past distinguished visiting professor at Swarthmore College in 2009, supports respect for language diversity and language rights among Latino youth in U.S. campuses.

12 • PASSING STRANGE

Embodying and Negotiating Difference in Academia

DAPHNE LAMOTHE

Access to higher education has transformed my sense of self and life's possibilities. Likewise, I believe that taking part in institutions of higher education has transformed those spaces, making them more open to people of varied racial, ethnic, and class backgrounds. The insights I've gained have been hard won, because the diversification of colleges and universities—and my own participation in that process—has been produced through acts of witnessing, self-inquiry, and analysis.

For me, as the product of a Haitian immigrant community in New York City, the path through life in the earliest years was apparently clear: good behavior and studiousness would lead to marriage; remaining in New York close to my large extended family; and reliable employment, perhaps as a nurse or teacher, possibly as a doctor or lawyer if I proved to be that ambitious. One could argue that I followed that map perfectly because I am a teacher (teaching being among the various other responsibilities of a college professor), am in a marriage that meets my birth community's unspoken heteronormative expectations, and have birthed two children.

Yet this cursory narrative obscures a number of detours I ended up taking: choosing to partner with a man who has no Haitian heritage, and who was raised neither Catholic nor on the East Coast, brought to our marriage its own set of cultural differences. My extended sojourn in California for graduate school opened up the possibility that I might at other points in my life choose to live away from my Haitian "village within the city" in southern

Queens. And my commitment to and success within academia has afforded me the upward social mobility that my parents strove to attain, while at the same time introducing a new set of ideas, values, and demands that run counter to their socially conservative, communitarian (though they would never have called it that), and religious views. In other words, my education and my assumption of a role within the higher educational establishment have pulled me away from my family of origin in multiple ways, even as this very education has reinforced my core sense of self. It has also made tangible for me the premise that identities are composed of multiple, sometimes contradictory, selves.

In the seventies and eighties, I was a student in the city's Catholic schools from first through twelfth grade. At that time, Irish American and Italian American nuns and laypeople took on the responsibility of educating children even as the racial demographics of the neighborhoods they served underwent a steady transformation.[1] Each year brought fewer white ethnics and more black and Latino students into the classrooms. As part of the first wave of that change, I and the other black and brown students were still a minority, albeit a growing one, in those classrooms. My classrooms had not yet entered the era of celebratory multiculturalism, nor were they paragons of racial enlightenment. The topics of racial difference and inequality either were off limits or were met with nervous laughter, when, for example, my tenth-grade English teacher, Sister Brigid, read the part of Jim, the enslaved protagonist in *Adventures of Huckleberry Finn*, in an exaggerated *Negro* dialect. Incidents such as these were relatively infrequent. For the most part, our education emphasized memorization, repetition, and discipline (this last a synonym, I instinctively knew, for *obedience*). I was a quiet girl who found it easy to meet these expectations. Thus, my teachers rewarded me with the highest compliment: the assumption that I would go to a four-year college. For students like me, our teachers' vision of our futures remained largely unchanged from where they steered previous generations of students. After high school, those of us who were academically inclined would go on either to the local Catholic universities or perhaps to the great public City University system of New York. These institutions had done a commendable job of educating and increasing the life prospects of generations of poor and working-class New Yorkers, and my reputation as a hardworking and quiet student made it almost inevitable that I would follow this path.

My guidance counselor encouraged me to fill out my college applications for schools with familiar names. Yet for some reason still unknowable to me, I chafed against the perception that my horizon should be so limited. I had paid attention when a classmate, another black "bookworm" like me, made the decision a year earlier to apply to an Ivy League college and had got in. This idea came to her because of her friendship with the conductor of our school orchestra, and I recall thinking to myself, "If she was capable of doing that, why couldn't I?" I followed Deidre's lead and let her initiative pull me along and into the Ivy League.

In my first years of college, I worked my way through several possible majors, trying on sociology, history, and political science for size, fueled by the desire to major in something "useful" that would lead to a well-compensated career. I was, in other words, a typical undergraduate from a working-class background who saw higher education through a pragmatic lens as a gateway into the middle class. Lacking any idealistic notions of the ivory tower, I nonetheless settled on an English major simply because those were the classes I enjoyed the most and in which I acquired the best grades. More important, it allowed me to answer (with a measure of honesty) the question I frequently faced from home: "What are you going to do with that major?" I could imagine myself becoming a journalist, a teacher, or a lawyer, all respectable answers to anyone who questioned my mother's sanity in allowing me to leave home for school.

The idea of becoming an academic wormed its way into my consciousness just as unexpectedly as had the idea of applying to Yale. My decision was impulsive, fueled by two impressionable moments, one of perceived failure and the other of unexpected clarity. The first moment took place the summer after my junior year as I attempted to prepare for the law school admission test in a similar fashion to the way I prepared for the SATs. Taking practice tests from an exam preparation book had worked well enough the first time, and it was much more economical than paying for an expensive review course, so I committed myself to the task once again. My resolve lasted long enough for me to get to the logical reasoning section of the first practice test, which I found incomprehensible. Feeling backed in a corner, I wondered why I was putting myself through this hassle when I wasn't even sure that I had any interest in the law outside the fact that it sounded respectable.

Putting the book aside, I recommenced my quest to imagine my future. The answers proved elusive until several months later, when I found myself sitting at the seminar table of a respected professor of Renaissance literature. I had taken two of her Shakespeare surveys the year before, and my awe of and appreciation for her brilliant lectures and lucid analyses brought me to yet another class. That day, as the class discussed the assigned text, I offered an interpretation that went somewhat against the grain of the discussion that had preceded. The details of that discussion—the focus of the conversation, the name of the play—have receded in time, but what remains entrenched in my memory is my professor's turning toward me, her pupils widening slightly, and her appreciative response: "I have never thought of it that way." The world stopped for an instant, and I had a moment of clarity. I was good at this! And so, at this particular fork in the road, my decision to apply to graduate school in English was not a dramatic departure from my predestined path, but it did feel as though I was participating in self-determination.

These stepping-stones, isolated moments when a supportive remark or a helping hand created an opportunity for self-reflection, happened periodically. There was the dinnertime conversation with my residential college dean, who encouraged me to consider the University of California–Berkeley because "it's good to explore the world, and you can always come back home when you're ready." He gave me tacit permission to venture even further from my Queens home, even though I knew that my decision to attend a residential college as an undergraduate had already caused my parents much emotional turmoil. The graduate student instructor in my senior year, whose gentleness I found reassuring, agreed to write me a letter of recommendation. I didn't yet know enough to distinguish between adjunct instructors, teaching assistants, and professors, so his confession that his word as a graduate student would carry less weight than that of his wife, a professor, was invaluable advice. His further encouragement that I ask his wife (my Shakespeare professor!) for not one but two letters was gratefully accepted. Looking back on it now, I imagine that they must have discussed my cluelessness, because when I gathered up the courage to go to her office hours, she took the time to walk me through the process of applying for graduate school. I had never spent so much time in her office before, nor would I ever again. But at that meeting, she guided me on how to decide where to apply; whom else to ask for letters of recommendation; and how to present myself as a serious scholar, as opposed to merely a book lover with a good work ethic.

Moments of serendipity such as these followed me into graduate school and have continued to do so throughout my career. Only a few of the individuals to whom I'm so indebted looked like me, yet all responded generously when I was in need of necessary advice or feedback. Notably absent in all these memories is a mentor in the sense that the word is traditionally invoked: a single individual who takes you under her wing, dispensing wisdom and guidance and providing a gateway to her own network and contacts. The word carries with it the suggestion of a sustained relationship.

Once I entered the pre-professional world of graduate school, I was constantly reminded of the importance of having a mentor to guide me through the convoluted and often unspoken expectations of the profession. At national conferences for young scholars, I heard again and again about the significant role that mentors play in one's career development. How-to-succeed books sang the importance of drawing upon the wisdom and counsel of a trusted teacher. But throughout, my experience has been in equal parts (a) a struggle to figure out the social codes of the institutions in which I found myself, (b) a receptiveness to those moments when certain individuals proved willing to share their knowledge and insights with me, and (c) a combination of tenacity, curiosity, and openness to new ideas and experiences. I consider whatever professional success I've managed to achieve as much a product of my good fortune as a matter of meritocracy at work. At the time, I had no idea that the teaching assistant from whom I asked for a letter of recommendation happened to be married to a professor who was familiar with me. Although my residential college dean ate in the dining hall every evening of my four years at Yale, I had never shared a meal with him until fall semester, senior year, when he asked me about my plans for the future and planted the seed of the idea that I might give California a try. The classmate who inspired me to apply to Yale was mentored by our orchestra conductor and was encouraged by him; if not for *their* relationship, I would not have applied. I was lucky, I worked hard, and I paid attention.

ORIENTATION AND ASSIMILATION: INTEGRATING
DIFFERENCE WITHIN THE ACADEMY

When I enter the classroom these days, students and colleagues read my unaccented English and my visibly black and female body in particular ways. Until I reveal certain facts about myself, most assume that I am African American with cultural roots in the American South, and with an attendant experiential knowledge of southern history and culture. They assume that I grew up in a monolingual household and that I am either Protestant or not religious. Occasionally, I find myself wanting or needing to resist the impulse to pass as fully culturally American, whereas my experience in Haitian circles is typically one of failing to prove myself Haitian *enough*. To other Haitians and Haitian Americans, my New York City birthplace is less of an issue than my inability to speak Creole well, the rarity of my visits to my parents' birthplace, and the amateur quality of my Haitian cooking. And while I was acutely aware of American society's disdain and contempt for Haitian people, particularly during the influx of immigrants during the seventies and eighties who bore the stigma of the label "boat people," I suffered none of the insults and jabs directed at my cousins, who had just arrived. My Haitian identity is embedded in my Haitian American upbringing in an immigrant community in Queens, New York, more than it is in the immediate memory of a lived experience on the island. My African American identity is rooted in the same. For me, as a cultural in-betweener with a hybrid subjectivity, strangeness or outsiderness is the state in which I feel most at home.

In my junior year of college, I participated in a march through the central campus organized by the Black Student Association. As we walked, most sang the words to "Lift Every Voice" (what I would learn later is informally known as the Negro National Anthem) by James Weldon Johnson (lyrics, 1899) and Rosamond Johnson (music, 1900). Moved by the song's stirring rhythms and victorious message of unity, I turned to the person standing next to me and said, "I love this song. I wish I knew what it is called." She stared at me with incomprehension and then turned away and continued to walk in unison with the crowd. Although I also continued the march, I lost that momentary sense of cohesion, because I had revealed myself to be an outsider to this great African American tradition. While the experience was relatively minor, the memory of it remains major, for I experienced it as a failure of an unspoken test of authenticity. Today, I recognize that, like most of my classmates, I was and am as much a citizen of "African America" as I am a U.S. citizen, and both involve learning expectations and customs along the way.

To be a black student at Yale in the eighties, much as it is to be a black professor at Smith College in the first half of the twenty-first century, is to be considered a part of a monolithic group that shares the same language, culture, and references. The irony is of course that as a scholar of the Harlem Renaissance, among other subjects, I now introduce students to the prodigious output of the Johnson brothers and other great African American artists. My job now is to transfer knowledge about this history and culture and these traditions to yet another generation of students. I consider these traditions to be as much a part of my legacy as is Caribbean culture and history, but my pedagogy and scholarship are necessarily grounded in book learning as much as lived experience.

I am the product of multiple histories and cultural influences. This fact doesn't make me special or unique, yet my experiences as a second-generation American make the processes of identity formation that much more acute and transparent, because the parts of the self do not line up seamlessly. Here W.E.B. DuBois's (1903) formulation of double-consciousness proves illuminating for his description of the condition as "this sense of always looking at one's self through the eyes of others, of measuring one's soul by the tape of a world that looks on with amused contempt and pity" (11) and is an apt description not only of growing up black and American but also of having partial claims to and histories of exclusion from all of my identities: black/African/American/Haitian/daughter/mother/wife/professor. (This list is presented in no particular order or hierarchy other than one that I believe would make sense to readers of this essay. My point here is that the context determines how I perceive and present myself. There is no "I" except as conceptualized in response to one's environment and or social context.) And as Gloria Anzaldúa (1999) articulated in her description of the development of a *mestiza* consciousness that growing up on the borderlands of Mexican and Anglo societies produces:

> Cradled in one culture, sandwiched between two cultures, straddling all three cultures and their value systems, *la mestiza* is a product of the transfer of the cultural and spiritual values of one group to another. Being tricultural, mono-lingual, bilingual, or multilingual, speaking a patois, and in a state of perpetual transition, the *mestiza* faces the dilemma of the mixed breed: which collectiv-ity does the daughter of a darkskinned mother listen to (100)?

Anzaldúa's description of the hybrid subject in a state of continual transition resonates with my own sense of movement between the poles of Haitian/African/American. Yet I've also discovered that institutions, organizations, and communities struggle to acknowledge and accept the hybrid subject because their presence introduces an instability that disrupts the group's sense of wholeness. This is true on both micro and macro levels.

Occupying the borderlands, or the hyphenated space of the cultural in-betweener, has made me deeply familiar with the feeling of moving through the world as the "stranger," Georg Simmel's (1908) sociological formula-tion, based on observations of the European Jew of which he was one, of the individual who lives and participates in a community yet who is viewed as a partial insider, someone who is in the group, but not of it. The distances between national, cultural, social, and epistemological spheres can be vast, particularly for the young and unformed mind. While my upbringing made me unhappily yet intimately familiar with being a "stranger," my postsec-ondary education gave me the vocabulary, the analytical tools, and the per-spective to make sense of those experiences.

DuBois's, Anzaldúa's, and Simmel's theoretical insights have provided the foundation for a deep and rich body of critical and theoretical literature on identity and cultural formation, yet they are at odds with how institutions of higher learning operate in their attempts to integrate students and faculty who represent cultural, ethnic, and racial diversity. These institutions typi-cally construct notions of a monolithic group that embodies "difference" while also needing to assimilate the community's (white, upper-middle-class) norms. This approach often fails to account fully for the possibility of multiplicity and heterogeneity within the marginalized group. One way that colleges achieve this goal is by creating programs designed to meet the per-ceived needs of minority students, such as orientation activities intended to create opportunities of in-group bonding, and introducing students to the rigors of the college classroom. Of course, not all minority students come from challenged public schools and neither do all minority students need or want opportunities to bond with other minority students. But such programs do acknowledge that these activities are helpful to a majority of minority students. Another strategy is the creation of student organizations devoted to the pursuit of cultural awareness, social bonding, and political action. These efforts play an important role in the diversification of college campuses, yet they also have the potential to fracture the fragile bonds they attempt to create, particularly when they fail to account for heterogeneity within particular groups.

My own teaching and counseling of students reflect these insights about the complexities of cultural formations and identity. On my syllabi, I feature prominently essays by theorists such as DuBois and Anzaldúa and literature, music, and film that illuminate the insights of the hybrid subject and cultural in-betweener and articulate the complexity and multiplicity of black identities and cultures. I've found that students can have a mixed response to this pedagogical approach. Some welcome the introduction to a new analytical and theoretical framework; others look on these discussions of intragroup dynamics as a distraction from what they view as the real struggle: to gain an understanding of antiblack racism and oppression. My refusal to view these choices as either/or, but rather as both/and, grows from my conviction that there are multiple approaches to the study of African American history and culture that merit consideration. The discipline of African American studies is strong enough to allow for teaching and research that takes not only an activist approach but also theoretical, philosophical, and aesthetic approaches. More productively, putting different critical frames in conversation with each other can lead to a greater measure of insight and understanding. For example, African American feminist critics' insistence on the necessity of an intersectional approach to the study of race has created space for analyses of gender, sexual orientation, and class that deepen and complicate our understanding of racial formations. On a more personal level, just as I was empowered as an undergraduate student by my introduction to ideas and a critical vocabulary that enabled me to think through my experiences, so do I aspire to create a classroom environment that endows students with the analytical capacity and critical distance to make sense of their world(s).

Colleges and universities create diversity and mentoring programs to increase the retention rates of students and faculty of color. Many individuals benefit greatly from these efforts to transform the academy into a more intimate and familiar space that feels welcoming, a symbolic home. The construction of any community, however, presupposes the drawing of boundaries that encircle some while excluding others. In my years as a professor, I have encountered black students who are bicultural, biracial, queer, adoptees raised by parents of a different race, and disabled, who feel pressured to hide or erase some crucial part of themselves in order to be accepted by the school's African American community. As we in our respective institutions work on creating more inclusive spaces, we must also emphasize the critical work we do in the classrooms to theorize and make transparent the complexities of how communities are built, as well as the politics of belonging and not belonging. Some of us have no choice but to be strangers. Some of us choose to be strangers, in the sense of seeking out unfamiliar territories and experiences. All of us need to develop the emotional and intellectual capacities to identify, name, navigate, and negotiate these intricate communal and social structures.

THE EMBODIED INTELLECTUAL

When in my late twenties, within the course of four years, I gave birth to my first daughter, finished my dissertation and earned my doctorate, started my first tenure-track job, and gave birth to a second daughter. I had no role models of how to balance these tremendous and labor-intensive responsibilities other than my own parents, neither of whom graduated from college but both of whom set a high standard of industriousness with their long commutes and work days and their strong sense of familial obligation. My circumstances as a young (female) parent professor forced me to cross multiple social spheres in just a few years, from Haitian to American, lower-middle/working class to upper-middle class, and African American to predominantly Anglo-American spheres. The realities of my entrée into a new and elevated professional class brought different challenges: not only a workweek that stretched well beyond the traditional forty hours but also the intrusions of e-mail and other digital media that brought the office into the home, on vacation, and on the sidelines of soccer fields and dance academy waiting rooms. Moreover, while I was a proverbial latchkey kid of the seventies, my generation of (middle-class) mothers carried with us raised expectations for active participation in our children's recreational lives and at school. I struggled with the choice either to contribute to my children's social ostracization if I failed to engage in the rituals of arranged play dates that were the norm in these social circles or to suffer the inevitable loss of precious time for class preparation, research, or writing when I chauffeured my children to their after-school commitments. The few fathers who sat on the sidelines or in the waiting rooms could slip away unmolested to take a conference call or finish reading a report for work; mothers, however, felt a clear and persistent pressure to contribute to the teams' and schools' community bonding. These domestic, professional, and social expectations compounded the challenges of my learning how to transform my thesis into a book and secure a publisher under the tyranny of the tenure clock's relentless ticking. My strongest impression of those earliest years as a junior faculty member can be described in two words: *overwork* and *exhaustion*. I rarely brought my children to the office, because I never saw another child in the building that housed my department. And at the same time, I always brought my office to my home and struggled mightily to keep the load from collapsing on me.

Colleagues who might have acted as mentors to me failed to offer immediate practical advice on how to juggle work and family. In some cases, they were simply too overwhelmed by work themselves to reach out to a junior scholar who didn't feel entitled to reach out first. In other cases, the particulars of how they managed when their own families were young and their careers were undeveloped had receded too far back in memory to be of any practical use. Circumstances as far ranging as day care arrangements in our town and the state of the academic publishing industry had changed so drastically since they had been assistant professors that they felt they could not offer useful, concrete advice, or so they told me. Being a professor, a mother, or both is demanding enough, but never more so when one has no role models or examples to follow. As I struggled to find my place and my voice within academia, one could convincingly argue that I suffered from a classic case of impostor syndrome in which I convinced myself that my professional successes were the result of luck and other external circumstances, and had little to do with my own innate talents (see Clance and Imes 1978). Yet it is also inarguable that the markers of my physical body—black, female, slight of stature, young, and occasionally pregnant—lent credence to the perception that I did not belong. In my first years as a professor, I was asked repeatedly if I was a student, and sometimes by my own colleagues! Alternately, when I am asked what I do for a living, my reply is often met with a murmur of surprised approval: "Good for *you*!"

Armed with the critical, analytical, and theoretical tools that I needed to comprehend the contingency and intersectionality of identity, the constructedness of imagined communities, and the way that power inhabits social structures, I am able to recognize that my state of not-belonging has changed from one of alienation to one of critical distance and engagement. In laypersons' terms, I have grown from feeling like a "stranger" to having a critical capacity to act quite purposefully like a "stranger," in Simmel's sense of being a member of the collective, endowed with the capacity to interrogate and confront the group's unexamined and unspoken assumptions.[2] If pushed, I might even go so far as to say that my status as stranger or in-betweener is an intrinsic part of why I found myself drawn to the life of the mind, because it cultivated within me the tendencies toward observation, critical detachment, and self-reflection, all key attributes of a scholar and critic.

Now in the middle stages of my career, I find myself more often than not in the position of supervising and guiding junior faculty and students of color. Rather than beginning from the assumption that I have the answers for how to best navigate the tricky waters of academia, I offer up my own stories of when I've failed or succeeded, and my thoughts about the reasons for these outcomes. I emphasize the emotional, personal, and situational conditions that informed the choices I've made and caution such people who speak with me to consider their own unique circumstances. I try also to render institutional structures and practices transparent and hope that this gives them the tools to discern their own pathways and goals. I hope that my contributions prove meaningful, but I'm OK with the possibility that they may be meager. The one truth that I've come to recognize is that sometimes a passing comment or interaction can be enough to lift a veil, open a door, and potentially transform a life. I offer my own pedagogical and mentoring practices, not as an example of the best model for responding to the diversification of institutions of higher learning, but to encourage college faculty and administrators to conceptualize, promote, and advocate for diverse student and faculty representation by placing ideas such as pluralism, heterogeneity, intersectionality, and hybridity at the center of their institutions' mission.

NOTES

1 In 1976, PBS presented a Bill Moyers–hosted documentary on my hometown titled *Rosedale: The Way It Is*. The film chronicled the sometimes violent struggles of the town's six thousand white residents in 1974 to keep Caribbean and African American people from moving into Rosedale. By the time my family moved there in 1976, Rosedale's white residents had effectively lost that battle. There were only two or three white families who still lived on my block, and within less than a decade, they too would flee.

2 "The unity of nearness and remoteness involved in every human relation is organized, in the phenomenon of the stranger, in a way which may be most briefly formulated by saying that in the relationship to him, distance means that he, who is close by, is far, and strangeness means that he, who also is far, is actually near. For, to be a stranger is naturally a very positive relation; it is a specific form of interaction. . . . His position as a full-fledged member involves both being outside it and confronting it" (Simmel 1950, 402).

13 ◆ A DEAN'S WEEK

"Trapdoors and Glass Ceilings"

THERESA TENSUAN

It's late on a Monday afternoon and I am standing at the threshold of my office, a suite that I share with the dean of first-year students and the coordinator for international student services. My title is associate dean of the college, dean of multicultural affairs, and director of the Office of Multicultural Affairs. There's a relationship between these myriad responsibilities and the everything-but-the-kitchen-sink contents of my purse. I find myself rummaging for keys that I am convinced are buried somewhere between the folder that has the minutes from last week's Educational Policy Committee meeting and my worn copy of *Fun Home: A Family Tragicomic*, a graphic memoir by the American writer Alison Bechdel (2006), that I'm having the students in my writing seminar read, and—ugh—the napkin with the half-eaten brownie from last Friday's reception for the student leaders who had participated in our leadership program.

MONDAY: WHAT'S IN A NAME?

At the moment I realize that I had left the keys someplace else altogether, I hear a soft knock at the door to the outer suite. It's Lawrence (I am using pseudonyms), who is smiling apologetically as he asks me if I have just a couple of minutes to talk with him. I quickly work through the mental equation that takes into consideration the fact that I promised the third grader in my household that I would help her with her spelling words, plus the fact that I was planning on making a quick stop at the office supply store that has a sale on composition books to pick up forty for the diversity retreat that my office is co-sponsoring this weekend, plus the fact that I'm supposed to pick up rice, chicken, broccoli, and seltzer to counterbalance the fast food dinners of the previous week. I balance all this against the fact that Lawrence looks a little tense and that it is unusual for him to stop by unannounced— he's the kind of student who makes appointments over a week in advance, shows up five minutes ahead of time with an agenda in hand, and follows up our meetings with a thank you note that outlines the action steps that he's drawn up based on our discussion.

It is in part because of this kind of focus, drive, and initiative that Lawrence is one of the two students sitting on the search committee for a new assistant professor in the department of their major. One of the professors on the committee is the second reader for Lawrence's thesis and has been mistakenly sending e-mails meant for Lawrence to Jeremy, another senior major in the department—something Jeremy discerned from the fact that the source material that the professor had listed as must-read material had everything to do with Lawrence's project on post–World War II city planning in Germany and not much to do with Jeremy's project on urban landscapes and the civil rights movement in the American South. They are the only two black male students in the department's cohort of senior majors, and Lawrence is looking for advice on how to approach the professor tactfully, given that they are currently sitting on the same committee and that the man will have a substantive impact on Lawrence's senior seminar grade.

From one perspective, the situation verges on the absurd. Jeremy is compact, has a *café au lait* complexion, sports an Afro of Sly Stone–like proportions, is well known on campus as a motormouth, and has a nervous, kinetic energy that serves him well as a performer with the campus's improv troupe. Lawrence is at least a foot taller than Jeremy, wears his hair high and tight as befits the son of a Marine sergeant, is dark skinned, and is circumspect—the kind of student who chooses his words with great care whether in person or on the page. I remember the very first conversation I had with Lawrence, which came early in his sophomore year when he was taking an introductory course with the professor in question. The teaching assistant (TA) for the course suspected Lawrence had cheated on the midterm just because Lawrence and Jeremy, the two black students in the class, had both received grades well above the class curve. The TA would have had no way of knowing that both Lawrence and Jeremy were in the top 10 percent of the sophomore class as a whole—indeed, given that the college culture eschews any talk about grades, Lawrence and Jeremy themselves probably weren't aware of that ranking—but I wonder if the TA would have been so quick to jump to the suspicion of cheating if Lawrence and Jeremy were white.

Lawrence and I end up talking for half an hour about how to approach the situation—a real-life, real-time working through of the query James C. Scott (1990) poses at the outset of *Domination and the Arts of Resistance*: "How do we study"—or in this case, negotiate—"the power relations when the powerless are often obliged to adapt a strategic post in the presence of the powerful, and when the powerful may have an interest in overdramatizing their reputation and mastery" (xii)? Lawrence and I both understand that drawing the professor's attention to his mistake will be awkward at best, and at worst could hobble a relationship that they both anticipate could one day become professional. We work through the question of whether approaching his major adviser would offer some useful pointers about how to broach the subject with the professor in question or if it will be seen as going over the professor's head, since Lawrence's adviser is also the departmental chair. Lawrence's familiarity with military hierarchies (a capacity that isn't often valued in our Quaker-founded college) attunes him to the nuances of hierarchical structures of academia, a capacity that has enabled him to negotiate dynamics that are invisible and discombobulating to many of his peers. Lawrence is by no means powerless in this situation, but neither does he fit what Audre Lorde (1984) calls "the mythical norm," within which "the trappings of power reside" (116). Lorde notes that in the United States, "this norm is usually defined as white, thin, male, young, heterosexual, Christian, and financially secure," a litany to which we might add able bodied and, particularly in academic contexts, neurotypical. Lawrence and I have both been well schooled in what Scott defines as the "hidden transcripts" that undergird the unspoken codes and expectations of both dominant and subordinate groups; he was actually introduced to Scott's work in the context of this professor's course. We talk a lot about what kind of language and tone can convey that Lawrence doesn't harbor any ill will and would just like to clear up the confusion—that ritual obeisance that a good student knows how to perform, even if (particularly if) the professor is in the wrong. Even as he is able to create a critical distance from and perspective on the situation, over the course of our conversation, Lawrence cycles through his anger and frustration: After all his accomplishments in—and contributions to—the department, he's being seen as interchangeable with Jeremy. I send him off with my best wishes and ask him to check back in with me after he has his conversations with the members of his department, and I finally lock the door behind me wondering if my encouragement to confront the issue directly was the best advice.

TUESDAY: A TALE OF TWO STUDENTS

It's one thirty and I'm forty minutes into a phone call with Frances's mother, following several futile attempts to get in touch with Frances herself; she's been on my radar since last spring when her name came up at the midsemester meeting where deans and advisers review the academic records of students who have been struggling academically. Frances had two failing grades on her transcript; it turns out that one is for a phantom fifth course that she had intended to drop after she had settled on her classes for the term, but she didn't follow through with the paperwork; for the other, though, she hadn't submitted the final essay despite repeated requests from the professor teaching the course.

Over the summer, Frances was diagnosed with clinical depression and her mother—herself the chair of psychology at a Research One (R1) university—tactfully and tactically shares her concern that Frances is not getting the support that she needs at the college. I find myself, as Frances's dean, feeling defensive as I enumerate the contacts that Frances has made with the college's counseling and psychological services as well as with the office of academic resources, and it occurs to me that part of the reason why Frances may not be responding to my e-mails is because the way I operate is actually a lot like her mother's. Frances has learned how to deflect the iron-hand-in-the-velvet-glove approach that usually works when I deploy it with her peers. Her mother and I both clearly place stock in the kind of social capital that Pierre Bourdieu (1986) describes as "the aggregate of the . . . resources which are linked to possession of a durable network of more or less institutionalized relationships of mutual acquaintance and recognition—or, in other words, membership in a group—which provides each its members with the backing of the collectively-owned capital, a 'credential' which entitles them to credit in various senses of the word" (248). When I recognize that simpatico relationship with Frances's mother, strained as it is, I am able to speak to the reason why I had contacted Frances's parents in the first place; in repeatedly missing classes—fully understandable as a symptom of her depression and a byproduct of her medication—Frances is heading toward failure in at least two of them, and if this course of events continues, she will be asked to take a leave from the college.

As this conversation unspools, I hear someone tapping on the door, and I realize that I'm supposed to be meeting with Mathilde for our "regular" one thirty appointment that we've managed to miss twice in the past three weeks. It takes me a full ten minutes to get off the phone, and by the time I get to the waiting area to greet Mathilde, Dawn Scribe, the administrative assistant, tells me that Mathilde was going back to her shift in the IT department. I make a mental note to e-mail Mathilde to reschedule our meeting for a time that doesn't conflict with her work schedule—Mathilde is also on my radar, since she had almost capsized herself at the end of her first year by deciding not to take one of her finals. Her logic, at once taking care of her parents and avoiding her own demons, was that if she failed out of school, her parents wouldn't have to worry about marshaling their slender resources to keep her in college, since they were trying to save money to hire an immigration lawyer who would be able to help them secure legal standing.

Before I can commit the mental reminder to a stick-on note, though, I see that Frances has actually stopped by, no doubt prodded by her mother, who has figured out what lever can get her daughter out of bed to see her dean. Frances and I spend the better part of the next hour mapping out her standing in the classes in which she's enrolled, ending up with a working plan for how she will approach the coming week as well as scheduling an appointment for two o'clock on Tuesday next week.

With Frances squared away, at least for the time being, I remember to send a quick e-mail to Mathilde asking her if she can stop by again between four and five, which should be right after her international politics class, when I'll be back in the office following a meeting for a group of co-workers that has taken on the task of figuring out how to convert a former gym into an arts and humanities center, which is itself followed by a meeting with a group that is assigned to figure out a centralized scheduling system, a project that has been in the work for the better part of a decade for reasons that have to be relearned by each new committee assigned to the task. That meeting runs over, and I'm behind schedule in getting back to the office and am worried that I'll miss Mathilde again—she doesn't stop by at all that afternoon, but sends an apologetic e-mail at the end of the day noting that she had agreed to pick up a friend's shift at the dining center where she works a second job. When we had spoken about her schedule at the beginning of the semester and I questioned the wisdom of her working two jobs, she explained that she sends part of her paycheck home. By contributing to the family's rent, Mathilde assuages some of the guilt that she feels as the eldest daughter who would otherwise be at home, contributing more to the family income, helping look after her two younger sisters, and figuring out how to alleviate her parents' immigration woes. Given her circumstances— having parents who both work more than one job while actively contending with the fear of discovery and deportation—Mathilde is unlike students who have the privilege of, in Terrell Strayhorn's (2010) words, the benefit of ample "'air time' to think aloud about their educational aspirations" (324) in the context of ongoing family conversations, whereas I have the strong suspicion that Frances has never been to a family gathering in which she *wasn't* asked about her educational aspirations. As I engage in this internal dialogue, I realize that in letting my phone conversation with Frances's mother run an extra ten minutes, I've effectively missed a week with Mathilde.

WEDNESDAY: TIME OUT

At the end of the summer, I was invited to share some reflections on issues of access at small liberal arts colleges for a conference of educators in a consortium who work with students who historically have been underrepresented in higher education. Six weeks later, with the conference less than seventy-two hours away, I shut the door to my office decisively, telling my assistant, Dawn, and the student interns in the office to knock only if it's a crisis. I decide that I'll talk about some missteps that I've taken in the twelve-person writing seminar that I'm teaching this fall, in which a third of the students in the class are the first in their immediate families to go to college, the students who self-identify as people of color outnumber other students two to one, and just under half speak a language other than English at home.

This extraordinary diversity is possible in large part because we currently have a student body that is entirely composed of students who applied to the college after our board of managers moved to make the school not only need blind but also loan free. That decision, in concert with the work of an extremely dedicated and visionary admissions team, created a sea change in the student body by making a highly selective small liberal arts college both worth the consideration and attainable for students from communities, perhaps most notably Latino and Latina students and other students from the American Southwest, that have been historically underrepresented here.

This particular set of students has the kind of chemistry that can make the instructor feel superfluous at times, and most days I find myself just very grateful for the intellectual vitality that is engendered by open exchanges among people from very different backgrounds and experiences. At other points, I am highly aware of the ways in which socioeconomic differences among students in the classroom create radically different kinds of access, and how moves that I have made to level the playing field at times end up only amplifying those differences.

For example, over the years, I've learned to be mindful of the cost of books, after a student brought to my attention the fact that a reading list I had composed would eat up over half of his book budget for the semester; thus I was particularly pleased to find out that one of the books that I was teaching, Jaime Cortez's *Sexile,* a work that had an initial print run of only five thousand volumes, was available from the creator as a free downloadable high-resolution PDF. As my students would say, "Sweet!" At the same time, we found that being able to view the PDF on a screen meant that a reader could see a level of detail and clarity that wasn't possible in the printed copies, and at this point differences in students' socioeconomic statuses became quite visible, given that some were toting the very latest in tablet technology while others were not.

We were able to work with the library and with our IT department to get students access to college-owned equipment, but in the days that it took me to get that together, I was reminded of the ways in which I unthinkingly maintain sets of assumptions and expectations that form the unspoken codes that structure community members' behavior, a set of codes that are, for some students, a comfortable structure in which they've lived their entire lives, and for others, a series of trapdoors, missing steps, and glass ceilings. Even as I congratulate myself for being mindful of students' access to technology, I think of Kristin Lindgren's (2005) acknowledgment and challenge:

> To those who are more informed, access also means making information available in multiple modes, hiring ASL interpreters familiar with academic discourse, using technology creatively, providing texts in large print and alternative formats, and so on. But once we begin to imagine what full access might look like, the possibilities seem endless, the concept elusive and protean. I like to think that providing access involves more than checking off a list of practical accommodations, though these practical matters are incredibly important. Access also involves a way of thinking about the world that challenges us to imagine how another body, another self, experiences it. What could be more intellectually engaging than imagining another's world? Isn't this something like what we do when we read a novel? Why are we so reluctant to imagine the different bodies and different lives of the *non*fictional people with whom we live and work?

I remember a conversation with a student in office hours who came from a town not far from the small town where I grew up in rural southwestern Pennsylvania, who, when asked if she was enjoying a class taught by a professor who has the reputation of being a brilliant raconteur, said, "It's weird—I've never been in a place where someone can speak for twenty minutes without being interrupted."

In reminding me of the values and practices of a community in which bodies of knowledge encompassed understandings of how to tend to a sick cow as well as how to predict when the rains would come based on the height and shape of the clouds, the student helped me understand the ways in which what we envision as a robust intellectual exchange can be, in fact, simply a one-way monologue. One of the challenges that my colleagues and I face is whether we can separate out such elitist assumptions and practices from our collective commitment to excellence whereby students can offer new models and modes of understanding and animating the world, and can literally as well as figuratively articulate new—

I'm interrupted by a knock at the door. My protected time is over. As a full-time professor (which I was for a decade before moving into this position), I was sometimes able to finish a thought, or speak or write for twenty minutes without being interrupted, but for me now as a dean, crises seem to come every seventeen minutes.

THURSDAY: FACULTY MEETING

I'm listening to the debate surrounding a new summer bridge-and-mentoring program for high-achieving students from underrepresented communities, a program that some colleagues see only as a drain of resources and faculty time. In the meetings where I've sat with the colleagues who have been crafting the program, we've been seeing it not only as an opportunity to support promising scholars but also as a matrix in which we can learn what kind of mentoring enables students to thrive, particularly those who come in without the cultural capital that is evident in advanced placement credits or that is manifest in the advice from family members who are familiar with the practices and protocols that lead to success in college.

When my colleague Ruth Alvarez inaugurated the position of first-year dean at the college, she was the first to point out to advisers that the students who were coming from the underresourced public high schools were the students who were taking the most difficult classes they could get into because this was the strategy they had used in high school to get the best education that they could, whereas the students who had gone to independent schools or public schools in wealthier communities were practiced in the art of figuring out how to balance their schedules with classes that would be a real challenge and classes in which they would have to work less hard.

Given the research that shows how productive such bridge-and-mentoring programs can be, I'm trying to figure out why one faculty member is trembling with rage as he condemns the program for providing a healthy stipend to the professors who elect to teach a course in the summer program.

When I take a couple of steps back from my own investment in the program in question, I appreciate that this faculty member is simply noting that the coin of the realm for tenure is the literal weight of one's scholarship and that to promote summer teaching as valuable college service is disingenuous if such teaching and service isn't truly valued at such key points in a scholar's career.

I think about this in relation to an emerging conversation about how experiential learning and community engagement might be incorporated into the graduation requirements, thus ascribing value to a key aspect of community life in which there is a disproportionate number of students from underrepresented communities in leadership roles. This is especially important in campus communities where faculty labor is often cast hierarchically, in which scholarship is valued over teaching, which is valued over service, which is itself almost a dirty word. Indeed, could a reevaluation of the distribution requirements (which function as the curricular DNA of the college) be a springboard for reframing the values that undergird institutional practices such as the expectations for tenure?

I want to resist the faculty member's vision of the program as part of a zero-sum game in which resources put into one arena are resources denied another, where there are winners cakewalking down the center of the dance hall while the losers are leaning up against the wall, plotting their eventual revenge. What are the ways of understanding our common mission: how can excellence in scholarship be understood as having a dynamic relationship with innovative teaching? What does it mean to embrace the idea that the first-year, first-generation student from San Luis Obispo is as vital a member of the intellectual community as the full professor who is a third-generation University of Chicago PhD?

I wonder about this in relation to the conversation that the board of managers is opening regarding the need-blind, no-loan policy that it adopted right before the economic crisis of 2008, a policy that has sent financial aid expenditures skyrocketing at the precise moment that the college's endowment has dropped by a third. I see how the managers are wrestling with the question of how to steward the college's resources responsibly while maintaining access for those who have been most disenfranchised.

FRIDAY: WHAT'S IN A NAME?

The conference on access and higher education is both inspiring and sobering; it is energizing to be in the company of people who have made it their profession to find avenues for access for deserving students. The keynote speaker reminds us that all students are deserving, and shows us the direct connection between resources devoted to public school education and the eventual success of the students who go through the system and speaks to the sea change that happens at schools to which resources are granted or from which resources are taken away.

I have to leave before the afternoon sessions because I'm getting a number of e-mails about a developing crisis on campus. Hoping against hope that it is a tempest in a teapot, I return to the college to get briefed on the situation that is unfolding. Back in my office, as I puzzle over how to open up spaces in my calendar to schedule a meeting (which will be the first in a series that will, all told, take over forty hours—more than a full workweek, if any of us actually worked only forty hours a week), I hear a knock on my half-open door. It is Lawrence, who has stopped by to let me know that the conversation with the professor went well.

To celebrate, we walk down the hallway to the café, where I see Mathilde, and as she pulls an espresso for me and pours a coffee for Lawrence, she and I figure out a time when we can actually meet the following week. I see a couple of students from my writing seminar—one from Accra, Ghana, the other from the Bronx, New York—working together on a problem set for chemistry, and I acknowledge a curt nod from my colleague who had raised objections about the summer bridge-and-mentoring program, thinking that I should probably figure out a time to sit down with him and other faculty members who had raised concerns—but giving myself until at least next week to do so.

And I'm surprised when I run into a faculty colleague whose eyes light up when he sees me—he had chaired a search committee in the social sciences for which I was the token humanist, and he had offered me some extremely useful advice at a moment when I was trying to get a program off the ground. He calls me by the name of one of the few other Asian American women on campus—a senior colleague who is about a head taller and twenty pounds lighter and who favors tailored suits over my bright, flowing thrift store tunics. I could go on about our differences: she is a first-generation Taiwanese immigrant, whereas I'm second-generation Filipina American; she's graceful and gracious and would know, I fantasize, how to respond in such a moment. As it is, as I am, I turn to Lawrence and ask him, quite seriously, "So tell me. What exactly *did* you say in that meeting?"

CONCLUSION

Theorizing the Transformation of the Twenty-First-Century Campus

SARAH WILLIE-LEBRETON

In the introductory chapter, I asserted that the essays in this volume were an attempt to take what had been private conversations and bring them into a more public space. The contributors and I hope they serve as a springboard to serious and sustained conversations about difference and diversity, about the challenges and extraordinary possibilities of higher education in the United States, and about the normative expectations we have of campus communities that hold up ideals of inclusion and fairness but also occasionally benefit from challenges to the ways things have always been done.

At the start of Chapter 1, Michael Smith and Eve Tuck quote Charles Mills; in another quote, Mills writes, "White supremacy is the unnamed political system that has made the modern world what it is today" (1999, 1). This volume takes no issue with that observation; indeed, social scientists researching and writing the world over during the twentieth century gathered dramatic evidence to support it. White supremacy is one of many systems of domination and oppression, but remains one of the most powerful and obscure. It is the combination of power and opacity that make the racial system (in the form of white supremacy), the sex/gender system (in the forms of patriarchy and heteronormativity), and the class system (in the form of capitalism), among others, so challenging to analyze.

They are difficult to see, to name, and to understand for at least three reasons. First, these systems of oppression and privilege operate according to a tautology that justifies their rightness in the world. One aspect of that self-justification is a purposeful obfuscation of the distinction between individuals and ideology. To that end, many of us confuse frustration about systems with anger at individuals. As a scholar and a teacher, my charge includes (a) clarifying the difference between investigating and analyzing systems, (b) appreciating that not all systems are unfair, (c) working to undermine systems that are unfair, (d) challenging unfair practices, and (e) avoiding humiliating individuals who may not know that such systems exist, even if they regularly benefit from them.

A second reason that such systems are challenging to analyze is that most of us who are victims (and that occasionally includes teachers) of unfair systems are angry about it. Teachers, scholars, and professors—like other members of society—are confused, hurt, and frustrated when treated poorly, unfairly, stereotypically, or without compassion. It is a challenge to be rigorous and thoughtful, attentive, and clearheaded about one's analysis when one is the victim of such an unfair system. In addition, teachers, like clergy, social workers, and nurses are supposed to be cheerful, humble, and grateful. Our work is idealized as mission driven, so when we are angry it's difficult for many people to appreciate that mission-driven work is still done by individuals who occasionally have hurt and angry feelings.

Of course, to be privileged by one or more of these systems also inhibits good judgment during the process of conducting research and analysis. In other words, no one teacher is more or less likely to be good at social analysis; it takes good old-fashioned maturity, self-reflexivity, creativity, and a willingness to be engaged with others who can offer honest critique. Those who teach about social inequality, and the systems that uphold and defend its various forms, whether or not they benefit from them, have to negotiate their emotional responses regularly. When, as Iris Marion Young says, we offer complaint, insight, concern, or argument about them, our complaints and insights are dismissed as personality disorders or more evidence that we belong to groups that are overemotional, quick to anger, irrational, and nonintellectual. Thus, members of academia who respond to such issues are caught in a feedback loop: if you complain, you reveal that you are one of the complainers, and all the adjectives with which complainers are tarred are understood to be antithetical to the scholarly identity.

A third reason that such systems are difficult to analyze is that they are increasingly hard to see, expose, and challenge. The brilliant Italian sociologist Antonio Gramsci, who died in prison during Benito Mussolini's fascist regime in the first half of the twentieth century, observed that Western industrialized societies were becoming increasingly bureaucratic, rationalized, and legalistic. He argued that such a transformation went hand in glove with the abolition of slavery and serfdom, with greater rights for individuals, and with the putative development of democracy. With each push in particular regions of the world for group and individual freedom has come a pushback from those who have had a disproportionate amount of power. While some privilege is forfeited with each social movement toward liberation, other privilege is protected with even greater intensity. Thus, we have the paradoxical situation of more public, worldwide discussions of human rights, and more underground, private abuses of those same rights. Gramsci's understanding of the worldwide move of national governments toward coercion and consent and not just outright domination (what he called *hegemony*) helps to explain why, for example, the United States has more African American men in prison than at any other time in its history while simultaneously having an African American as its president; how four women have served as Supreme Court justices and three as secretary of state, yet most women still do not earn the same wages as their male counterparts, women do a disproportionate share of housework and child care, and women work disproportionately in the sex trade.

What does all this have to do with a book on college teaching? Today, college and university campuses are more diverse than ever; they also regularly erupt in protests because of dissatisfaction by faculty, students, and staff over serious issues. The protests of today are no less serious than the ones of fifty years ago when students protested for civil rights, against the war in Vietnam, for greater participation in the governance of their schools, against an unquestioned and automatic respect for authority, and against dress codes for women only. Nor are they less serious than the protests of thirty years ago when students protested against investments in companies that did business with South Africa. Today, students protest for greater diversity in the student body, on the faculty, among staff, and in the curriculum; they protest against rising costs and for more financial aid; they protest against the manipulation of statistics to obfuscate the existence of crimes on campus, especially crimes of power that disproportionately affect women, gay, and first-year students; they protest continued investment in and overreliance on fossil fuels, which has created dramatic and horrible weather conditions for everyone and may kill the planet; they protest for courses that have everything to do with knowledge of social inequality, justice, and conflict resolution. In other words, they are protesting to have an education that is relevant and centered around justice. Because campuses are more diverse than ever, however, it can seem both to outsiders—and to those who are charged with managing campuses—that no one is grateful for the changes, that no one accepts authority anymore, that claims and complaints are unreasonable and lack civility, and that while freedoms keep growing attendant responsibilities do not.

Against such a backdrop, if we are to understand the choices that today's faculty members make about their syllabi and their colleagues, their students and the dynamics of campus spaces—be they in classrooms, offices, faculty meetings, or departmental hallways, on campus greens, or at board meetings—we also need to appreciate the context in which these choices are taking place. And that context is rich, complex, multilayered, and always within the confines or against the backdrop of hegemonic social forces. In other words, the college or university campus is a site in which old and new assumptions about patronage, gratitude, meritocracy, and diversity are being argued and played out at exactly the same time that the college and university campus is opening up slowly but steadily to persons who had been excluded from it.

Our analysis, therefore, demands an appreciation that there is still resistance to this greater inclusion even as most of our universities and colleges have begun to embrace diversity, some more cautiously than others. And it demands an appreciation that even as we talk about systems and organizations, our everyday lives are made up of individuals, usually trying to do their jobs well, to play to their own strengths, to be seen as team players by their co-workers, and to espouse a level of mutually understood fairness.

In beginning to theorize what transformation means on college and university campuses in the twenty-first century, then, one observation I make from all the essays is that all the authors have a *heightened awareness of their positionality*—whether they are teaching assistants, assistant professors, associate professors, or full professors. They are aware not just of

their occupational rank but also of aspects of their identity that are important to them and salient and sometimes triggering for others. As persons
whose groups were once outsiders, they cannot escape such awareness. H.
Mark Ellis, author of chapter 3, recalls: "A student once wrote on my teaching evaluation that it was her first time having a Black teacher and that she
was 'pleasantly surprised' that I was so 'smart and articulate.' She [admitted]
that she could not hear a word I said for the first few weeks in the semester
because what was coming out of my mouth didn't match what she expected
to hear from a Black person." But faculty members like Ellis and like Anita
Chikkatur, author of Chapter 7, struggle with whether they are the right people to teach this material and how much they should or should not change:
"Some students questioned whether my curriculum is 'biased,'" wrote
Chikkatur, "[while] another student noted that I should be 'more radical' in
class." The authors in this volume, like faculty members all over the United
States, allow that heightened sensitivity to guide their self-reflection, their
choices in how to be most effective in the classroom, and their interactions
with colleagues. They even admit that they wrestle with these issues within
themselves. Cheryl Jones-Walker, who contributed Chapter 4, recounts a
day when she defended the efficacy of "working-class schools" to her students. When grilled about the kinds of schools she had attended, Jones-
Walker, who is African American and middle class, upended stereotypes by
sharing that she and her siblings are not first-generation college attenders
and that all matriculated at the country's most selective colleges and universities. "When I left class that day I did not know what to think, but I felt very
uncomfortable because I was not certain what had transpired. . . . While I
think it is important for me to acknowledge my class privilege, I was worried that I unconsciously wielded it in order to combat racial stereotypes."
In another version of this, Pato Hebert, author of Chapter 5, was able to
offer some of his students the bridge to feel comfortable sharing important
aspects of themselves by strategically sharing aspects of himself.

Being aware of their positionality led many of the authors to try different
things with different groups of students. Says Ghanaian Dela Kusi-Appouh,
contributor of Chapter 2, "After the first semester of being a TA for this class,
I was left with mixed feelings and unsettled questions about the weight
of my positionality on the types of interactions I had with students. . . .
Being offered the TA position again for the next semester represented an

opportunity to try things differently. . . . I proposed to the professor that we include a voluntary weekly discussion section as well as an ongoing group project." I don't know any good teacher who doesn't borrow tools from others to become more effective and to have an arsenal of ideas in his or her teaching knapsack. This self-awareness is a wonderful tool that we encourage our colleagues who had not necessarily been self-conscious about their positionality to acquire.

Another observation that contributes to theorizing transformation is that of *openness to difference*. In fact, being open to one kind of difference has the potential to make the classroom more inclusive for everyone. Celebrating the decisions that her school has made to become more inclusive, Theresa Tensuan, in Chapter 13, observes the dynamics of diversity and inclusion at work: "This particular set of students [in my class] has the kind of chemistry that can make the instructor feel superfluous at times, and most days I find myself just very grateful for the intellectual vitality that is engendered by open exchanges among people from very different backgrounds and experiences." Similarly, Anna Ward reminds us, in Chapter 9, that inclusion can humble us, not the way Tensuan describes the classroom, but the way that treating multiple systems of oppression can alter our own views: "Designing this course [on queerness and disability] put pressure on my nondisabled privilege, as I expected it would, but I did not anticipate the extent to which it would exert pressure on who and what travels as queer, particularly as that positionality is refracted in and through the lens of dis/ability."

Likewise, in Chapter 8, on disabilities and higher education, Kristin Lindgren expresses gratitude for the first student with traditional classroom challenges who was placed in her classroom: "It quickly became apparent that '*accommodating*' Peter created a richer learning environment for all of us. Because he absorbed information by reading lips, other students learned to face him when they spoke rather than mumbling into their notebooks. All of us began to articulate our ideas more clearly and to take our time in doing so." If we move away from the ways in which disabilities are *deficits*, we become mindful of the ways accommodating them becomes a *benefit* for all the students in the classroom. One pragmatic outcome of the transformed contemporary campus, then, is the opportunity to learn from those who are different.

Just because things are better, however, doesn't mean that they are easier. Painful conversations and confrontations are part of any change that undermines the status quo. Regardless of who the confrontations are between, it can sometimes feel like we will never reach that shining city on a hill, either within ourselves, as Daphne Lamothe candidly testifies in Chapter 12, or together, as Betty Sasaki, in Chapter 10, and Aurora Camacho de Schmidt, in Chapter 11, remember campus protests. At least three of these essays contain examples of the kinds of confrontations that fuel some of us with anger, make some of us stand up and cheer, and impel still others of us to run for cover and wish for the days when young people were seen and not heard, or junior faculty were silent until tenure, or discrimination laws didn't allow people to sue colleges and universities, or presidents never had opinions different from board members, or . . . well, you get the picture.

What the essay by Camacho de Schmidt, that by Sasaki, and my own reveal is that sometimes the most authentic confrontations are unavoidable and may be necessary when the architecture of the organization cannot support all the challenges that it is enduring. Such confrontations have the power to offer the organization—its official leaders and each of its constituent groups—the chance to press a reset button and explore its challenges more deeply. Marches, demonstrations, uncomfortable conversations, even lawsuits, do not necessarily mean that the place is falling apart. In fact, they may point to an organization healthy enough to withstand challenges from within and leadership strong enough to move forward in the midst of criticism. Camacho de Schmidt remembers this wisdom at the end of a recent year of protests: "'Something beautiful is emerging and growing,' said our [student] speaker . . . even as he warned us of the difficulties . . . still ahead. . . . We all need to recognize that accepting difference is not a seamless process but the first step in an arduous process of dialogue, accommodation, and mutual discovery." Protests may signal unhappiness, but their eruption points us toward places, persons, and situations that need attention. In fact, Sasaki contends, if we assert that we are mutually responsible for making the institution better, then we undermine the fault lines that invite us into separation. Sasaki concludes her assertion by quoting the political philosopher Iris Marion Young: "In a model that distributes responsibility to all community members across their differences, responsibility itself becomes one of the valuable bonds that brings us together, even as, at times, it requires us to dissent from widely held public opinion." She continues, "In contrast to the liability model of responsibility, which focuses on a single agent to blame for an injustice in our institutions, the social connection model asserts that 'we have the responsibility to try *to speak out* . . . with the intention of mobilizing others' (Young 2011, 93)."

Camacho de Schmidt and Sasaki bring us to a theoretical concept that is two pronged and difficult to achieve: once the process begins to diversify an organization, including voices that were once excluded, the road ahead is long and difficult and the model we need to accomplish the process is one of mutuality and shared responsibility rather than there being one person or one group in charge. Knowing this can allow us to be open to the kinds of places where such sharing happens, for example, the space of critique in the photography class that Pato Hebert describes. It can also remind us that when our colleges and universities go through painful protests that are the result of greater diversity and the inclusion of more voices, both the protests and the changes have the potential to keep us all moving toward the prize of more genuine community.

Finally, the transformation of the twenty-first-century campus also entails a level of commitment to education, to scholarship, and to a vision of faculty, staff, and students in shared governance. It includes nurturing the qualities of leadership and collaboration with which sometimes younger, adjunct, and previously marginalized faculty have more experience. It includes skill at riding what one might only call waves of greater compliance with federal regulations while strategizing appropriate resistance to injunctions that don't actually help the victims of crime, promote better teaching, or advance ethical scholarship. I use the metaphor of riding the waves because we know that leading such institutions as presidents, deans of students or faculty, chancellors, and directors on boards can be exciting, creative, or challenging to one's career. It's very difficult work when the larger American public isn't sure what the sticker price of higher education pays for and worries about a professorate that doesn't look like one they remember.

Theorizing twenty-first century higher education is based on new ideas in the classroom by professors who hadn't been there before and classes that hadn't been taught in the same way before. In his essay on teaching photography, photographer, activist, and conceptual artist Pato Hebert argues for new forms of art to upend authority and for criticism to be as compassionate as it is evaluative. Daphne Lamothe appreciates that although it is unlikely for students who are like her, the child of Catholic, Haitian immigrants, to major in English literature in the Ivy League, the things she learned along the way by imitating a fellow student here, or confiding to a teaching assistant there, led her to offer the kind of education that she once sought to current students. More than ever, we need the parents of current students to assume that their children have something to teach them and that today's students, in turn, will learn from their children the likes of which they never expected.

A NOT-SO-DISTANT PAST

Occasionally, we forget that the ways our society has moved ahead have not always been this way; we get amnesiac on ourselves and pretend we've always been the most just and inclusive place on the planet. Higher education in the United States is no less different. American campuses have transformed rather dramatically, in both form and content, during the twentieth century, from expanded physical plants to curricula that have mushroomed beyond Latin and Greek, agriculture and home economics. Although higher education in the United States originally targeted, indeed in many cases was restricted to, young men of European descent and Protestant affiliation, it has become more open and diverse over the past century. It has not become as diverse as most young people believe it to be (Gallagher 2011), and the diversity that has been achieved has been won at a high cost that both student and faculty protesters paid to force its doors open (Thelin 2004). Still, with all that remains to be achieved, there are more women, people of color, people with a variety of religious backgrounds and sexual identities, people with a range of physical and mental challenges, people who grew up in the United States speaking a language other than English in their homes, and people from countries outside the United States sitting in the classrooms and serving on the faculty and staff of American colleges and universities than at any other time in the nation's history.

These changes exist in large part as a result of social movements that included outright demonstrations, paternalistic and courageous responses to those demonstrations, pragmatism, and legal challenges to discriminatory admissions policies. And they included long, hard conversations among people who had lots in common and much that was not. They included the willingness to face not only the denial of tenure for faculty but also the possibility of expulsion from college of students—students whose parents had given everything to get them there. They included the willingness to be arrested and the shock that some of them would be killed in pursuit of their ideals. It's important that we avoid sugarcoating these recent histories.

After the Civil War, both black and white Christians set up teaching and vocational colleges for African Americans. After the first wave of European immigration to this country in the late 1800s, Jews, excluded from many private colleges and universities, enrolled in public colleges and universities and then sued to fight quotas meant to keep them out in the early 1900s (Steinberg 2001). African Americans, too, sued historically white institutions, continually doing so from the late nineteenth century through to the landmark *Brown v. Board of Education* decision, for the right to apply to and attend what had been racially exclusive schools (Franklin 2000). Similarly, from the mid-nineteenth century through the 1960s, white women either sued to be included in all-male institutions or created their own schools (Thelin 2004). Catholics and Jews also founded their own colleges and universities, not only, like their Protestant counterparts, to educate students in their religious traditions but also as counterbalances to the discrimination that members of their faith, traditions, and ethnic backgrounds faced at schools quietly reserved for the progeny of Protestant, British-descended, and affluent families. Many Protestant denominations set up colleges to train clergy and protect their young people from temptations outside the faith. The inclusion of groups that had been previously underrepresented slowly followed, especially at the nation's elite institutions, as campus administrators realized (with the help of lawsuits and social protest) that education is at its most vigorous when it draws on the experiences of persons from many backgrounds.

This consciousness among mostly Euro-American university administrators about the relationship between diversity and intellectual vibrancy was not reached easily or voluntarily; it was largely a by-product of the civil rights and black freedom movements, the second-wave women's movement, and the New Left student movement, all of the late 1960s. The American Indian movement, the Chicano movement, the LGBTQ (lesbian, gay, bisexual, trans*, queer) movement, and movements for and by people who were physically and intellectually challenged followed suit, using both protest and legal advocacy to push for change.

These movements, largely promoted by young people on college and university campuses, were also cross-generational and often cross-occupational, as working-class employees at colleges and universities and neighboring church congregations, women's clubs, and local activists met with and supported students who questioned the privileges of whiteness; the commonsense wisdom of sex-segregated education; the indisputability of one canon in different disciplines; the ways that the American university was complicit in warmongering, from scientific research for defense to ROTC; the cultural conformity of the cold war; and the assumption of adult omniscience and its corollary of unquestioned respect for authority. Student protesters even challenged what has become common wisdom that integration and cosmopolitanism are always the best-case scenarios for every group in every situation.

Conversations on today's campuses have to do with these things as well as with fiduciary responsibility, technology, governance, and admissions. Our institutions of higher education struggle with preparing students to be educated about the fields they enter and educated about the wider world in which they'll participate. Most liberal arts colleges and even research universities advocate some measure of inclusive and participatory process within the organization, even as they are beholden to a variety of governance structures that are patently undemocratic. The challenges that students of the 1960s raised about authority and participation are still with us, albeit in different form today. In many ways, this volume explores the new clothes the challenges wear, and allows readers to pull up a chair to the conversations that contemporary faculty and staff pose to themselves and to each other every day on the contradictions, options, and opportunities for growth and reconciliation on today's campuses.

A tremendous amount is at stake as we wrestle with the ideas shared in the essays in this volume. As once private conversations become public and as we move from aspiring to greater diversity to living with its consequences, those of us who belong to groups that were once kept outside the doors of academia, or ignored if we were inside, are—together with our students and our staff colleagues—transforming our campuses. As Smith and

Tuck observe in Chapter 1, however, it is happening with, on, and sometimes against our bodies. I would add that it is also requiring our spirits and
our minds and our physical and emotional stamina, and thus it is always
and every day larger than the debates about higher education. Not one of us
would have contributed an essay if we were not committed to our students
in particular and higher education in general, and willing to work with our
colleagues. We assume that of our readers as well, and we welcome the conversation that follows.

REFERENCES

Abe, Hideko, Lisa Arellano, James Barrett, Jim Behuniak, Catherine Besteman, Adrian
Blevins, Lyn Mikel Brown, Debra Campbell, Lynne Conner, Julie de Sherbinin.
2013. "An Open Letter to Joseph R. Reisert, Harriet S. and George C. Wiswell, Jr.
Associate Professor of American Constitutional Law." *Colby Echo*, March 13.

Ackelsberg, Martha, Jeni L. Hart, Naomi J. Miller, Kate Queeney, and Susan Van Dyne.
2009. "Faculty Microclimate Change at Smith College." In *Doing Diversity in Higher
Education: Faculty Leaders Share Challenges and Strategies*, edited by Winnifred
Brown-Glaude, 83–102, New Brunswick, NJ: Rutgers University Press.

Ahmed, Sara. 2010. *The Promise of Happiness*. Durham, NC: Duke University Press,
———. 2012. *On Being Included: Racism and Institutional Life*. Durham, NC: Duke
University Press.

Alexander, Michelle. 2012. *The New Jim Crow: Mass Incarceration in the Age of Color-
blindness*. New York: New Press.

Allport, Gordon W. 1954. *The Nature of Prejudice*. Garden City, NY: Doubleday
Anchor Books.

Anyon, Jean. 1980. "Social Class and the Hidden Curriculum of Work." *Journal of
Education* 162, no. 1:67–92.

Anzaldúa, Gloria. 1999. *Borderlands/La Frontera: The New Mestiza*. San Francisco:
Aunt Lute Books. First published 1987.

Bechdel, Alison. 2007. *Fun Home: A Family Tragicomic*. New York: Mariner Books.

Bennet, William. 1994. *The Devaluing of America: The Fight for Our Culture and Our
Children*. New York: Simon and Schuster.

———. 2013. *Is College Worth It? A Former Secretary of Education and a Liberal Arts
Graduate Expose the Broken Promise of Higher Education*. With David Wilezol. Nash-
ville, TN: Thomas Nelson.

Boice, Robert. 2000. *Advice for New Faculty Members: Nihil Nimus*. New York: Pearson.

Bonilla-Silva, Eduardo. 2013. *Racism without Racists: Colorblind Racism and the Persistence of Racial Inequality in America*. 4th ed. Lanham, MD: Rowman and Littlefield.

Bourdieu, Pierre. 1986. "The Forms of Capital." In *Handbook of Theory and Research for
the Sociology of Education*, edited by J. Richardson. New York: Greenwood Press.

Bowen, William G., and Derek Bok. 2000. *The Shape of the River: Long-Term Consequences of Considering Race in College and University Admissions*. Princeton: Princeton University Press.

Bright, Susan. 2010. *Auto Focus: The Self-Portrait in Contemporary Photography*. New
York: Monacelli Press.

Brown, A. H., R. M. Cervero, and J. Johnson-Bailey. 2000. "Making the Invisible Visible: Race, Gender, and Teaching in Adult Education." *Adult Education Quarterly* 50, no. 4:273–288.

Bryson, Mary, and Suzanne de Castell. 1993. "Queer Pedagogy: Praxis Makes Im/Perfect." *Canadian Journal of Education* 18 (3): 285–305.

Butler, Judith. 2004. *Precarious Life: The Powers of Mourning and Violence.* New York: Verso.

BUTT. "About." 2013. Accessed September 3. http://www.buttmagazine.com/information/.

Byrd, Jodi A. 2011. *The Transit of Empire: Indigenous Critiques of Colonialism.* Minneapolis: University of Minnesota Press.

Calhoun, Craig. 1995. *Critical Social Theory.* Hoboken, NJ: Wiley.

Caughie, Pamela L. 1994. "Passing as Pedagogy: Feminism in(to) Cultural Studies." In *English Studies/Culture Studies: Institutionalizing Dissent,* edited by Isaiah Smithson and Nancy Ruff, 76–93. Urbana: University of Illinois Press.

Clance, Pauline R., and Suzanne A. Imes. 1978. "The Impostor Phenomenon in High Achieving Women: Dynamics and Therapeutic Intervention." *Psychotherapy: Theory, Research, and Practice* 15, no. 3:241–247.

Clifford, James. 2012. "Feeling Historical." *Cultural Anthropology* 27, no. 3:417–426.

Colby Bicentennial. 2013. "With Love, Peace, and Without Fear." Video of student protest, bicentennial convocation, Colby College, February 27. http://www.youtube.com/watch?v=h8k3af3YaiI.

Collins, Patricia Hill. 1990. *Black Feminist Thought: Knowledge, Consciousness, and the Politics of Empowerment.* 1st ed. Boston: Unwin Hyman.

Cortez, Jaime. 2004. *Sexile.* New York: Institute for Gay Men's Health, http://www.apla.org/news-and-multimedia/publications/documents/sexile_web.pdf.

Davis, Lennard J. 2011. "Why Is Disability Missing from the Discourse on Diversity?" *Chronicle of Higher Education,* September 30, B38–B40.

———. 2013. *The End of Normal: Identity in a Biocultural Era.* Ann Arbor: University of Michigan Press.

Delbanco, Andrew. 2012. *College: What It Was, Is, and Should Be.* Princeton: Princeton University Press.

Delgado Bernal, Dolores, and Octavia Villalpando. 2005. "An Apartheid of Knowledge in Academia: The Struggle over the 'Legitimate' Knowledge of Faculty of Color." In *Critical Pedagogy and Race,* edited by Zeus Leonardo, 185–204. Malden, MA: Blackwell.

D'Souza, Dinesh. 1991. *Illiberal Education: The Politics of Race and Sex on Campus.* New York: Free Press.

DuBois, W.E.B. 1999. *The Souls of Black Folk.* New York: W. W. Norton. First published 1903.

Duster, Troy. 1991. "They're Taking Over! Myths about Multiculturalism; One Soldier's Notes from the Affirmative Action Front." *Mother*

Jones, August 31. http://www.motherjones.com/politics/1991/09/
theyre-taking-over-myths-about-multiculturalism.

Ellis, H. Mark. Forthcoming. "Free to Speak, Safe to Claim: The Importance of Writing in Online Sociology Courses in Transforming Disposition." In *Writing in Online Courses: How the Online Environment Shapes Writing Practices*. Edited by Christopher Weaver and Phoebe Jackson. Manuscript under review.

Ellsworth, Elizabeth. 1989. "Why Doesn't This Feel Empowering? Working through the Repressive Myths of Critical Pedagogy." *Harvard Educational Review* 59:297–309.

Feldman, Christina. 2008. "Long Journey to a Bow: Overcoming the Last Great Obstacle to Awakening; The Conceit of Self." *Tricycle*, Fall. http://www.tricycle.com/dharma-talk/long-journey-bow.

Ferguson, Roderick A. 2012. *The Reorder of Things: The University and its Pedagogies of Minority Difference*. Minneapolis: University of Minnesota Press.

Ferrall, Victor E., Jr. 2012. *Liberal Arts at the Brink*. Cambridge, MA: Harvard University Press.

Fletcher, M. Jason, and Marta Tienda. 2011. "High School Quality and Race Differences in College Achievement." Princeton University's Office of Population Research. http://theop.princeton.edu/reports/wp/FletcherTienda_2011.pdf.

Fox, Catherine. 2006. "Reprosexuality, Queer Desire, and Critical Pedagogy: A Response to Hyoejin Yoon." *Journal of Advanced Composition* 26 (1/2): 244–253.

Franklin, John Hope. 2000. *From Slavery to Freedom: A History of African Americans*. 8th ed. Edited by Alfred Moss Jr. New York: McGraw-Hill. First published 1947.

Freire, Paulo. 2000. "Pedadgogy of the Oppressed." *Bloomsbury Academic*. First published 1968; first English translation 1970.

Gallagher, Charles. 2011. *Rethinking the Color Line: Readings in Race and Ethnicity*. 5th ed. New York: McGraw-Hill.

Gee, James. 2005. *An Introduction to Discourse Analysis: Theory and Method*. 2nd ed. New York: Routledge.

Goffman, Erving. 1961. *Asylums: Essays on the Social Situation of Mental Patients and Other Inmates*. 1st ed. Anchor/Doubleday.

Gramsci, Antonio. 1971. *Selections from the Prison Notebooks*. Reprint. New York: International. First published 1936.

Groys, Boris. 2010. "The Fate of Art in the Age of Terror." In *Concerning War: A Critical Reader in Contemporary Art*, edited by Maria Hlavajova and Jill Winder, 88–103. Utrecht: BAK.

Hames-García, Michael. 2011. *Identity Complex: Making the Case for Multiplicity*. Minneapolis: University of Minnesota Press.

Hannah-Jones, Nikole. 2011. "In Portland's Heart, 2010 Census Shows Diversity Dwindling." *Oregonian*, April 30. http://www.oregonlive.com/pacific-northwest-news/index.ssf/2011/04/in_portlands_heart_diversity_dwindles.html.

Harlow, Roxanna. 2003. "'Race Doesn't Matter, but . . .': The Effect of Race on Professors' Experiences and Emotion Management in the Undergraduate College

Classroom." In "Race, Racism, and Discrimination." Special issue, *Social Psychology Quarterly* 66, no. 4:348–363. http://www.jstor.org/stable/1519834.

Harris, Cheryl I. 1992. "Whiteness as Property." *Harvard Law Review* 106:1707–1791.

Holland, Sharon Patricia. 2012. *The Erotic Life of Racism*. Durham, NC: Duke University Press.

Hooks, Bell. 1990. *Yearning: Race, Gender, and Cultural Politics*. Boston: South End Press.

———. 1994. *Teaching to Transgress: Education as the Practice of Freedom*. New York: Routledge.

Johnson-Bailey, Juanita, and Ronald M. Cervero. 1998. "Power Dynamics in Teaching and Learning Practices: An Examination of Two Adult Education Classrooms." *International Journal of Lifelong Education* 17, no. 6:389–399.

Johnson-Bailey, Juanita, and Ming-Yeh Lee. 2005. "Women of Color in the Academy: Where's Our Authority in the Classroom?" *Feminist Teacher* 15, no. 2:111–122.

Kafer, Alison. 2013. *Feminist, Queer, Crip*. Bloomington: Indiana University Press.

Kanter, Rosabeth Moss. 1977. *Men and Women of the Corporation*. New York: Basic Books.

Katz, Jackson and Sut Jhally. 1999. "Tough Guise: Violence, Media and the Crisis in Masculinity." Northampton, MA: Media Education Foundation.

Kendall, Frances. 2006. *Understanding White Privilege: Creating Pathways to Authentic Relationships across Race*. New York: Routledge.

Kerschbaum, Stephanie, and Margaret Price, organizers. 2013. Archives and commentary, "Disability and Disclosure in/and Higher Education Conference." Conference at the University of Delaware, Newark, October 25–27. http://www.udel.edu/csd/conference/.

Kishimoto, Kyoko, and Mumbi Mwangi. 2009. "Critiquing the Rhetoric of 'Safety' in Feminist Pedagogy: Women of Color Offering an Account of Ourselves." *Feminist Teacher* 19, no. 2:87–102.

Kohl, Herbert R. 1994. *I Won't Learn from You and Other Thoughts on Creative Maladjustment*. New York: New Press.

Kumashiro, Kevin K. 2002. *Troubling Education: Queer Activism and Antioppressive Pedagogy*. New York: Routledge Falmer.

Ladson-Billings, Gloria. 1995. "Toward a Critical Race Theory of Education." *Teachers College Record* 97:47–68.

———. 1996. "Silences as Weapons: Challenges of a Black Professor Teaching White Students." *Theory into Practice* 35, no. 2:79–85.

Lazarus, Margaret, and Renner Wunderlich, Patricia Stallone, and Joseph Vitagliano. 1979. "Killing Us Softly: Images of Women in Advertising."

Lazos, S. R. 2012. "Are Student Teaching Evaluations Holding Back Women and Minorities?" In *Presumed Incompetent:. The Intersections of Race and Class for Women in Academia*, edited by Gabriella Gutiérrez y Muhs, Yolanda Flores Niemann, Carmen G. González, and Angela P. Harris. Logan: Utah State University Press.

Lee, Ming-Yeh, and Juanita Johnson-Bailey. 2004. "Challenges to the Classroom Authority of Women of Color." In *Promoting Critical Practice in Adult Education*, edited by J. Sandlin and R. St. Clair, 55–64. New Directions for Adult and Continuing Education, no. 102. San Francisco: Jossey-Bass.

Leonardo, Zeus, and Ronald K. Porter. 2010. "Pedagogy of Fear: Toward a Fanonian Theory of 'Safety' in Race Dialogue." *Race, Ethnicity, and Education* 13, no. 2:139–157.

Lewis, Amanda E. 2008. " 'Even Sweet, Gentle Larry?' The Continuing Significance of Race in Education." In *Literacy as a Civil Right: Reclaiming Social Justice in Literacy Teaching and Learning*, edited by Stuart Greene, 69–86. New York: Peter Lang.

Lindgren, Kristin. 2005. "(S)paces of Academic Work: Considering the Temporal Dimensions of Access." Paper presented at the Conference on College Composition and Communication, San Francisco, March 16.

Lipsitz, George. 2011. *How Racism Takes Place*. Philadelphia: Temple University Press.

Lorde, Audre. 1984. *Sister Outsider: Essays and Speeches*. Trumansburg, NY: Crossing Press.

Lukasiewicz, Mark, Eugenia Harvey and Diane Sawyer. 1991 [2005]. "True Colors: Racism in Everyday Life." ABC News. Corvision Media.

Maher, F., and M. K. Tetreault. 1993. "Frames of Positionality: Constructing Meaningful Dialogues about Gender and Race." *Anthropological Quarterly* 66:118–126.

Marx, Karl. 1852. *"The 18th Brumaire of Louis Napoleon." in Die Revolution*. New York: Weydemeyer.
https://www.marxists.org/archive/marx/works/download/pdf/18th-Brumaire.pdf.

Massey, Douglas S., Camille Z. Charles, Garvey Lundy, and Marie J. Fischer. 2006. *The Source of the River: The Social Origins of Freshmen at America's Selective Colleges and Universities*. Princeton: Princeton University Press.

Matsuda, Mari J., Charles Lawrence, Charles, Richard Delgado, and Kimberlé Crenshaw. 1993. *Words That Wound: Critical Race Theory, Assaultive Speech, and the First Amendment*. Boulder, CO: Westview Press.

McIntosh, Peggy. 2003. "White Privilege: Unpacking the Invisible Knapsack." In *Understanding Prejudice and Discrimination*, edited by Scott Plous. New York: McGraw-Hill.

Mears, Bill. 2013. "Supreme Court Sidesteps Big Ruling on Texas Affirmative Action." CNN.com, June 24. Captured from http://www.cnn.com/2013/06/24/politics/scotus-texas-affirmative-action/.

Merritt, Deborah J. 2008. "Bias, the Brain, and Student Evaluations of Teaching." *St. John's Law Review* 82:235–287.

Mills, Charles W. 1999. *The Racial Contract*. Ithaca, NY: Cornell University Press.

Minikel-Lacocque, Julie. 2013. "Racism, College, and the Power of Words: Racial Microaggressions Reconsidered." *American Educational Research Journal* 50, no. 3:432–465.

Minow, Martha. 1990. *Making All the Difference: Inclusion, Exclusion, and American Law*. Ithaca, NY: Cornell University Press.

Mohanty, Chandra Talpade. 1994. "On Race and Voice: Challenges for Liberal Education in the 1990's." In *Between Borders: Pedagogy and the Politics of Cultural Studies*, edited by Henry A. Giroux and Peter McLaren, 145–166. New York and London: Routledge.

Moll, Luis C., and Norma González. 1994. "Lessons from Research with Language-Minority Children." *Journal of Reading Behavior* 26:439–456.

Monson, Connie, and Jacqueline Rhodes. 2004. "Risking Queer: Pedagogy, Performativity, and Desire in Writing Classrooms." *Journal of Advanced Composition* 24, no. 1:79–91.

Mostern, Kenneth. 1994. "Decolonization as Learning: Practice and Pedagogy in Frantz Fanon's Revolutionary Narrative." In *Between Borders: Pedagogy and the Politics of Cultural Studies*, edited by Henry A. Giroux and Peter McLaren, 253–272. New York and London: Routledge.

Moyers, Bill. 1976. "Rosedale: The Way It Is." *Bill Moyers Journal*, Public Broadcasting System, New York. http://www.paleycenter.org/collection/item/?q=all&p=175& item=T78:0632.

Munro, Petra. 1998. *Subject to Fiction: Women Teachers' Life History Narratives and the Cultural Politics of Resistance.* Philadelphia: Open University Press.

Niemann, Y. F. 2012. "Lessons from the Experiences of Women of Color Working in Academia." In *Presumed Incompetent. The Intersections of Race and Class for Women in Academic*, edited by Gabriella Gutiérrez y Muhs, Yolanda Flores Niemann, Carmen G. González, and Angela P. Harris. Logan: Utah State University Press.

Omi, Michael, and Howard Winant. 1994. *Racial Formation in the United States: From the 1960s to the 1990s.* 2nd ed. New York: Routledge.

Patai, Daphne. 1991. "Point of View: Minority Status and the Stigma of 'Surplus Visibility.'" *Chronicle of Higher Education*, October 30, A52.

Pérez, Emma. 1999. *The Decolonial Imaginary: Writing Chicanas into History.* Bloomington: Indiana University Press.

Pierce, C. M. 1969. "Is Bigotry the Basis of the Medical Problems of the Ghetto?" In *Medicine in the Ghetto*, edited by J. C. Norman. New York: Meredith.

———. 1970. "Offensive Mechanisms." In *The Black Seventies*, edited by F. Barbour, 265–282. Boston: Porter Sargent.

Pierre, Jemima. 2004. "Black Immigrants in the United States and the 'Cultural Narratives' of Ethnicity." *Identities: Global Studies in Culture and Power* 11:141–170.

Polkinghorne, Donald E. 1995. "Narrative Configuration in Qualitative Analysis." In *Life History and Narrative*, edited by J. Amos Hatch and Richard Wisniewski, 5–24. London: Falmer Press.

Price, Margaret. 2011. *Mad at School: Rhetorics of Mental Disability and Academic Life.* Ann Arbor: University of Michigan Press. Kindle edition.

Quijada, David Alberto. 2006. "Collegial Alliances: Exploring One Chicano's Perspective on Mentoring in Research and Academia." In *The Latina/o Pathway to the Ph.D.: Abriendo Caminos*, edited by Janet Castellanos, Alberta M. Gloria, and Mark Kamimura, 255–268. Sterling, VA: Stylus.

Ravitch, Sharon M. 2005. "Introduction: Pluralism, Power, and Politics: Discourses of Diverse Pedagogies and Pedagogies of Diversity." In Introduction to *Challenges of Multicultural Education: Teaching and Taking Diversity Courses*, edited by Norah Peters-Davis and Jeffrey J. Shultz. Boulder, CO: Paradigm.

Regents of the University of California v. Bakke (No. 7811). (1978). 438 U.S. 265. Legal Information Institute. https://www.law.cornell.edu/supremecourt/text/438/265.

Rinpoche, the Dzogchen Ponlop. 2006. "Contemplating Emptiness." In *The Best Buddhist Writing, 2006*, edited by Melvin McCleod, 232–248. Boston: Shambhala.

Rodriguez, Dylan. 2011. "White Supremacy as Substructure: Toward a Genealogy of a Racial Animus, from Reconstruction to Pacification." In *State of White Supremacy: Racism, Governance, and the United States*, edited by Moon-Kie Jung, João Costa Vargas, and Eduardo Bonilla-Silva, 47–76. Stanford, CA: Stanford University Press.

Sampaio, A. 2006. "Women of Color Teaching Political Science: Examining the Intersections of Race, Gender, and Course Material in the Classroom." *Political Science and Politics* 39, no. 4:917–922.

Sanchez-Casal, Susan, and Amie A. MacDonald. 2009. *Identity in Education*. New York: Palgrave Macmillan.

Scott, James C. 1990. *Domination and the Arts of Resistance: Hidden Transcripts*. New Haven, CT: Yale University Press.

Simmel, Georg. 1950. "The Stranger." In *The Sociology of Georg Simmel*. Translated by Kurt Wolff. Glencoe, IL: Free Press. First published 1908.

Singleton, Glenn Eric, and Curtis Linton. 2006. *Facilitator's Guide to Courageous Conversations about Race*. New York: Sage.

Solórzano, D. G. 1997. "Images and Words That Wound: Critical Race Theory, Racial Stereotyping, and Teacher Education." *Teacher Education Quarterly* 24, no. 3:5–19.

Spry, Tami. 2001. "Performing Autoethnography: An Embodied Methodological Praxis." *Qualitative Inquiry* 7:706–732. doi: 10.1177/107780040100700605.

Stanley, Christine A. 2006. "Coloring the Academic Landscape: Faculty of Color Breaking the Silence in Predominantly White Colleges and Universities." *American Educational Research Journal* 43:701–736.

Steele, Patricia E. and Thomas R. Wolanin. 2004. *Higher Education Opportunities for Students with Disabilities: A Primer for Policymakers*. Washington, DC: Institute for Higher Education Policy. http://www.ihep.org/research/publications/higher-education-opportunities-students-disabilities-primer-policymakers.

Steinberg, Stephen. 2001. *The Ethnic Myth: Race, Ethnicity, and Class in America*. 3rd ed. Boston: Beacon Press.

Strayhorn, Terrell. 2010. "When Race and Gender Collide: Social and Cultural Capital's Influence on the Academic Achievement of African American and Latino Men." *Review of Higher Education* 33, no. 3:307–332.

Sue, Derald Wing. 2010. *Microaggressions and Marginality: Manifestation, Dynamics, and Impact*. Hoboken, NJ: Wiley.

Sue, Derald Wing, Christina M. Capodilupo, Gina C. Torino, Jennifer M. Bucceri, Aisha Holder, Kevin L. Nadal, and Marta Esquilin. 2007. "Racial Microaggressions in Everyday Life: Implications for Clinical Practice." *American Psychologist* 62, no. 4:271–286.

Tatum, Beverly Daniel. 1997. *Why Are All the Black Kids Sitting Together in the Cafeteria? And Other Conversations about Race.* New York: Basic Books.

———. 2007. *Can We Talk about Race? And Other Conversations in an Era of School Resegregation.* Boston: Beacon Press.

Thelin, John R. 2004. *A History of American Higher Education.* Baltimore: Johns Hopkins University Press.

"This Year's Freshmen at 4-Year Colleges: A Statistical Profile." 2010. *Chronicle of Higher Education*, January 22, A23.

Thompson, Rosemarie Garland. 1996. *Extraordinary Bodies: Figuring Physical Disability in American Culture and Literature.* New York: Columbia University Press.

Tuck, Eve, and K. Wayne Yang. 2012. "Decolonization Is Not a Metaphor." *Decolonization: Indigeneity, Education &and Society* 1, no. 1:1–40.

U.S. Bureau of Labor Statistics. 2011. "How Many Jobs Do Americans Hold in a Lifetime?" Posted on 5/18/2011 and captured on1/25/2015 at: May 18. https://www.mindflash.com/blog/2011/05/how-many-jobs-do-americans-hold-in-a-lifetime/.

U.S. Census Bureau of the Census. 2008. "Money Income of Families—Percent Distribution by Income Level in Constant (2007) Dollars: 1980–2007." *Current Population Reports*, Table 680.

U.S. Department of Education. N.d. "Building the Legacy: IDEA 2004." idea.ed.gov.

U.S. Department of Justice, Civil Rights Division. 2007. *Enforcing the ADA: A Status Report from the Department of Justice.* October–December. http://www.ada.gov/octdec07.pdf.

U.S. Government Accountability Office. 2009. *Higher Education and Disability: Education Needs a Coordinated Approach to Improve its Assistance to Schools in Supporting Students.* October. For highlights of GAO-10-33, a report to the Chairman, Committee on Education and Labor, House of Representatives. See http://www.gao.gov/assets/300/297433.pdf.

Valdés, Guadalupe, Sonia V. González, Dania López García, and Patricio Márquez. 2003. "Language Ideology: The Case of Spanish in Departments of Modern Languages." *Anthropology and Education Quarterly* 34, no. 1 (March):3–26.

Wah, Lee Mun. 1994. "The Color of Fear: A Film." Oakland, CA: Stir-Fry Productions.

Wilderson, Frank B., III. 2010. *Red, White, and Black: Cinema and the Structure of U.S. Antagonisms.* Durham, NC: Duke University Press.

Williams, Patricia. 1991. *The Alchemy of Race and Rights: Diary of a Law Professor.* Cambridge, MA: Harvard University Press.

Williams College. 2015. "History of Latino/a Studies." Accessed September 7. http://latino-studies.williams.edu/academics/history.

Winant, Howard. 2004. "'Behind Blue Eyes: Whiteness and Contemporary US Racial Politics." In *Off White: Readings on Power, Privilege, and Resistance,* edited by Michelle Fine, Lois Weis, Linda Powell-Pruitt, and April Burns, 3–16. New York: Routledge.

Wolfe, Patrick. 2006. "Settler Colonialism and the Elimination of the Native." *Journal of Genocide Research* 8, no. 4:387–409.

Yalom, Irvin D., 1995. *The Theory and Practice of Group Psychotherapy.* Boston: Basic Books.

Yoon, K. Hyoejin. 2005. "Affecting the Transformative Intellectual: Questioning 'Noble' Sentiments in Critical Pedagogy and Composition." *Journal of Advanced Composition* 25, no. 4:717–759.

Yosso, Tara J., William A. Smith, Miguel Ceja, and Daniel Solórzano. 2009. "Critical Race Theory, Racial Microaggressions, and Campus Racial Climate for Latina/o Undergraduates." *Harvard Educational Review* 79, no. 4:659–690.

Young, Iris Marion. 1986. "The Ideal of Community and the Politics of Difference." *Social Theory and Practice* 12, no. 1:1–26.

———. 1990. *Justice and the Politics of Difference.* Princeton: Princeton University Press.

———. 2001. "Activist Challenges to Deliberative Democracy." *Political Theory* 29, no. 5:670–690.

———. 2002. *Inclusion and Democracy.* New York: Oxford University Press.

———. 2011. *Responsibility for Justice.* New York: Oxford University Press.

CONTRIBUTORS

AURORA CAMACHO DE SCHMIDT studied philosophy at the Universidad Iberoamericana in Mexico City. She received an MA and PhD in Latin American literature from Temple University. Before coming to Swarthmore, from which she retired as professor of Spanish in the Department of Modern Languages and Literatures, Aurora directed the Mexico-U.S. Border program of the American Friends Service Committee, and was engaged in Mexico-U.S. relations as a policy analyst, immigrants' rights advocate, and writer. Her two most recent articles explore the connections between pictorial and photographical images and the written word, including poetry. With her husband, Temple University historian Arthur Schmidt, Aurora edited and translated Elena Poniatowska's *Nothing, Nobody: the Voices of the Mexican Earthquake* (1995), and Alberto Ulloa Bornemann's *Surviving Mexico's Dirty War* (2007).

ANITA CHIKKATUR is an associate professor of educational studies at Carleton College. She earned her BA in sociology and educational studies at Swarthmore College and her MA and PhD in the Education, Culture, and Society program at the Graduate School of Education at the University of Pennsylvania. Chikkatur taught English at a junior high school in a small town in Japan for two years. Her dissertation research, conducted at an urban public high school in the United States, examined processes of racialization as an integral part of creating American national identity, a project being reconfigured as a result of new immigration patterns. Chikkatur's research and teaching interests include student and teacher perspectives on race, gender, and sexuality and issues of diversity and difference in educational institutions.

H. MARK ELLIS received his BA from Montclair State University and his MA and his PhD from Northwestern University. He has studied classical piano performance at the Oberlin Conservatory of Music, the Manhattan School of Music, and at the Peabody Institute of Music. He is associate professor of sociology at William Paterson University in New Jersey. His field of research and teaching interests include the sociology of culture, police work, art and music, occupations and professions, education, theory, methodology, race, gender, and the sociology of the body. Ellis is the recipient of the Robert F. Winch Memorial Award for Outstanding Graduate Lecturer in Sociology at Northwestern University and the William Paterson University Provost Award for Excellence in Teaching. He is the author of "Looking Ahead in the Here and Now: Your Major and Profession" (2008) in *Off to College; Educational Guidance Research Group.*

PATRICK "PATO" HEBERT received his BA from Stanford University and his MFA from the University of California at Irvine. An artist based in New York and Los Angeles, his work explores the aesthetics, ethics, and poetics of interconnectedness. Hebert's practice shifts across a range of media. He received a 2010 Mid-Career Fellowship for Visual Artists from the California Community Foundation and the Excellence in Photographic Teaching Award from Center in Santa Fe, New Mexico, in 2008. Hebert has been working in HIV prevention since 1994, collaborating with the communities most affected by HIV/AIDS. Exhibitions include Museo de Las Artes, Guadalajara; Kunsthal Charlottenborg, Copenhagen; Orange County Museum of Art, Newport Beach; and Longwood Arts Project, the Bronx, New York.

CHERYL JONES-WALKER, on-leave from Swarthmore College, is currently Visiting Associate Professor in the Teacher Education department at the University of San Francisco. She began her professional career as a fourth grade teacher in the Bronx, NY, and she continued teaching in a Boston-area independent school and then internationally in Gabon, Central Africa. Prior to completing her doctoral work at the University of Pennsylvania, she worked at the Center for Collaborative Education in Boston, a non-profit organization committed to improving urban K-12 education. Jones-Walker's research is focused on the examination of identities on macro and micro levels in order to design the best supports for learners and to address larger socio-historical issues that undermine opportunities for individuals who have been marginalized. She is the author of *Identity Work in the Classroom: Successful Learning in Urban Schools* (2015), Teachers College Press.

DELADEM "DELA" KUSI-APPOUH attended Agnes Scott College, where she received a BA in sociology and anthropology, as well as Cornell University, where she received an MA and PhD in development sociology and social demography. Her primary research interests are in adolescent health, family dynamics, international development, and social network analysis. Kusi-Appouh has been the Fred H. Bixby Post-doctoral Fellow at the Population Council, working in its Zambia Office on the Adolescent Girls Empowerment Program. Select publications include "The Specter of Divorce: Views from Working- and Middle-Class Cohabitor," in *Family Relations* 60 (2011), coauthored with A. J. Miller and S. Sassler, and "Ideology and the Experience of Poverty Risk: Views about Poverty within a Focus Group Design," in *Journal of Poverty* 15 (2011), coauthored with T. A. Hirschl, and M. R. Rank.

DAPHNE LAMOTHE received her BA from Yale University and her PhD in English from the University of California at Berkeley. She is an associate professor of African American studies at Smith College. Lamothe's research interests center on the intersection of ethnography and the African American imagination, the construction of cultural memory in contemporary black fiction, and narratives of migration and diaspora. She teaches on African American literature of 1746–1900 and the Harlem Renaissance. Her book, *Inventing the New Negro: Narrative, Culture, and Ethnography*, was published in 2008 by University of Pennsylvania Press.

KRISTIN LINDGREN is the director of the Writing Center and a visiting assistant professor of writing at Haverford College, where she teaches courses in literature, writing, and disability studies. She earned a BA at Dartmouth College, an MA at Columbia University, and a PhD at Bryn Mawr College. She is coeditor of two books on Deaf culture, *Signs and Voices* and *Access*, and author of numerous articles and essays on illness and disability. Her work appears in several collections, including *Gendering Disability; Illness in the Academy, Disability and the Teaching of Writing, The Patient*, and *Disability and Mothering*. Most recently, Lindgren co-organized the symposium "In/Visible: Disability and the Arts" (2011) and sponsored an art exhibition at Haverford titled "What Can a Body Do?" in conjunction with a series of related residencies by scholars and artists (fall 2012).

BETTY G. SASAKI is an associate professor of Spanish, specializing in Renaissance and Baroque literature, at Colby College, where she has chaired the Department of Spanish many times. Along with language classes, she has taught a variety of Golden Age literature courses, ranging from ideology and ethics to the identity politics of the picaresque novel. Sasaki's research interests include sixteenth- and seventeenth-century Spanish poetry; women writers of the Golden Age; and representations of race, class, and gender in the literature of that period. She has written articles on Luis de Góngora, Francisco de Quevedo, Sor Juana Inés de la Cruz, and multicultural biography. She is currently preparing articles on Quevedo's sermons; Miguel de Cervantes's *Novelas ejemplares*; and multiculturalism, assimilation, and affirmative action. Double majoring in Portuguese and Spanish as an undergraduate, Sasaki earned her doctorate from the University of California–Berkeley.

MICHAEL D. SMITH is an assistant professor of education at the State University of New York at New Paltz. He received a BA in psychology from Elon College and an MEd in educational psychology from the University of North Carolina at Chapel Hill. He began his career as a research associate at the American Institutes for Research in Washington, DC, and decided to continue his education. In 2009 he completed his PhD from the University of South Florida–Tampa in curriculum and instruction with an emphasis on special education. His research interests include teacher preparation for diversity, issues of power and privilege in education, and the influence of race and ethnicity on identity and pedagogy. Smith has a published chapter on phenomenological research methods and has published two articles on the intersection of race, culture, and teacher preparation.

THERESA TENSUAN received her BA from Haverford College in English and women's studies and her doctorate from the University of California–Berkeley. After fourteen years in the classroom, she has submitted her book, *Breaking the Frame: Comics and the Art of Social Transformation,* for review and has made a transition from classroom to student personnel administration, becoming the director of the Office of Multicultural Affairs at Haverford College in the summer of 2011. She writes about the interrelations between contemporary culture and practices of social transformation. In the context of her work as an assistant professor of English, she was a coordinator of the Gender and Sexuality Studies Concentration; she is currently involved with the interfaith mentoring program Word and World, which fosters emerging activists in peace-building movements.

EVE TUCK (Unangax̂) is a member of the Tribal Government of St. Paul Island, in Alaska. She is Associate Professor of Critical Race and Indigenous Studies at OISE, University of Toronto, and a mother. Tuck is author of *Urban Youth and School Pushout: Gateways, Get-aways and the GED* (2012), co-author with Marcia McKenzie of *Place in Research: Theory, Methodology and Methods* (2015), and co-editor with K. Wayne Yang of Youth Resistance and Theories of Change (2014). She is interested in decolonization, Native feminist theories, participatory research, and Indigenous futurities.

ANNA WARD teaches courses in queer and LGBT studies, visual and popular culture, embodiment, and disability studies. Before joining Smith College, she was a Mellon Postdoctoral Fellow at Swarthmore College from 2010 to 2012 and coordinator of the Gender and Sexuality Studies Program in 2012–2013. She received her PhD in women's studies from the University of California–Los Angeles. Her work has appeared in *Camera Obscura, Social Psychology Quarterly, American Quarterly*, and *The Scholar & Feminist*. Works in progress include a book project titled *Ecstatic Bodies: The Queer Life of Orgasm*.

SARAH WILLIE-LEBRETON is a professor of sociology at Swarthmore College, where she has also served as chair of the Department of Sociology and Anthropology, coordinator of the Black Studies Program, associate provost of the college, and chair of the Task Force on Sexual Misconduct. She received her BA from Haverford College and her MA and PhD from Northwestern University in sociology. She is the author of *Acting Black: College, Identity, and the Performance of Race*, published by Routledge in 2003, and is at work on a book about American librarians.

INDEX

Ackelsberg, Martha, 125–126
activism/political action, 144–147, 148–151, 158, 204–206. *See also* student dissent
administrators, 160; difficulties faced by, 203; diversity, role in facilitating, 34, 35, 89, 96, 155, 167, 205–206; as faculty mentors, 95, 107–108; student dissent and, 131, 141–148, 151–152, 154, 164
admissions. *See* affirmative action; diversity
affect: course evaluations as evidence of, 67; faculty positionality and, 25, 47, 69, 135, 197; identity formation and, 88; marginalized identities and, 129–132; online learning and, 53, 56; safety/safe spaces and, 21–22, 55–56
affinity groups, 63
affirmative action, 41, 85–86, 91, 96n2, 155
African American studies, 179
Ahmed, Sara, 106, 130, 132, 134
Allport, Gordon W., 35
Alpes, Augustus Maximilian, 154
Americans with Disabilities Act (ADA), 115, 116–117
Anyon, Jean, 61–62
Anzaldúa, Gloria, 161–162, 177–178
Asian Americans, 96n2, 101
assignments, 38, 75, 78, 80, 81–82, 109n3
Association for Higher Education and Disability (AHEAD), 116

Bechdel, Alison, 184
Bennett, William, 165
blackness: African American experience, 3, 176–177; "angry Black" stereotype, 26, 51, 61; power relations, experiences of, 185–187; as problem, 46–47; in visual art, 78–79; whiteness construction and, 17–18, 19–20. *See also* competence/authority, challenges to

body/bodies: chattel slavery and, 19, 20; disability and, 120, 191; in visual art, 75–77, 80
Boice, Robert, 71
Bok, Derek, 165
Bourdieu, Pierre, 164, 187–188
Bowen, William, 165
Bright, Susan, 75, 76, 78, 80
Bryson, Mary, 127–128
Butler, Judith, 148

Calhoun, Craig, 84, 88
Camacho de Schmidt, Aurora, 202–203
Caughie, Pamela, 128, 134
Cervero, Ronald M., 41
Chikkatur, Anita, 200
class status/socioeconomic background, 3–4; access to elite education and, 86–87, 101; disability and, 117; family obligations for some students, 188–189; Latin American/Latino distinction and, 162; "low-tier" institutional designation and, 61–62; need-blind, loan-free admissions policies, 190, 193–194; parenting expectations and, 180–181; preparation for college and, 157–159, 192–193; technology and course material access and, 190–191; white students' ability to think about, 52
Clifford, James, 6
Collins, Patricia Hill, 37
color-blind ideology: difficulties talking about race/racism and, 16, 33; reproduction of white privilege in classroom and, 64; safe spaces and, 21; student resistance to antiracist course material and, 28, 29. *See also* white supremacy
community: complexity of, 180; dissent/conflict and, 130, 136–137, 140–146, 148–150, 202–203; erasure of difference and,

CPSIA information can be obtained
at www.ICGtesting.com
Printed in the USA
LVOW13s1816290718
585288LV00017B/168/P